Strangers
to
Ourselves

Strangers to Ourselves

Unsettled Minds and the Stories That Make Us

Rachel Aviv

FARRAR, STRAUS AND GIROUX

New York

Farrar, Straus and Giroux
120 Broadway, New York 10271

The chapter "Laura" was originally published, in much different form, in
The New Yorker in 2019 as "The Challenge of Going Off Psychiatric Drugs."

Grateful acknowledgment is made for permission to reprint lines from
Jane Kenyon, "Having It Out with Melancholy," from *Collected Poems*.
Copyright © 2005 by The Estate of Jane Kenyon. Reprinted with the
permission of The Permissions Company, LLC, on behalf of Graywolf Press,
Minneapolis, Minnesota, graywolfpress.org.

Library of Congress Control Number: 2022021878
ISBN: 978-0-374-60084-6

Our books may be purchased in bulk for promotional, educational, or business
use. Please contact your local bookseller or the Macmillan Corporate and
Premium Sales Department at 1-800-221-7945, extension 5442, or by email at
MacmillanSpecialMarkets@macmillan.com.

www.fsgbooks.com
www.twitter.com/fsgbooks • www.facebook.com/fsgbooks

1   3   5   7   9   10   8   6   4   2

To my parents

CONTENTS

Strangers
to
Ourselves

"Someone better than me"

In the early weeks of first grade, I made a friend named Elizabeth. She was the oldest child in our class but tiny, with thin, knobby limbs. We connected over the game mancala, dropping marbles into a wooden board with fourteen shallow holes. I avoided other classmates so I'd be ready when Elizabeth asked me to play. Somehow she always did. I felt that I had willed our friendship into being.

I asked my mom why Elizabeth's house, in Bloomfield Hills, a wealthy suburb of Detroit, smelled so different from ours. I was disappointed that her answer—laundry detergent—felt so ordinary. Elizabeth's house was so large that I was sure she got lost in it. She had a yellow canopy bed, a walk-in closet, a swimming pool. She showed me how when she brushed her blond hair it got even lighter. Her family had a refrigerator in their basement devoted just to sodas, and one day Elizabeth proposed that we feed Coke to our knees. We tried the experiment in her babysitter's car and laughed as Coke dripped onto the seats. It seemed incredible that there was only one way to drink.

At home, I sometimes pretended I was Elizabeth. I walked into rooms and imagined I didn't know where they led. It seemed like a fluke, a bit of bad luck, that I had been born as me rather than as Elizabeth. I remember waking up forlorn after a dream: I was given the chance to become Elizabeth if I picked the right seat on the school bus. I walked past thirteen rows, overwhelmed by the opportunity, and chose the wrong seat.

I had just turned six, and the boundaries between people felt porous. During music class, I was assigned a seat between two boys: On one side was Sloan, the tallest kid in first grade. He had a perennially runny nose, the snot greenish. On the other side was Brent, who was chubby and breathed so heavily that I sometimes checked to see if he'd fallen asleep. Their physical attributes seemed contagious. To protect myself, I tried to sit at the centermost point of my chair, as far away as possible from both boys. If I moved toward Sloan, I felt I'd grow too tall. If I inched toward Brent, I'd become fat. My older sister, Sari, and I had watched a news segment about an obese man who had a heart attack in bed and then had to be removed from his apartment by a crane. We tried to imagine the logistics: Did they have to knock down the walls? How did they attach the man to the machine? I decided to err on the side of Sloan.

At lunch, everyone in my class was required to take at least a "mouse taste" of each dish—one noodle, a single pea. Many years later, my first-grade teacher, Ms. Calfin, told me, "You'd just sit there looking at your mouse tastes pensively, and I'd be like, 'Go ahead! We only have twenty minutes! Keep going!' But it was a slow roll." Two weeks into the school year, I asked for permission to visit the bathroom after lunch. "Do you have to go potty?" Ms. Calfin asked. She said that I told her that I just wanted to look in the mirror.

A few days later, I wouldn't touch the mouse tastes that Ms. Calfin had put on my plate. She asked if instead I'd be going to the salad bar, where I sometimes got croutons. I tried to hide my grin when I said no. She looked at me carefully and made an expression that I didn't know how to classify—it looked like a frown and a smile at the same time. I could feel her contemplating who I was, and her focus was exhilarating. I loved her and worried that my feelings were unreciprocated. It seemed to me that she preferred the stolid children whose mothers volunteered at school.

For the next two days, I mostly refused to eat or drink. I don't remember my reasoning, only the reactions of the adults and my vague sense of pride. I got the idea from Yom Kippur, the day of atonement, which we'd celebrated the week before. It was the first time I realized that it was possible to say no to food. The decision retained the religious energy from the holiday and carried an aura of martyrdom.

I went to Hebrew school three times a week and liked to entertain the idea that I had some invisible channels of communication with God. Several times a day, I prayed for my family to be healthy until we were "eighty-seven years or older," repeating "me and Mom" several times, because our survival felt most important. I remember walking on the pebbles in my dad's girlfriend's backyard and realizing that every step had been preordained by God. But the epiphany was eclipsed by self-consciousness; I felt that maybe I was having my burning-bush moment. The content of the revelation was secondary to my desire to distinguish myself as someone capable of having one.

On September 30, 1988, I told my mom that I was so dizzy I felt I would bump into a wall. I had barely eaten for three days. She took me to the pediatrician. "I was thinking, 'Well, they'll give you some fluids, and then I'll take you home,'" my mom later told me. She described me as an exuberant and silly six-year-old. But my dad's girlfriend, Linda, who became my stepmom, recalled that in her presence I was the saddest child she had ever known. When presented with activities that she assumed would excite me, I often replied with the same phrase: "What's so big about that?" Linda observed that I had an unusual ability to sit completely still while silently crying, often at the kitchen table. My dad would tell me to eat and I would refuse, sometimes for more than an hour, until he gave up and drove me to school.

My doctor noted that I had lost four pounds in the last month. Until recently I'd had a normal diet, he wrote, "consisting mostly of pizza, chicken, cereal." He described my "current accomplishments" as "running, jumping, riding two-wheeler." For "personal/social," he noted that I was bored. He advised my mom to take me to Children's Hospital of Michigan, in Detroit, where I was admitted for "failure to eat." A psychiatrist there described me as a "well developed but very thin female in no acute distress."

After interviewing my mother and father, who had divorced a year earlier and were still fighting over custody, one doctor at the hospital wrote, "Her mother states that her father pokes fun at obese individuals, and the father did not protest this statement." My father, on the other hand, proposed that my problem originated with my mother, who was "overly concerned with foods." She did stockpile so many whole-grain breads that, when we opened the freezer door, loaves bought at farmers markets around Detroit would sometimes topple out. But she had a relatively normal, if passionate, relationship with food. Like many women her age, she occasionally tried to diet, with flagging conviction.

The week before my hospitalization, my mom kept a journal for me—I couldn't write yet, so she transcribed as I talked—but I shared no details about my state of mind, only chronological accounts of my days interspersed with questions like, "Where does a snake's diarrhea come out of?" and "Why don't people have tails?" My mom, who had recently broken up with her boyfriend, kept her own journal too. That week, she recorded a dream—she was always documenting her dreams—in which she asked a gardener to take apart our house brick by brick. "All that remains is dirt and the cement shape of the house," she wrote.

On my first evening at the hospital, a nurse presented me with a tray of food, which I refused. My mom was hungry, so she ate it instead. "They got very mad at me," she told me. "I was not to confuse what I ate with what you ate." The next day, the nurses gave me an IV, because I'd become dehydrated.

My medical records do not present a coherent picture of why I wasn't eating or drinking. One psychologist wrote, "Clearly, her symptoms are an expression of the pathology in the relationship between her mother and father." Another observed, "Rachel attempts to look inside herself to understand and resolve her intense feelings related to her external world" but struggles with an "over-complicated thought process," leading to a "self-condemning attitude (i.e., I must be the problem)." Although the description could apply to almost anyone, the doctors concluded that I had "an unusual case of anorexia nervosa."

Anorexia has often been described as a "reading disorder," brought on by uncritical consumption of texts that present thinness as the feminine ideal. I was only starting to learn to read. I had never heard of anorexia. When my mom told me the diagnosis, it sounded to me like a species of dinosaur. The Japanese scholar Takayo Mukai, a former anorexic, describes a similar sense of disorientation when encountering the word in the 1980s, before anorexia was well-known in Japan: "The eight-letter-word was just an empty envelope, unstamped and unaddressed."

My father and Linda went to our local library and read the only book they could find on the subject: *The Golden Cage* by Hilde Bruch, published in 1978. Bruch, a psycho-analyst known as "Lady Anorexia," began writing about anorexia in the sixties, when the illness was obscure. She hypothesized that novelty was essential to the disease, which she described as a "blind search for a sense of identity and selfhood." She predicted (inaccurately) that, once a critical mass of girls became anorexic, the incidence of the illness might decrease, because it would no longer feel special. "The illness used to be the accomplishment of an isolated girl who felt she had found her own way to salvation," she wrote. "Each one was, in a way, an original inventor of this misguided road to independence."

My mom also read about the illness, mostly from the psy-choanalytic perspective that was dominant at the time, and internalized a common message: the mother was to blame. "It's I who has caused all the pain—and the original injury," she wrote in a spiral-bound journal that she often carried in her purse. She turned this realization into an indictment of her own character. "I must own that I have a propensity to be mean and to hurt," she wrote. "What I do, sometimes, to my children, is mean—though I think I try very hard to protect them." Neither my sister nor I remember her doing anything approaching mean, but she believed what these books told her about herself. In notes for a conversation with my doctors, she reminded herself to be "humble," and not to "claim to understand what's happening."

The word "anorexia" felt so powerful that I was afraid to say it. I was learning to sound out letters, and words felt like tangible entities that somehow embodied their meaning. I would not say the names of any foods because pronouncing the words felt like the equivalent of eating. "If such terms were used in her presence," a psychologist wrote, "she would cover her ears." I wouldn't say "eight," because the number sounds like "ate." I was upset when one of the nurses, frustrated by my stubbornness, told me that I was a "tough cookie." My mother was more sensitive to my concerns, and when I asked about the condition of my hospital roommate, a girl with diabetes, my mom avoided the word "sugar." She explained, "It's like the opposite of what you have."

I was assigned a young psychologist, Thomas Koepke, who was soft-spoken and nurturing. I answered his questions with as few words as possible. I had a vague fear that, even when I stayed silent, my thoughts were being transcribed and printed from the back of my head, like pages released from a printer. In an evaluation that today makes me self-conscious about the career I have chosen, another psychologist wrote, "Rachel handled herself in a way that she appeared to very consciously be aware of her ability to control the interview."

Koepke told my parents that the doctors on his team had no evidence of a child as young as six having ever been diagnosed with anorexia. Nevertheless, they moved me out of the room that I shared with the girl with diabetes and to the fifth floor of the hospital, which, as far as I could see, was racially divided. At the end of the hall were Black children with sickle cell anemia. In the center, where I was placed, was a small group of white girls, all older than me. Due to malnutrition, some of their faces and arms were covered with lanugo, the soft, feathery hair that coats the skin of newborns. Every morning, we were weighed while wearing our hospital gowns, our backs to the scales.

The girls often spoke of their "privileges." If we completed one meal, delivered on a tray to our beds, and the nurses didn't find any large crumbs on our laps, we could call our parents. If we finished two meals in a day, our parents could come to the hospital for an hour-long visit. But the consequences for abstaining from food were severe: skip two meals, and we were assigned to bed rest. To use the bathroom, we had to page a nurse, who would record our "output." We lost our freedom to watch television or visit the game room, where children with other illnesses played. The threat of a feeding tube—the punishment for losing too much weight—hovered over every meal. I didn't realize that the tube would go inside my nostrils. I imagined a huge tube, like a covered slide, that I would live inside.

ON THE ANOREXIA UNIT, I was assigned a new roommate, Carrie, a twelve-year-old with straw-colored hair. I asked her, "Do you think I'm weird?" so many times that she eventually said, "If you ask me one more time, I will say yes." She knew all the nurses on our floor and had become close with other patients. I viewed her and her friend Hava, who lived in the room next to us, as mentors. Hava was twelve and beautiful, with sharp features and long brown hair that she didn't brush. There was something rugged and wild about her that reminded me of heroines of books about settling the American frontier. She kept a detailed journal of her hospital stay that was inflected by the therapeutic language through which she was learning to understand herself. A precocious student of her surroundings, she entered a rhapsodic mode after meeting me: "For god's sake the girl's only 6," she wrote. "Look at her!" She went on, "Let her trust an adult and release her childish behaviors hidden somewhere within that taut, stiff body. I bet she is just waiting for somebody to reach out their hand for her to clasp on to!"

Hava may also have been unduly influenced by the spirit of Yom Kippur. She went to a Jewish day school and was terrified, she wrote in her journal, that she would not "be written in the book of life"—God's record of those who deserve to live another year. She blamed herself for "not achieving a state of holy perfection."

There were other similarities between us: Hava's parents were also involved in a prolonged and hostile divorce, and they, too, joked about obese family friends. They "always made fun of the Ornsteins and called them the Oinksteins," she wrote. She had a friend like Elizabeth, too: a girl she not only admired but wanted to become. When she played at the friend's house, she wrote in her journal, she liked to imagine that she lived there and would never go home. Her handwriting was so similar to mine that recently, when reading certain passages of her journal, I became briefly disoriented and assumed I was reading my own words.

When I met Hava, she had been hospitalized for nearly five months. Her mother, Gail, visited Hava's sixth-grade class and tried to explain Hava's extended absence. "Even though Hava's very thin," she told the class, "she thinks she's very fat."

Hava, who weighed seventy pounds, seemed conflicted about whether her mother's explanation improved her social status. In her journal, she listed "what I wish I could like about myself," which included "my personality," "my intelligence—my grades," and "my feelings." She had dreams in which she was "pleading with my peers and suddenly I received their total acceptance and understanding," she wrote.

In the playroom, where everyone vied for the one *Pac-Man*

game, Hava befriended a thirteen-year-old who was pregnant with twins. When Hava complained about the strict eating rules on the anorexia unit, the pregnant girl's mother casually mentioned that Hava could burn off calories through exercise. "She's the one who made up my mind that I'd do jumping jacks tonight," Hava wrote.

I was in awe of Hava and Carrie's friendship, which solidified around mutual goals. "Carrie and I compared our bones, skin, color and thinness," Hava wrote. "If Carrie weren't here I don't know where I'd be!" They seemed to go through cycles of weight loss and gain together. When they were on the upswing, the nurses let them visit the labor-and-delivery unit, where they gazed at the newborns. Some of the babies had "needles and everything stuck in them, so it made me real thankful," Hava wrote. "I just wish it could be easier to have a meal without the feeling of guilt." When the nurses weren't watching, Hava and Carrie paced the halls until Hava had trouble breathing; they also volunteered to distribute lunch trays to other patients—"that was my exercise for the day," Hava wrote.

I hadn't known that exercise had anything to do with body weight, but I began doing jumping jacks with Carrie and Hava at night. I no longer let myself sit down, so as not to be a "couch potato," a term they taught me. Nurses came to each room on the anorexia unit with a rolling cart of young-adult novels. After I arrived, they began including books for younger readers, like the Berenstain Bears, the Clifford books, and the Mr. Men and Little Miss books, including *Mr. Strong*, a book about a man who ate eight poached eggs for breakfast, a detail I found monstrous. I learned to read in my hospital room while standing up. When nurses entered our room, I tried out my new skill by stringing together the five or six letters on their name tags.

The older girls seemed to consider me a kind of mascot, an anorexic-in-training. My ideas about food and the body were even more magical than theirs. I would eat a bagel but refuse a small bowl of Cheerios—one big O seemed preferable to three hundred or so tiny Os. When Hava and Carrie let me watch them play Go Fish, I wanted to know (but was ashamed to ask) what sort of fish they were referring to: Fish in the ocean? Or cooked on a plate? I didn't understand that fish in the ocean became the type cooked on the plate, and, if they meant the latter kind, I didn't want anything to do with the game.

I couldn't keep up with Hava and Carrie, who spoke about their weight not just in pounds but in ounces, too. Although anorexia has a reputation as a reading disease, perhaps it is just as much about math. Mukai, the Japanese scholar, recalled that when she was anorexic she entered a "'digitalized' world, where everything was understood in terms of meters, centimeters, kilograms, calories, times, and so forth." She wrote, "I no longer shared culture, nor social reality, nor even language with anybody. I was living in a closed reality where things did make sense to me, but only to me."

I wasn't sophisticated enough to do the math that the disease required, but I was drawn to the way that Hava and Carrie had adopted a new value system, a foreign mode of interpreting their physical sensations and assessing their worth. Whenever a new patient arrived on our unit, Hava noted the girl's height and weight in her journal. "I need to wait my urges out for food and experience the high of accomplishment," Hava wrote. "The high is so wonderful." It seemed that she was disciplining her body for some higher purpose that she never named.

In her 1995 essay "The Ascetic Anorexic," the anthropologist Nonja Peters, who was anorexic, proposes that the disease unfolds in distinct phases: In the beginning, the anorexic is propelled by the same cultural forces that inspire many women to diet. The process can be sparked by a trivial remark. Mukai decided to diet after she asked her mother if she would grow up to be fat like her grandmother. "Maybe, yes," her mother replied. Mukai fixated on the comment, even though she recognized that her mother "was laughing. She was joking. I knew." In her journal, Hava described the pivotal moment when a friend described her size as "medium." Hava's parents urged her not to listen to her friends, but Hava wrote, "If they think I'm fat then I'm fat."

Eventually, an impulsive decision gathers momentum, becoming increasingly hard to reverse. "Once the ascetic path is taken, ascetic behaviour produces ascetic motivations— it is not the other way around," Peters writes.

Several scholars have studied the parallels between anorexia nervosa and anorexia mirabilis, a condition of the Middle Ages in which young religious women starved themselves as a way of freeing their spirits from their bodies and becoming one with the suffering of Christ. Their loss of appetite, it was said, was a miracle. Their bodies became such powerful symbols of faith and purity that they struggled to begin eating again, even when their lives were at risk.

The historian Rudolph Bell has named this condition "holy anorexia," concluding that these women had a disease. But the opposite argument also seems true: anorexia can feel like a spiritual practice, a distorted way of locating some nobler self. The French philosopher René Girard describes anorexia as being rooted in "the desire not to be a saint but to be regarded as one." He writes, "There is great irony in the fact that the modern process of stamping out religion produces countless caricatures of it." Once the course has been set, it is difficult to change the terms of engagement.

In a diary that I kept in second grade, I wrote, "I had some thing that was a siknis its cald anexorea." I explained that "I had anexorea because I want to be someone better than me."

I WENT TWELVE days without seeing my parents. My mom did come to the hospital once to drop off pajamas, after I'd bled through my old ones when the IV needle fell out of my arm. I heard my mom's voice and, though I'd been restricted to bed rest, I ran out of my room and down the hall toward her. Both of us were crying, but when I got within a few feet of her, the nurses held me back.

Three times a day, a nurse sat with me for thirty minutes while I looked at my meals without eating more than a few bites. Each tray of food contained three hundred calories. When the tray was taken away, the nurse monitored me for forty-five more minutes, to make sure I didn't throw up. I hadn't even realized that voluntary vomiting was physically possible.

After nearly two weeks, I finished breakfast and then lunch. I enjoyed what was served, macaroni and cheese, and found myself finishing the meal without realizing it. "I kind of look forward to the meals because sometimes I may forget myself and start to enjoy it," Hava wrote in her journal. Perhaps I was caught by the same accidental pleasure. The nurse monitoring my meal congratulated me and told me I'd earned a privilege: I could call my parents. I remember walking to the telephone beside my bed and dialing my mother's number. Once I heard her voice, I was so relieved that I couldn't speak. I just laughed.

When my parents visited me, they were dismayed to discover that I had acquired a repertoire of anorexic behaviors. In addition to doing jumping jacks, I refused to sit or lie down until 9:00 p.m., my bedtime. My sister, who was eventually allowed to visit me, too, grasped the appeal of my new friends. "I had a little crush on Carrie," she told me years later. "She was very pretty and cool, and I remember she had nice, smooth hair." She added, "Those girls took care of you."

My parents were angry that I had fallen under the sway of older girls versed in the illness. "Until then, it had been pure mental process—it was so internal to you," my stepmom told me. "You weren't reading magazines and didn't have an image of what an ideal thin person looked like." My mom said, "I don't think you even understood 'thin.' You just, I think, didn't want your stomach to protrude—as all children's stomachs do."

My father was the only one who rejected my diagnosis. "From a very young age you used to say, 'You're not the boss of me,'" he said. "That was the behavior that you brought to the table." In an "Eating Attitudes List" that my dad was told to complete, one question asked whether "my teenager thinks about burning up calories when she exercises." My dad crossed out the word "teenager" and wrote in the margins, "Did not know it then, now she does."

ONCE MY PARENTS began visiting me, it was as if the spell had been broken. My goals realigned. To continue seeing them, I began eating everything on my trays. My mom and dad were allowed to visit separately every day, for a half hour each, as long as I ate my meals.

The windowsill in my room filled up with figurines from *Pee-wee's Playhouse*, a show that my sister and I had watched every weekend. My dad brought a new character almost every time he visited: Chairry, the armchair; Reba the Mail Lady; Miss Yvonne, whom Pee-wee called the "most beautiful woman in Puppetland." I now understood, thanks to Carrie and Hava, that television was for couch potatoes, and I no longer permitted myself this indulgence. But during my dad's visits, I allowed myself to watch as he sat on my hospital bed, held a figurine in each hand, spoke in a high-pitched nasal voice, and acted out the show.

I had to reach fifty pounds to be released from the hospital—nine pounds more than I'd weighed when I was admitted. At night I went to the nurse's station and requested small boxes of frosted shredded wheat. When I picked my nose, I put the boogers back in, so I wouldn't lose extra weight. "Rachel began eating 900 calories on the twelfth day of hospitalization, and gradually increased her consumption to the point that she had little problem consuming in excess of 1,800 calories per day," Koepke wrote.

My sister said that the last time she visited me at the hospital "they had fattened you up to the point that it looked like your sweatshirt was tucked in—it was just your body, but somehow it looked like extra material." Carrie had also gained enough weight that she was preparing to go home. Hava's recovery was more halting. "I feel so crazy and weird after I eat—but nobody would understand if I can't even explain it myself," she wrote. "I wish someone could help me and just change my mind about everything."

I was discharged from the hospital on November 9, 1988, six weeks after I arrived. Koepke seemed pessimistic about my prospects for recovery. "Given the intense hostility"—between my parents—"and severity of the disease, we are extremely guarded regarding the prognosis," he wrote. He and his team suggested that a psychiatric hospital would be the "appropriate placement for Rachel." But he wrote that my parents decided to hold off on "this recommendation for the time being." My mom was shocked by the suggestion. "I feared once you'd gone into that system of psychiatric institutions, it may have been very difficult to pull you out," she told me.

I returned to school the day after I was discharged. I asked my mom if I could tell my classmates that I had been hospitalized for pneumonia, but she wouldn't let me lie. On my first day back, my mom came to the classroom with me and, as the other children sat in a circle on the rug, we explained that I'd been in a hospital. "It wasn't a long discussion," my mom said. "No one insinuated that you were different or sick in a mental way. I think the children probably understood it as sick in a physical way. And, indeed, you were in need of nourishment."

Afraid of being a couch potato, I refused to sit at my desk or on the rug where we had circle time. Ms. Calfin allowed me to stand. "The way you would stand is with one of your arms at your side and the other holding your elbow," Elizabeth, who is now a marriage counselor, told me. Sometimes students asked me to step to the side when I was blocking their view of the chalkboard, and I remember thinking that I wasn't actually in their line of sight—that they just wanted to call attention to my unusual behavior. But I was never mocked, as far as I can recall, and after a month I began sitting down like all the other children. "You kind of blended right back into the mix," Ms. Calfin said, adding, "I just wanted you to feel that you were part of this community again." That spring, a psychologist wrote that my symptoms had lifted. Anorexia, he concluded, was a "coping style in dealing with the pressures that she has felt."

Elizabeth and I began playing mancala again. Soon we called each other best friends. She often invited me to sleep over at her house and we started a New Kids on the Block club in her walk-in closet. Somehow in my memory Hava merges into Elizabeth: they both wore silky nightgowns, were thin and fragile, and were described by my mother as "ethe-real." "I want to be Elizabith," I wrote in my journal. "I want to have a biger house. I want evry body to like me."

When I was in fifth grade, my mom told me that she saw a girl who looked like Carrie, wearing camouflage pants, sift-ing through a garbage can in downtown Birmingham, where we lived. I can't track down Carrie's last name—our doctors don't remember it either—so I've never been able to confirm if the person was her. I didn't learn anything about Hava for several more years, until she was featured in an article in *The Detroit News* about identifying early signs of mental illness in adolescence. A photograph showed her standing in front of a lake, her hair down to her waist. She was still beautiful, but she looked slightly ravaged. The article said that she had spent her adolescence and early adulthood in and out of psy-chiatric hospitals. She'd had to drop out of high school. She considered her eating disorder the defining fact of her life.

~~~~~~~~~

A few years ago, I went to Sweden to report a story about a condition known as "resignation syndrome." Hundreds of children from former Soviet and Yugoslav states who had been denied asylum in Sweden had taken to their beds. They refused food. They stopped talking. Eventually, they seemed to lose the ability to move. Many had to be given feeding tubes. Some gradually slipped into states resembling comas. One child told me that during his months in bed he'd felt as if he were in a glass box with fragile walls, deep in the ocean. If he spoke or moved, it would create a vibration, which would cause the glass to shatter. "The water would pour in and kill me," he said.

Psychiatrists proposed that the condition was a reaction to both the stress of the migration proceedings and the trauma in the countries the children's families had fled. But they couldn't understand why the illness occurred only in Sweden—not in any neighboring Nordic countries, where refugees from the same countries had resettled. As I interviewed families, I discovered that many of the children diagnosed with resignation syndrome had known someone who suffered from the disorder, too. There were allegations in the Swedish press that the children were malingering, especially after Sweden established resignation syndrome as grounds for granting residency. But when I met the children, I felt sure that they were not pretending. They took weeks, sometimes months, to emerge from a nearly catatonic state, even after their families were told they could stay in Sweden. What began as a protest seemed to take on its own momentum. The children had become martyr figures, a role that at first seemed freeing, but it began to destroy them.

My conversations with families and doctors in Sweden made me reconsider my early experience with anorexia. Something about the mute, fasting children in Sweden felt familiar to me. For a child, solipsistic by nature, there are limits to the ways that despair can be communicated. Culture shapes the scripts that expressions of distress will follow. In both anorexia and resignation syndrome, children embody anger and a sense of powerlessness by refusing food, one of the few methods of protest available to them. Experts tell these children that they are behaving in a recognizable way that has a label. The children then make adjustments, conscious and unconscious, to the way they've been classified. Over time, a willed pattern of behavior becomes increasingly involuntary and ingrained.

The philosopher Ian Hacking uses the term "looping effect" to describe the way that people get caught in self-fulfilling stories about illness. A new diagnosis can change "the space of possibilities for personhood," he writes. "We make ourselves in our own scientific image of the kinds of people it is possible to be." In an essay about the children diagnosed with resignation syndrome in Sweden, Hacking refers to Pascal's wager: to avoid the possibility of eternal Hell, we should behave as if God is real even though we lack proof of his existence. Over time, we may internalize the faith we'd been simulating; our belief will become sincere. Hacking proposes that for some illnesses a similar process is at work. We find a way to express our distress through imitation, until, eventually, we "have 'learned' or—better—'acquired' a new psychic state."

AT SIX YEARS OLD, it still seemed possible that I could become someone else through sheer will. Had I stayed in the hospital longer or returned to a less welcoming school, I may have followed Hava's path. "Labels aren't so bad," she wrote in her journal. "They at least give you a title to live up to . . . and an identity!!!!"

My stepmom, the most practical person in my family, has told me she was once doubtful that I'd make it to adulthood. I do have certain traits that make me susceptible to fasting for no reason, like an amorphous sense that self-restraint is a moral good. But I also wonder if I ever had anorexia in the first place. Maybe my limited exposure to the ideal of thinness prevented me from wanting it badly enough. To use the terms of the historian Joan Jacobs Brumberg, who has written eloquently about the genesis of eating disorders, I was "recruited" for anorexia, but the illness never became a "career." It didn't provide the language with which I came to understand myself.

This sense of narrow escape has made me attentive to the windows in the early phases of an illness, when a condition is consuming and disabling but has not yet remade a person's identity and social world. Mental illnesses are often seen as chronic and intractable forces that take over our lives, but I wonder how much the stories we tell about them, especially in the beginning, can shape their course. People can feel freed by these stories, but they can also get stuck in them.

Psychiatrists use the term "insight"—a pivotal, almost magical word in the field—to evaluate the truth of people's stories about what is happening to their minds. In a seminal 1934 paper in *The British Journal of Medical Psychology*, the psychiatrist Aubrey Lewis defined insight as the "correct attitude to a morbid change in oneself." A patient with the "correct attitude" recognizes, for instance, that spirits of dead people are not suddenly talking to her; rather, the voices are symptoms that medication can silence. Insight is assessed every time psychiatric patients are hospitalized, and it looms large in decisions about whether to treat them against their will. But the concept largely ignores how the "correct attitude" depends on culture, race, ethnicity, and faith. Studies show that people of color are rated as "lacking in insight" more often than those who are white, perhaps because doctors find their mode of expressing distress unfamiliar, or because these patients have less reason to trust what their doctors say. In the starkest terms, insight measures the degree to which a patient agrees with his or her doctor's interpretation.

Fifty years ago, at the height of the psychoanalytic era, insight described a kind of epiphany: unconscious desires and conflicts became conscious. A patient was said to have insight if she could recognize, say, her repressed hatred for her father and the way that this forbidden emotion had formed her personality. Eventually, though, it became apparent that gaining insight into interpersonal conflicts, though intellectually rewarding, did not provide a cure.

Biomedical explanations of illness, which began to dominate in the eighties and nineties, did away with the need for this sort of insight. The "correct attitude" came to rest on a new body of knowledge: patients were insightful if they understood that their disorders arose from diseases of the brain. The biomedical approach solved a moral problem—that patients and their families were being blamed—and it has been celebrated for its potential to reduce stigma. The surgeon general's first-ever report on mental health, in 1999, proposed that stigma arises from "the misguided split between mind and body first proposed by Descartes." At a press conference, the surgeon general announced that there is "no scientific justification for distinguishing between mental illness and other forms of illness."

That may be, but the biomedical framework doesn't seem to have actually reduced stigma. Studies show that people who see mental illness as biological or genetic are less likely to blame mental conditions on weak character or to respond in punitive ways, but they are more likely to see a person's illness as out of her control, alienating, and dangerous. The disease comes to seem unyielding, a strike of lightning that can't be redirected. In her memoir *The Center Cannot Hold*, Elyn Saks, a professor of law, psychology, and psychiatry at the University of Southern California, writes that when she was diagnosed with schizophrenia she felt as if she were "being told that whatever had gone wrong inside my head was permanent and, from all indications, unfixable. Repeatedly, I ran up against words like 'debilitating,' 'baffling,' 'chronic,' 'catastrophic,' 'devastating,' and 'loss.' For the rest of my life. *The rest of my life*."

Hava had excellent insight—in her journal she referred

frequently to her "chemical imbalances"—whereas I, at six, had basically none. When I began eating again, it felt like a random choice. But perhaps the decision was possible because my doctors' explanations meant little to me. I wasn't bound to any particular story about the role of illness in my life. There are stories that save us, and stories that trap us, and in the midst of an illness it can be very hard to know which is which.

Psychiatrists know remarkably little about why some people with mental illnesses recover and others with the same diagnosis go on to have an illness "career." Answering the question, I think, requires paying more attention to the distance between the psychiatric models that explain illness and the stories through which people find meaning themselves. Even if questions of interpretation are secondary to finding effective medical treatment, these stories alter people's lives, sometimes in unpredictable ways, and bear heavily on a person's sense of self—and the desire to be treated at all.

~~~~~~~~~~

I have always been drawn to the genre of the case study while also bristling at the picture it presents of a closed world, limited to one person and one explanation. I wonder if those of us who write about mental illness have too often taken our cues from psychiatry. Stories about psychiatric illness are often deeply individual; the pathology emerges from within and is endured that way, too. But these stories neglect where and how people live, and the ways their identity becomes a reflection of how others see them. Our illnesses are not just contained in our skull but are also made and sustained by our relationships and communities. Although a purely psychiatric model of the mind may be essential to the survival of people with mental illness, the title of this book, *Strangers to Ourselves*—a phrase that comes from Hava's journal—is a reminder that this framework may also estrange us from the many scales of understanding required, especially in periods of illness or crisis, to maintain a continuous sense of self.

In an essay called "The Hidden Self," William James writes that "the ideal of every science is that of a closed and completed system of truth." Scholars achieve this goal, he writes, largely by neglecting what he calls the "unclassified residuum"—those symptoms and experiences that do not "wear just this ideal form." This book is about people whose struggles with mental illness exist outside of this "closed and completed system of truth." Their lives unfold in different eras and cultures, but they also share a setting: the psychic hinterlands, the outer edges of human experience, where language tends to fail. I have chosen subjects who have tried to overcome a feeling of incommunicability through writing; the book draws not only from conversations with them but from their diaries, letters, unpublished memoirs, poems, and prayers. They have come up against the limits of psychiatric ways of understanding themselves and are searching for the right scale of explanation—chemical, existential, cultural, economic, political—to understand a self in the world. But these different explanations are not mutually exclusive; sometimes all of them can be true.

At times, I contemplated devoting the entire book to each life I have written about here, but I wanted to emphasize the diversity of experiences of mental illness, the fact that, when questions are examined from different angles, the answers continually change. The book begins by telling the story of a man torn between the twentieth century's dominant explanations for mental distress—the psychodynamic and the biochemical. The rest of the chapters move beyond these two prevailing frameworks: one character tries to understand who she is in relation to her guru and gods; another is reckoning with her country's racist history and how it has shaped her mind; a third has been so defined by psychiatric concepts that she doesn't know how to explain her suffering on its own terms. In this sense, the book is about missing stories, the facets of identity that our theories of the mind fail to capture. It's impossible to go back in time and uncover what baseline feelings existed before a story was told—when a person's angst and loneliness and disorientation had yet to be given a name and a vessel—but I find myself searching for the gap between people's experiences and the stories that organize their suffering, sometimes defining the course of their lives.

In creating a shared language, contemporary psychiatry can alleviate people's loneliness, but we may take for granted the impact of its explanations, which are not neutral: they alter the kinds of stories about the self that count as "insight" and how we understand our potential. Ray Osheroff, the subject of the first chapter, is trying to make sense of two conflicting models of the mind, neither of which has made his suffering legible. "Am I really this?" Ray asks. "Am I not this? What am I?"

WHEN I WAS a teenager, my mom, a high school English teacher, proposed that we write a book together, a series of alternating chapters about my experience as the country's youngest (as far as we knew) diagnosed anorexic. I dismissed the idea, which I found embarrassing. My mom was surprised when I informed her, two decades later, that I had written about that episode now. I have also been surprised by the intellectual hold that this experience has had on me. A strange sense of abyss opens up when I think about the life I have now, and how easily it might have gone another way, as it did for Hava, to whose story I return in the epilogue. The divide between the psychic hinterlands and a setting we might call normal is permeable, a fact that I find both haunting and promising. It's startling to realize how narrowly we avoid, or miss, living radically different lives.

RAY

"Am I really this? Am I not this? What am I?"

In 1979, Raphael "Ray" Osheroff walked eight hours a day. Breathing heavily through pursed lips, he paced the corridors of Chestnut Lodge, one of the most elite hospitals in the country. "How many miles are you going to pace today, Ray?" a nurse asked him. Ray calculated that he walked about eighteen miles a day, in slippers. Another nurse wrote that he frequently bumped into people but "doesn't even seem to realize he had physical contact."

As he paced, Ray, who had a mustache and bushy black hair, recalled the lavish vacations that he and his wife had enjoyed. They were both doctors in northern Virginia, and they dined out so frequently that when they entered their favorite restaurants they were immediately recognized. They were the most popular medical couple in the Washington area, Ray decided. The motion of his legs became a "mechanism of self-hypnosis in which I would concentrate on the life I once had," he wrote in an unpublished memoir. Ray's feet became so blistered that orderlies at the Lodge took him to a podiatrist. His toes were black with dead skin.

In his medical notes, Ray's psychiatrist, Manuel Ross, wrote that Ray suffered from "a form of melancholia, not mourning"—a reference to Freud's 1917 paper "Mourning and Melancholia." In the essay, Freud had proposed that melancholia arises when a patient is mourning something or someone but "cannot see clearly what it is that has been lost." Ray, a forty-one-year-old nephrologist, had founded a once thriving dialysis company, but the business had faltered, and he was consumed by his missteps. Ross concluded that Ray's obsessive regret was a way of staying close to a loss he was unable to name: the idea of a parallel life in which "he could have been a great man." Ray ruminated over the details of his downfall, because he was still in denial, clinging to an idealized version of himself.

From a phone in the hallway of the Lodge, Ray often called his colleague Robert Greenspan, who was running Ray's business in his absence, to share his regrets. In the background, Greenspan sometimes heard other patients shouting in "sort of unusual tones." A young man wandered the halls saying, "Hyperspace, hyperspace, hyperspace." Greenspan called a social worker at the Lodge to ask why Ray seemed to be deteriorating. The social worker explained that Ray "would get worse and that was part of the therapy. His personality had to be restructured. There had to be some tearing down and rebuilding."

After Ray had been at the Lodge for half a year, his mother, Julia, visited him for the first time. She was alarmed by his appearance. His hair had grown to his shoulders. He was using the belt of his bathrobe to hold up his trousers, because he'd lost forty pounds. Ray had once been a prodigious reader, but he had completely stopped. He was also a musician—he was in a jazz band and played banjo, trumpet, clarinet, piano, drums, and trombone—and, although he had packed sheets of music in the suitcase he brought to the

Lodge, he almost never looked at the pages. When a nurse called him Dr. Osheroff, he corrected her: "Mr. Osheroff."

Julia asked the Lodge psychiatrists to give her son anti-depressants. But at the time, the use of antidepressants was still so new that the premise of this form of treatment—to be cured without insight into what had gone wrong—seemed counterintuitive, even cheap. Drugs "might bring about some symptomatic relief," Ross, Ray's psychiatrist, acknowledged, "but it isn't going to be anything solid in which he can say, 'Hey, I'm a better man. I can tolerate feelings.'" Ross concluded that Ray was simply searching for a drug that would buy him the "return of his former status," an achievement that, Ross believed, had always been illusory.

THE LODGE ONCE had the atmosphere of a Southern plantation. Its main building, a brick mansion, had previously been the Woodlawn Hotel, the fanciest resort in Rockville, Maryland, catering to wealthy guests from Washington, D.C., twenty miles away. The building was designed in a French revival style, with a slate mansard roof, six chimneys, and roughly eighty white-framed windows. Surrounding the building were colonial bungalows scattered on a hundred acres of land shaded by sixty-foot trees.

The Lodge was founded in 1910 by a doctor named Ernest Bullard, and two decades later, his son, Dexter, took over the family business and transformed it into an institution where doctors believed they were finally uncovering the mysteries of the mind. Dexter had grown up on the first floor of the hospital, playing croquet and baseball with patients. "I knew the psychotic as a person long before I knew what the implications of the word 'patient' were," he said. The idea that patients were beyond empathy "just never became part of the experience." He found it frustrating to see them "labeled and put on the shelf."

After reading Freud in his father's library, Dexter decided that Chestnut Lodge could do what no other American hospital had done: psychoanalyze every patient, no matter how far removed from reality they were (as long as they could pay the admission fee). The Lodge would leave "no therapeutic stone unturned," he wrote. His goal was to create an institution that expressed the ethos of the analyst's office. "We don't know enough yet to be able to say why patients stay sick," he told a colleague in 1954. "Until we know that, we have no right to call them chronic."

At the Lodge, the goal of all conversations and activities was *understanding*. "No single word used at the hospital is more charged with emotional meaning, or more slippery in its cognitive implications," Alfred Stanton, a psychiatrist, and Morris Schwartz, a sociologist, wrote in *The Mental Hospital*, a 1954 study of the Lodge. The hope of "getting better"—by gaining insight into interpersonal dynamics— became its own kind of spirituality. "What occurred at the hospital," the authors wrote, "was a type of collective evaluation in which neurosis or illness was Evil and the ultimate Good was mental health."

Other hospitals were giving patients barbiturates, a sedating drug, as well as electroconvulsive therapy and lobotomies. But Dexter believed that "pharmacology has no place in psychiatry." At a medical society conference, when Dexter's colleague reported that he had lobotomized a patient and cured her in ten days, Dexter objected to the idea of a treatment that didn't even require self-knowledge. "You can't say that!" Dexter shouted.

The "queen of Chestnut Lodge," as people called her,

was Frieda Fromm-Reichmann, a founder of the Frankfurt Psychoanalytic Institute who lived on the grounds of the Lodge in a cottage that had been built for her. She sometimes took her patients to lunch at a country inn, or to an art gallery or a concert. She would imitate their posture, to more readily understand their perspective. The phrases "we know" and "I am here"—uttered at the right time, in a sensitive tone—"may replace the patient's desolate experience of 'nobody knows except me,'" she wrote.

Fromm-Reichmann described loneliness as "one of the least satisfactorily conceptualized psychological phenomena, not even mentioned in most psychiatric textbooks"—a state in which the "fact that there were people in one's past life is more or less forgotten, and the possibility that there may be interpersonal relationships in one's future life is out of the realm of expectation." Loneliness was such a deep threat, she wrote, that psychiatrists avoided talking about it, because they feared they'd be contaminated by it, too. The experience was nearly impossible to communicate; it was a kind of "naked existence."

Fromm-Reichmann and other analysts at the Lodge were described as "substitute mothers"; younger therapists vied for their attention, working through what they called sibling rivalries. The doctors, all of whom had undergone analysis themselves, felt that they had been incorporated into the Bullard household—as one psychiatrist put it, they were "part of a dysfunctional family." As patients walked down the hallway to their appointments, others shouted, "Have a good hour!" Alan Stone, a former president of the American Psychiatric Association, described the Lodge as "the most enlightened hospital in North America." He told me, "It seemed like Valhalla, the residence of the gods."

At the time, faith in the potential of psychology and

psychiatry seemed boundless. The psychological sciences provided a new framework for understanding society. "The world was sick, and the ills from which it was suffering were mainly due to the perversion of man, his inability to live at peace with himself," declared the first director of the World Health Organization, a psychiatrist. Following the war, at the 1948 meeting of the American Psychiatric Association, President Truman sent a message of greeting: "The greatest prerequisite for peace, which is uppermost in the minds and hearts of all of us, must be sanity." War was not just about power or resources—it arose from insecurity, neuroses, and other mental wounds. The psychologist Abraham Maslow said, "The world will be saved by psychologists—in the very broadest sense—or else it will not be saved at all."

Chestnut Lodge embodied the utopian promise of psychiatry, but the story that the institution told about itself was unable to survive the demands of a patient like Ray. In 1982, Ray sued Chestnut Lodge for failing to make him better. In the lawsuit, the twentieth century's two dominant explanations for mental distress collided. The psychiatrist Peter Kramer, the author of the landmark book *Listening to Prozac*, compared the case's significance to *Roe v. Wade*. As *Psychiatric Times* put it, the case created a "showdown between two forms of knowledge."

BEFORE ENTERING THE LODGE, Ray had been the kind of charismatic, overworked physician whom we have come to associate with the American dream. He had opened three dialysis centers in northern Virginia and felt within reach of something "very new for me, something that I never had before, and that was the clear and distinct prospects of success," he wrote in his memoir. He loved the telephone, which signified new referrals, more business—a sense that he was vital and desired. In the waiting room of his office, he installed plush theater seats. He befriended his patients, buying them air conditioners, paying their rent, or funding their funerals. He bought one patient, who had just immigrated, his own taxi.

But his "energies seemed to be so devoted to and focused on my training and career," he wrote in his memoir, that he neglected his wife and their two young sons. Eventually, she filed for divorce. Ray moved on quickly, falling in love with a glamorous and ambitious medical student named Joy. Sometimes he took Joy to business meetings, and they held hands under the table. He and Joy married in 1974. "Life was a sky-rocket," he wrote.

But after the wedding, he lost his momentum. He agreed to let his ex-wife move to Luxembourg with their sons for a year but immediately regretted the decision. His own father, who had run a deli in the Bronx, had been neglectful and absent—then died young—and Ray worried that he was reproducing the same sense of abandonment for his own boys. He could no longer be "consoled by the mystical thought that closure was possible," he wrote in his memoir, by being the "good father that I had lost."

Ray's thinking became circular. In order to have a conversation, his secretary, Dotty, said, "we would walk all the way around the block, over and over." He was so repetitive that he started to bore people. He couldn't sit still long enough to eat. "He would take a few bites and then get up, and then go to the men's room, go outside," Dotty said.

Joy gave birth to a baby less than two years after their wedding, but Ray had become so detached—he seemed to care only about the past—that he behaved as if the child wasn't his. He felt increasingly incapable of handling the stress caused by rivals in the dialysis field, and he sold a portion of his interest to a larger dialysis corporation. Although he retained a managerial role, supervising thirty-five people, he once again became convinced he had made the wrong choice. After finalizing the sale, he wrote, "I went outside and sat in my car and I realized that I had become a piece of wood." The air felt heavy, like some sort of noxious gas.

IN A DRUGSTORE that year, Ray came across *From Sad to Glad*, a 1974 book by Nathan Kline, one of the most prominent psychiatrists in America. In the book, which Ray immediately read, Kline attributes depression to "some disarray in the biochemical tides that sweep back and forth within the body." Kline was not curious about why his patients had become ill. "Do not try to dredge up reasons," he told his patients. On the cover of the book was the motto, "Depression: you can conquer it without analysis!"

Kline had become famous by studying the tuberculosis drug iproniazid, which had the unanticipated side effect of making patients feel too good. They became incautious, overexerting themselves. At a sanitarium on Long Island, patients who took the medication felt so lighthearted that they danced in the corridors. An Associated Press photograph from 1953 shows a semicircle of patients wearing long patterned skirts, looking dazed but pleased, smiling and clapping. One woman later told her psychiatrist that she had experienced happiness only once, when she had a religious conversion while recovering from tuberculosis. "I couldn't quite bring myself to tell her," her psychiatrist told *The New York Times*, "that her ecstatic experience might not have come from the Lord, but may have been instead a biochemical reaction to the medication."

Kline tried iproniazid on his patients and discovered that they became more competent and lively. When he gave iproniazid to a young married woman, he reported, she started "caring for her household efficiently and doing full time graduate work." When he prescribed the pills to a nurse, "even her physical appearance changed. The scowling brow and the drawn mouth were replaced by a relaxed and smiling appearance, which incidentally made her look twenty years younger." For another patient, an artist who had been unable to paint for more than a year, iproniazid lifted him out of the impasse: "He produced a profusion of oil paintings, water colors, and sketches totaling more than a hundred," Kline wrote.

The antipsychotic Thorazine had been developed a few years earlier, in a lab in France, and for the first time many psychiatrists were confronting the possibility that people didn't have to understand their childhood conflicts to get well. But the view was still unpopular. Kline said colleagues took him aside to warn him that, by claiming a drug could relieve depression, he was risking humiliation. "There was a large and adamant body of theoretical opinion that held that such a drug simply could not exist," Kline wrote. The neuroscientist Solomon Snyder has written that, at the time, a psychiatrist engaged in biological research was "regarded as somewhat peculiar, perhaps suffering from emotional conflicts that made him or her avoid confronting 'real feelings.'"

But Kline presented a new story about what sorts of feelings were "real." One of the epigraphs to his book was a quote by Epictetus: "For you were not born to be depressed and unhappy." When Kline tried iproniazid himself, he found that the drug produced a uniquely American kind of transcendence: he could work harder, faster, and longer.

Inspired by *From Sad to Glad*, Ray traveled to New York to see Kline at his office, a town house on East Sixty-Ninth Street in Manhattan. Ray promised Joy that after he took Kline's medications he would "be a new man." In Kline's waiting room, patients told stories of miraculous recoveries. They were so devoted to Kline that they "felt he was God," a colleague recalled. Kline was said to have more depressives in his private practice than any other doctor in New York, but he spent little time with them and much of the work was done by assistants. In a paper in the *Proceedings of the American Philosophical Society*, Kline boasted that it was now possible for psychiatrists to see four patients in an hour. "The chemicals produce their effects, as elsewhere in medicine, without the psychiatrist necessarily being present," he wrote.

Ray's appointment with Kline lasted ten minutes. Kline prescribed Ray a low dose of Sinequan, an antidepressant developed shortly after iproniazid. Ray tried the medication for a few weeks, but when it didn't seem to improve his outlook, he stopped. He dismissed Kline's clinic as a "cookbook-type operation."

RAY FELT THAT he'd carefully built a good life—the kind he'd never imagined he could achieve but, on another level, felt secretly entitled to—and with a series of impulsive decisions had thrown it away. "All I seemed to be able to do was to talk, talk, talk about my losses," he wrote.

He found that food tasted rotten, as if it had been soaked in seawater. Sex was no longer pleasurable either. He could only "participate mechanically," without "a sense of enjoyment or transportation," he wrote in his memoir.

Ray and Greenspan, his colleague, used to browse music stores together after work, trying out different instruments. Greenspan's wife, Bonnie, told me, "He wouldn't just play the notes of the song—he really played beautifully, and nothing else he did in life had that nuance." But even music gradually lost its appeal.

Ray began to threaten suicide. Worn down by his help-lessness, Greenspan and Joy gave him an ultimatum: if he didn't check into a hospital, Joy would file for divorce and Greenspan would leave the practice. Ray reluctantly agreed. He decided on Chestnut Lodge, which was then run by Dex-ter Jr., the founder's grandson. Ray had read about the hospi-tal in Joanne Greenberg's bestselling 1964 autobiographical novel, *I Never Promised You a Rose Garden*, which tells the story of her treatment with Fromm-Reichmann. The book is a kind of ode to the power of psychoanalytic insight. "The symptoms and the sickness and the secrets have many rea-sons for being," Greenberg, who had been diagnosed with schizophrenia, wrote. "If it were not so, we could give you a nice shot of this or that drug." But, she wrote, "these symp-toms are built of many needs and serve many purposes, and that is why getting them away makes so much suffering."

RAY TOOK A leave of absence from his business and checked into the Lodge on January 2, 1979—a time of year, following the loneliness and forced joy of the holidays, when many psy-chiatric admissions occur. It was a damp, overcast day. Ray's stepfather drove him up a road lined with white rocks, past fields dotted with garden gnomes. In the parking lot, carved wooden signs for each psychiatrist's car gave "the overall ef-fect of a row of crosses," Ray observed. "Almost like a ceme-tery." The building's exterior was stately, but inside the floors were linoleum, and the windows were lined with iron bars. Ceiling lamps were covered in wire cages. In a loud and frantic voice, Ray told his stepfather, "I don't care to stay here." But his stepfather said he could not allow him to go home.

Ray's roommate, who was being treated for sexual perversions, told Ray that he was lucky: Manuel Ross, the psychoanalyst to whom Ray had been assigned, was considered one of the best analysts at the Lodge. Wiry, with a graying mustache and a widow's peak, Ross had worked at the Lodge for sixteen years.

During Ray's first few weeks of therapy, Ross tried to reassure him that his life was not over, but Ray would only "pull back and become more distant, become more repetitive," Ross later told his colleagues. Hoping to improve Ray's insight, Ross interrupted Ray when he became self-pitying. "Cut the shit!" he told him. When Ray described his life as a tragedy, Ross said, "None of this is tragic. You are not heroic enough to be tragic."

During one analytic session, when Ray began to grasp that the problems in his life were of his own making, he was "just in utter pain at the idea that it wasn't external forces but was inside himself," Ross said. "And he called out in a very dour voice, 'I'm lying midway between Eros and Thanatos on my bed and trying to decide whether I want to live or die.'"

ALTHOUGH THE LODGE'S philosophy was that every patient deserved understanding, Ray's medical records suggest that his doctors did not like him. At a staff conference a few months after he arrived, a psychologist, Rebecca Rieger, said that after spending time with Ray (who described his upbringing as "a caricature of a Jewish immigrant family"), she had a pounding headache. "The time that I spent with the patient left me more exhausted than I have been, I think, with any other patient," she said. Ray was so agitated that, in order to administer a Rorschach test, she had to walk beside him as he paced.

"He is like ten patients in one," a social worker complained.

Rieger wondered if Ray had a "possible delusion," because "he kept talking about the brain, as though he might have some thoughts that there was something wrong with his brain in a physical sense."

Robert Gruber, the director of admissions, said that Ray had come to the Lodge only because he'd been pressured by his wife, whom Gruber had met once and liked. "If she has any sense, she probably will not maintain" the relationship, Gruber said at the meeting. "I guess what I am trying to bring out is the destructive element and that maybe this is how he will do with us—destroy our availability to him as he has destroyed her availability to him."

Ross agreed. "He treats women as if they are the containers for his anxiety and are there to indulge him and pat his hand whenever he's in pain," he said. "And he does that with me, too, you know—'You don't know what pain I'm in. How can you do this to me?'" Ross said that he had already warned Ray, "With your history of destructiveness, sooner or later you are going to try to destroy the treatment with me." Nevertheless, Ross was confident that if Ray "does stay in treatment for five or ten years, he may get a good result out of it."

"Five to ten years is about right," another psychiatrist said.

The hospital's clinical director said he hoped staff members weren't treating Ray with disdain. "I had some sense hearing people talk today that people think he is in some way kind of a bad person who talks like he's a big shot and sort of feel that he really isn't very important and big and to hell with him." He said that Ray seemed to him "very much a genuine little boy."

"I like him very much and I like working with him," Ross clarified. "He is quite a creative person. Perhaps he is so creative he won't even—he can't even be nailed down to one diagnosis. But it is mixed because, for example, he will say, 'You've got to tell me what to do.' And I say, 'Your main job is to sit on your ass and not do anything at all. Just sit here and don't do anything. Let us take care of you. Don't move at all.'"

A FEW YEARS before Ray entered the hospital, Dexter Bullard III, the great-grandson of the founder of the Lodge, hanged himself in his parents' house. He was a senior in high school and would have been the next in line to take over the family business. At the time, he had been seeing a psychoanalyst. Dexter Jr. once said, "If only I'd had my son with a modern psychiatrist, instead of an analyst who didn't believe in medications, he might still be alive," Ann-Louise Silver, a psychiatrist at the Lodge, recalled.

The doctors at the Lodge were split into two camps: Dexter Jr. was part of a contingent that was ready to embrace medications, but Ross and others there wanted to preserve the Lodge's original vision. Ross believed that, if Ray just worked harder to understand himself, he could start to recover. But over the course of more than half a year at the Lodge, Ray's losses became increasingly concrete. Joy had stopped returning Ray's calls months earlier, and she had filed for divorce. His ex-wife, who was still in Europe with their sons, had petitioned a judge to restrict his visitation rights. According to his contract, a new director of his dialysis clinic would be installed if he was absent for more than a year. Given his pace of improvement, it was unlikely he would meet the deadline.

In therapy, Ray felt as if "a mirror was being held up to me . . . a mirror for me to look and see what I was," and he was dismayed by the image. He asked Ross, "Will I ever grow old with my children around me?" In his memoir, he wrote that Ross replied, "You, a patriarch? How absurd. How utterly absurd. You, a patriarch? Ha, ha ha."

DISILLUSIONED BY THE LODGE, Ray's mother decided to transfer him to Silver Hill, a hospital in New Canaan, Connecticut, that had embraced the use of antidepressants. On August 1, 1979, she and her husband drove Ray to the airport, accompanied by two orderlies from the Lodge. At the airport, his mother cried quietly, covering her mouth with her handkerchief. According to the orderlies, Ray continued to talk about his losses at the airport and on the plane, even when his stepfather told him to wait until they landed, because he was inaudible above the engine's noise.

Surrounded by rolling green hills, the grounds at Silver Hill were "elegantly, beautifully manicured," Ray wrote in his memoir. Patients lived in cottages with white clapboard walls, flagstone paths, and trellises covered with wisteria. According to a 1964 paper in *Trends in Psychiatry*, the hospital was populated by business executives, surgeons, artists, and a "sprinkling of under-achieving and guilt-ridden college students of good family" who were encouraged "to find nonpathological topics of conversation." But, the article added, "here or there, to be sure, one sees other things: a beautiful woman whose beauty is spoiled by tic-like blinking, a tall fine-looking young man who bursts into boisterous and meaningless laughter."

Ray's new psychiatrist at Silver Hill, Joan Narad, immediately prescribed him two medications: Thorazine, to calm his agitation and sleeplessness, and Elavil, an antidepressant discovered in 1960. Her impression of him, she said, was as a "vulnerable person who desperately wanted a relationship with his boys."

On Ray's first evening at Silver Hill, he gave a nurse his wedding ring. "I don't need it anymore," he said. He described himself as "a homeless man with only a mother." The next morning, he called his mom and said, "This institution and a lot of pills can't change things." He felt like he was "floating in space in no definite direction." At times, he lost his balance; he had to hold on to furniture and walls.

On his seventh day, he told the nurses he wished to change his name and disappear somewhere. On his eighth day, he said, "I give myself another year or two to live. I hope to die quickly of a coronary in my sleep."

After three weeks there, he woke up in the morning, sat in an armchair, and drank a mug of steaming coffee. He read the newspaper. Then he called his psychiatric aide into his room. "Something is happening to me," he told her. "Something has changed." He felt a "terrible sadness," an emotion that he realized had previously been inaccessible. He hadn't seen his sons in almost a year, and he started to cry—the first time he'd done so in months. He thought he'd already been grieving his separation from his sons, but now he realized that what he'd been experiencing wasn't anything as alive as grief: it was "beyond feeling," he wrote. "It is a total absence of feeling."

THE FIRST EXTENDED report of a patient responding to anti-depressants was written by Roland Kuhn, a Swiss psychiatrist, in 1956:

> For three days now, it is as if the patient had under-gone a transformation. All of her restlessness and ag-itation has vanished. Yesterday, she herself observed that she had been in a complete muddle, that she had never acted so dumb in all her life. She did not know what had caused her behavior, but she was just glad to be better.

Kuhn was Nathan Kline's rival in the race to develop antidepressants. In the mid-1950s, working in a public hospital in a remote Swiss village, Kuhn began experimenting with a compound known as G22355 (later called imipramine). He gave it to some of his patients with schizophrenia, but instead of becoming peaceful, as he'd hoped, they were agitated and excited. One escaped from the hospital at night, still wearing pajamas, and rode a bike into town, singing loudly.

Kuhn concluded that the drug induced a state of euphoria, so he tried giving it to depressed patients instead. Six days later, he noticed that his patients were developing new interests "whereas previously they were continually tortured by the same fixed idea." When he asked them about their preoccupations, they told him, "I don't think of it anymore," or "The thought doesn't enter my head now." It appeared to

Kuhn that the drug "completely restores . . . what is of prime importance, the power to experience."

Kuhn was part of the phenomenological school of psychiatry, a movement, inspired by philosophers like Martin Heidegger and Edmund Husserl, that aimed to study the experience of mental illness on its own terms—without the interference of preexisting theories. Instead of focusing on signature signs of mental illness, like hallucinations or fatigue, these psychiatrists focused on the slippery sorts of experiences that can't be easily named: the way that illness changes one's sense of time and space (for instance, the ability to trust that a sidewalk is solid and won't simply dissolve into air). Their project was to describe, rather than to explain. Kuhn defined the method as "letting the things themselves speak." "Only when this happens," Kuhn wrote, can there be "a true relationship between patient and physician, a relationship between two human beings."

Kuhn was skeptical of the way that other psychiatrists measured mental experiences with questionnaires, narrowing mental life to a set of symptoms. He criticized Nathan Kline for treating the brain as if it were "a machine that just runs faster or slower." A psychiatrist, Kuhn wrote, must understand that he is "not dealing with a self-contained, rigid object, but with an individual who is involved in constant movement and change." Sometimes, Kuhn said, after taking medications his patients realized they had been ill for much longer than they had known; they began to reassess who they had been all along.

But Kuhn's perspective did not gain traction. Nicholas Weiss, the author of one of the few English-language papers on Kuhn, told me, "There was a moment at the beginning of psychopharmacology when there was an attempt to create a capacious perspective—to study the lived world of the suffering individual, and the way psychopharmacology changed it—but mainstream medicine in America cut out that perspective. And the cutting out of that perspective was presented as scientific progress." Doctors left behind the study of less measurable aspects of human experience—a parallel life for psychiatry itself.

ONCE RAY TOOK ANTIDEPRESSANTS, he regained his sense of humor, his generosity, and his passion for literature and music. A nurse wrote that he had "a warm, sensitive aspect to his disposition—especially towards his children." Narad, his psychiatrist, said, "A new human being began to emerge."

The poet Jane Kenyon describes a similar metamorphosis. After years of feeling as if "a piece of burned meat / wears my clothes, speaks / in my voice," her doctor proposed that she try an antidepressant. "With the wonder / and bitterness of someone pardoned / for a crime she did not commit / I come back to marriage and friends," she wrote. "What hurt me so terribly / all my life until this moment?"

Ray began spending time with another patient, a woman his age. He felt as if he and the woman were characters in *David and Lisa*, a 1962 movie about a tender relationship between two adolescents at a school for the mentally ill—one is afraid of touch, the other speaks only in rhymes. With a day pass from the hospital, Ray took a bus to downtown New Canaan, bought a bottle of champagne, and knocked on the woman's door. They spent the night together. "The act of making love," he wrote, "was not so much sexual or biological, but it was an act of defiance, a reaching out, a groping, a grabbing back of our humanness."

Ray began spending hours reading in the hospital's psychiatric library. He was shaken by a 1975 memoir, *A Season in Hell,* by Percy Knauth, a former *New York Times* correspondent who was suicidal until he took antidepressants. "Within a week the miracle began to happen," Knauth wrote. "No fears, no worries, no guilt feelings. I looked out of my window at a gray November day and I thought I had never seen a more beautiful world. For the first time in more than a year I felt good!" He added, "There is little doubt that I had been suffering from a norepinephrine imbalance," which was at the time a theory for the source of depression, one that has since been largely discarded.

The chemical-imbalance theory was first described in 1965 by Joseph Schildkraut, a scientist at the National Institute of Mental Health, in what became the most frequently cited paper in *The American Journal of Psychiatry.* Reviewing antidepressant studies and clinical trials in both animals and humans, Schildkraut proposed that the drugs increased the availability of the neurotransmitters dopamine, norepinephrine, and serotonin—which play a role in the regulation of mood—at receptor sites in the brain. He reasoned backward: if antidepressants worked on those neurotransmitters, then depression may be caused by their deficiency. He presented the theory as a hypothesis—"at best a reductionistic oversimplification of a very complex biological state," he wrote.

Nevertheless, the theory gave rise to a new way of talking about the self: fluctuations in brain chemicals were at the root of people's moods. The framework redefined what constituted self-knowledge. "The new style of thought," wrote the British sociologist Nikolas Rose, "not only establishes what counts as an explanation, it establishes what there is to explain. The deep psychological space that opened in the twentieth century has flattened out." He went on, "This is a shift in human ontology—in the kinds of persons we take ourselves to be."

At Chestnut Lodge, Ray had been lacking in insight, but at Silver Hill, where a different model of illness prevailed, he was an eager student of his condition. He began working on a memoir of his illness. On one page of the manuscript, he drew an annotated illustration of his floor at the Lodge. "My pacing path is delineated by the arrows," he explained. To research the book, he read medical literature on depression, a disease he now saw as "exquisitely curable." He felt relieved by the idea that the past two years of his life could be explained with one word.

After a month at Silver Hill, Ray reconsidered his plan to give up his dialysis business. "Somehow, some alteration in my chemistry, was giving me the will to fight," he wrote in the memoir. One night, he got out of bed at 2:30 a.m., paced around the room, and then put on a suit and tie. He asked an aide, "Do I look like a doctor?"

He called his colleague Robert Greenspan, who had doubled his own salary while Ray was gone, to share his news: He was ready to return to work. He no longer wanted to sell the business. On the phone, Ray said that he heard a "funny strange hesitating silence."

~~~~~~~~~~

Ray was discharged from Silver Hill after three months of treatment. It had been nearly a year since he had lived outside the confines of an institution. He returned to an empty house. Joy had already moved out with their son, taking most of the furniture. His other sons were still in Europe.

Ray showed up unannounced at his dialysis clinic. Patients embraced him and shook his hand; some of the nurses kissed him. But newer employees, hired by Greenspan while Ray had been away, kept their distance. Word had spread that he'd been in a mental institution. In the break room, the head nurse described Ray as a "lunatic" and "incompetent." A secretary observed that he asked rudimentary questions about how to work a dialysis machine. "People were coming to me saying, 'Did you see what he did? Did you see what he did?'" Greenspan said. "I would say, 'Write it down.'"

Greenspan was upset that Ray had failed to complete his course of treatment at the Lodge. He assumed that Silver Hill had merely done a "patch-up job." He quit and opened a competing practice in the same building. Many of Ray's patients and employees migrated there, too. News of Ray's illness—and the rift with Greenspan—spread throughout the medical community, and he stopped getting referrals. Sometimes, he didn't have enough patients to fill a day of work. Separated from his sons and barely working, Ray felt as if he'd lost the "trappings that identified me as a person existing in the world."

IN 1980, the year after he was released from Silver Hill, Ray read the entire *Diagnostic and Statistical Manual of Mental Disorders*. The third edition had just been published. The first two editions had been slim pamphlets, not taken particularly seriously. Diagnoses were unreliable and variable, depending on doctor and context. But for the new version, a committee appointed by the American Psychiatric Association worked to make the manual more objective and universal by cleansing it of psychoanalytic explanations, like the idea that depression is an "excessive reaction" to an "internal conflict." Now that medications had been shown to be effective—lithium helped for mania, Thorazine for schizophrenia, and imipramine and other drugs for depression—the experiences that gave rise to a condition seemed less relevant. Mental illnesses were redefined according to what could be seen from the outside, a checklist of behavioral symptoms. Melvin Sabshin, the medical director of the American Psychiatric Association, declared that the new *DSM* represented a triumph of "science over ideology."

The clinical language of the *DSM-III* relieved Ray's sense of isolation; his despair had been a disease, which he shared with millions of people. Ray was so energized by the new way of thinking about depression that he scheduled interviews with leading biological psychiatrists as research for his memoir, which he titled *A Symbolic Death*. He subtitled the memoir, *The Untold Story of One of the Most Shameful Scandals in American Psychiatric History (It Happened to Me)*.

But Ray despaired that he didn't even have the "literary legerdemain to evoke sympathy" for himself. "Who wants to hear a Horatio Alger story in reverse?" he asked. Throughout his memoir, he repeatedly gave himself pep talks. "You must tell this story," he reminded himself. "Others will listen and there will be between you, the teller and others—the listeners—a bond, a sense of community, that will make you once again feel like you are walking in step with the human race."

Ray sent a draft of his memoir to the psychiatrist Gerald Klerman, who had recently stepped down as the head of the federal government's Alcohol, Drug Abuse, and Mental Health Administration. Klerman had written disparagingly of what he called "pharmacological Calvinism": the belief that "if a drug makes you feel good, it's either somehow morally wrong, or you're going to pay for it with dependence, liver damage, chromosomal change, or some other form of secular theological retribution." Ray said that Klerman told him that his manuscript was "fascinating and compelling."

Emboldened by Klerman's approval, Ray decided to sue

Chestnut Lodge for negligence and malpractice, and he began looking for experts to testify on his behalf. He mailed part of his memoir to Frank Ayd, who had conducted the first clinical trial of Elavil, the antidepressant that Ray was taking. Ayd had described the emergence of psychopharmacology as a "blessing for mankind," one of the "most important and dramatic epics in the history of medicine itself." In his book *Recognizing the Depressed Patient*, from 1961, which became a bestseller, Ayd wrote that "no advantage is gained by an intellectual understanding of the psychological aspects of the illness."

After meeting Ray, Ayd felt confident he was "dealing with a sincere honest individual who was in remission from depression" and agreed to serve as an expert for a lawsuit. Not long after, Ray filed the suit, arguing that, because the Lodge failed to treat his depression, he had lost his medical practice, his reputation in the medical community, and custody of his children. Ray's friend Andy Seewald told me that Ray often compared himself to Ahab in *Moby-Dick*. "The Lodge was his white whale," he said. "He was searching for the thing that had unmanned him."

NO PSYCHIATRIC MALPRACTICE lawsuit has attracted more prominent expert witnesses than Ray's, according to Alan Stone, the former president of the American Psychiatric Association. The case became "the organizing nidus" around which leading biological psychiatrists "pushed their agenda," he told me.

In addition to Klerman and Ayd, Ray recruited Bernard Carroll, a professor of psychiatry at Duke who had invented a test (which is no longer used) for diagnosing depression by measuring adrenal-gland function. Ray also persuaded Donald Klein, a psychiatrist who served on the committee that wrote the *DSM-III*, to testify. Klein believed that the Lodge psychiatrists had, like many in the field, failed to rise to the demands of science. "If the diagnosis and treatment of patients is not an applied science, then what is it?" he asked at a conference. "An art form? A philosophical construction? A ballet?"

At a hearing before an arbitration panel, which would determine whether the case could proceed to trial, Ray's experts tried to define the new space that biological psychiatry had claimed.

"Psychiatrists have become—I refer to ourselves sometimes as 'medical intranauts,'" Ayd said.

"Medical what?" said a lawyer for the Lodge.

"Intra-nauts," Ayd said. "We're exploring the inner spaces of man."

"You're still in an exploratory area, aren't you?"

"We will, I'm sure, be exploring for the next hundred years," Ayd said. "We've been exploring for two thousand or so."

"Doctor, you can tell me yes or no," another Lodge lawyer asked. "Isn't it correct that one of the benefits of psychotherapy is trying to make persons look at themselves?"

"To make a person look at himself when he's in no condition to do so," Ayd said, "can be a very dangerous thing to do."

THROUGHOUT THE HEARING, which lasted two weeks, the Lodge presented Ray's attempt to medicalize his depression as an abdication of responsibility. In a written report, one of the Lodge's expert witnesses, Thomas Gutheil, a professor of psychiatry at Harvard, observed that the language of the lawsuit, much of which Ray had drafted himself, exemplified Ray's struggle with "'externalization,' that is, the tendency to blame one's problems on others." Gutheil concluded that Ray's "insistence on the biological nature of his problem is not only disproportionate but seems to me to be yet another attempt to move the problem away from himself: it is not I, it's my biology."

The Lodge's experts attributed Ray's recovery at Silver Hill at least in part to his romantic entanglement with a female patient, which gave him a jolt of self-esteem.

"It's a demeaning comment," Ray responded when he testified. "And it just speaks to the whole total disbelief in the legitimacy of the symptomatology and the disease." He said, "I'm not going to deny that I have had difficulties in living. I have looked at myself and examined myself from the viewpoint of a man who knows a lot about psychiatry now. Am I a narcissist? Am I really this? Am I not this? What am I?"

The Lodge lawyers tried to chip away at Ray's description of depression, arguing that he'd shown moments of pleasure at the Lodge, like when he played piano.

"The sheer mechanical banging of ragtime rhythms on that dilapidated old piano on the ward was almost an act of agitation rather than a creative pleasurable act of producing music," Ray responded. "Just because I played Ping-Pong, or had a piece of pizza, or smiled, or may have made a joke, or made googly eyes at a good-looking girl, it did not mean that I was capable of truly sustaining pleasurable feelings." He went on, "I would say to myself, 'I am living, but I am not alive.'"

Manuel Ross testified for more than eight hours. He had read a draft of Ray's memoir and he rejected the possibility that Ray had been cured by antidepressants. He was not a recovered man, because he was still holding on to the past. "That's what I call melancholia as used in the 1913 article," he said, referring to Freud's "Mourning and Melancholia."

Ross said that he had hoped that Ray would develop insight at the Lodge. "That's the true support," he said, "if one understands what is going on in one's life." He wanted Ray to let go of his need to be a star doctor, the richest and most powerful in his field, and to accept a life in which he was one of the "ordinary mortals who labor in the medical vineyard."

Ray's lawyer, Philip Hirschkop, one of the most prominent civil rights attorneys in the country, asked Ross, "As an analyst, do you have to sometimes look inside yourself to make sure you're not reacting to your own feelings about someone?"

"Oh yes," Ross said. "Oh yes." He took off his glasses and rested a tip of the frame between his lips.

"You who've locked yourself into one position for nineteen years with no advancement in position other than salary, might you be a little resentful of this man who makes so much more money, and now he's here as your patient?" Hirschkop asked.

"That's possible, sure," Ross said. "You have to take that into account—there's no question about that. I think that's your own kind of psychological work that you do on yourself. Am I being envious of this? Or am I describing the grandiosity just out of envy and spite? But I don't think I was doing that."

"Would you infer, fairly, that someone who locked themself into the same job for nineteen years might lack some ambition?"

"No, Mr. Hirschkop," Ross said. "I like the work I'm doing. I find it continually stimulating."

ON DECEMBER 23, 1983, the arbitration panel concluded
that Chestnut Lodge had violated the standard of care. The
case could proceed to trial. Joel Paris, a professor of psychiatry at McGill University, wrote that "the outcome of the
Osheroff case was discussed in every academic department
of psychiatry in North America." *The New York Times* wrote
that the case shook "the conventional belief, held even by
some doctors, that chronic depression is not an illness, but
merely a character flaw." According to *The Philadelphia Inquirer*, the case could "determine to a great extent how psychiatry would be practiced in the United States."

But shortly before the case was to go to trial, in 1987,
Chestnut Lodge offered to settle for $350,000. By then, Ray
was dating a high school classmate, Mauricette, who was the
widow of a psychoanalyst. She didn't like the way that Ray's
case pitted one school of psychiatry against the other. "It's
much too simplistic," she told me. "One school does not sup-
plant the other." Ray decided to settle the case and move on.

The country's most prominent psychiatrists continued to
treat the case as psychoanalysis's final reckoning. In a 1990
paper in *The American Journal of Psychiatry*, Gerald Klerman,
one of Ray's expert witnesses, wrote that psychiatrists had
an obligation to tell patients their diagnosis and to explain
treatment decisions by citing randomized studies. This duty
would function, Klerman said, as the medical equivalent of a
"Miranda rule"—the law requiring police to read suspects
a list of their rights so they can make an informed choice
about whether to speak.

Klerman was an advocate of what was then a fledgling

movement for evidence-based medicine, a model requiring that clinical decisions be based on randomized trials of treatment methods. The concept was first sketched out in the 1972 book *Effectiveness and Efficiency* by the Scottish epidemiologist Archibald Cochrane, who argued, as one textbook put it, that "nothing could be said of any treatment until the first patient had been randomized in a scientific study." Within the decade, randomized clinical studies emerged as the most trusted form of medical knowledge, supplanting the authority of individual case studies. When the director of the Centre for Evidence-Based Medicine in Oxford, England, was asked by *The New York Times* to explain how this new emphasis might transform the art of medicine, he responded, "Art kills."

Ray's doctor at Silver Hill, Joan Narad, told me that she was pained by the conclusions that people drew from Ray's story. "The case was used to increase polarity," she said. In his memoir, Ray wrote, "Although a 'cottage industry' devoted to commenting on the meaning of the world-famous Osheroff case continues to flourish, not one of the scholars had sought to interview the living primary source—me!"

The American Psychiatric Association held a panel on Ray's case at its annual conference in 1989, and Ray showed up with his oldest son, Sam, with whom he had reunited, to watch. Narad was there too, and she showed Sam pages of Ray's medical records where he had expressed his longing to see his children. "I told him, 'I just want you to know that your father tried to reach you—he loved you and was desperate to see you,'" Narad said.

But Sam and his younger brother, Joe, did not forgive their father. They believed he had latched on to the wrong explanations for why his life had gone off course. "My father had this gregarious, kind, brilliant side to him, but he never addressed his problems," Joe told me. "He kept telling the same repetitive story." As Joe saw it, his father would have been less depressed had he been able to pursue his childhood dream of becoming a musician, rather than studying medicine, the field that Ray's father had chosen for him. Sam and Joe wanted to devote their careers to theater, and they found it ironic when their father urged them to find a more respectable field, like business or law. Joe said, "Here's a guy who just wanted to play music—that's all he wanted to do—and he has two kids and all they want to do is plays. He perpetuated the patterning that he learned as a child."

AFTER RAY'S CASE, the Lodge began prescribing medication for nearly all of its patients. "We had to conform," Richard Waugaman, a Lodge psychiatrist, told me. "It wasn't always about whether it was going to help the patient. It was about whether it would protect us from another lawsuit."

The Lodge doctors felt chastened by a long-term study, published in 1984 in the *Archives of General Psychiatry*, that followed more than four hundred patients who had been treated at the Lodge between 1950 and 1975. Only a third of schizophrenic patients had improved or recovered—roughly the same percentage of patients shown at that time to recover in any treatment setting. What distinguished those who led productive lives from those who remained ill seemed unrelated to anything that had happened at the Lodge. At a symposium attended by five hundred doctors, the study's coauthor Thomas McGlashan, a psychiatrist at the Lodge, announced, "The data is in. The experiment failed."

For years, patients at the Lodge had their care covered through private insurance plans—there were also some, the so-called golden geese, who paid out of pocket—but in the early nineties, managed care came to dominate the insurance industry. To contain costs, insurance companies required doctors to submit treatment plans for review and show evidence that patients were making measurable progress. Long, elegant narratives of patients' struggles were replaced by checklists of symptoms. Mental-health care had to be treated as a commodity, rather than as a collaboration. Psychiatrists at the Lodge still held long meetings in which they analyzed each patient, but Kalyna Bullard, Dexter Jr.'s daughter-in-law, who worked as the hospital's general counsel, told me, "They were no longer getting paid for it."

The doctor–patient relationship, which the Lodge viewed as an enchanted bond—a cure for loneliness—was remade by the language of corporate culture. Psychiatrists became "providers" and patients were "consumers" whose suffering was summarized with diagnoses from the DSM. "Madness has become an industrialized product to be managed efficiently and rationally in a timely manner," wrote the anthropologist Alistair Donald, in an essay called "The Wal-Marting of American Psychiatry." "The real patient has been replaced by behavioral descriptions and so has become unknown."

As older analysts retired, the Lodge hired a new generation of doctors and social workers who were more enthusiastic about medications. But Karen Bartholomew, the former director of social work there, told me it was frustrating when staff members, dismissing the psychiatry of earlier eras, said, "We're so much better now." Increasingly, she said, patients showed up at the Lodge "on five or six different medications, and who knows what's working at that point?" She said, "I'm just waiting for the next opportunity to evolve, because this isn't working either—not in this country."

In 1995, Dexter Bullard Jr. died, and no one in the next generation of Bullards wanted to take over. The hospital was sold to a community-health nonprofit organization that soon drove the Lodge into bankruptcy. Ann-Louise Silver, the Lodge psychiatrist, believes that the suicide of Bullard's son and the changes it spawned—the turn to medications, the vacuum in leadership—"led to the death of the hospital." While Dexter Jr. was "grieving for his son," she told me, "many of us were grieving the old Lodge." By the late nineties, the buildings at the Lodge were falling apart. Silver said that one of her patients was on the third floor of the hospital when honey dripped on her face. On the ceiling were beehives.

By the hospital's final day, April 27, 2001, only eight patients remained. Some of the staff offered to forfeit their paychecks in order to keep the Lodge open a little longer. They also considered buying a property from the 1700s and creating a new hospital called Rosegarden Lodge, after *I Never Promised You a Rose Garden*. "We are not so different from our patients," Robert Kurtz, a psychiatrist at the Lodge, told *Psychiatric News* at the time. "We are rather chronic and stubborn and idealistic. We just don't give up!" But the plan never came to fruition. "A great listing lighthouse finally crashed into the advancing tide," Silver wrote.

Ray's psychoanalyst, Manuel Ross, worked at the Lodge until it shut down. Christopher Keats, the Lodge's director of psychotherapy in the late nineties, told me that Ross "remained himself: he kept working in the same way that he always had." When I called Ross, he told me he did not want to talk about Ray's case: "I have never discussed it—even privately," he said. "I think it's a cardinal principle of psychiatry, and even the priesthood: nothing is revealed."

The Lodge, like many mental asylums in the country, was abandoned. A local paper described the property as a gathering spot for "ghost hunters," driven by "tales of the paranormal and other hauntings." Then, in the summer of 2009, for reasons that were never determined, the Lodge's main building burned to the ground.

~~~~~~~~~

In 2013, I came across an article in *Psychiatric Times* titled "A Belated Obituary," a brief commemoration of Ray's life. He had died the year before the obituary was written, and his death had passed unnoticed. The author of the obituary could find almost no personal information beyond Ray's Facebook page: his profile image was the cover of a psychology book from 1986 called *Finding Our Fathers: How a Man's Life Is Shaped by His Relationship with His Father.*

I had seen brief references to Ray's case in psychiatric texts (in one, Ray was described as a man who, before his depression, had "everything in the world a person could want"), and I wondered how he made sense of the fact that his life and legacy had been defined by the clash between two opposing theories of his mind. I got in touch with Philip Hirschkop, Ray's former lawyer, and he invited me to his house in Lorton, Virginia, to read more than a dozen bankers boxes of Ray's files that he kept in his garage. Among the court and medical records, there were several drafts of Ray's unpublished memoir. He had revised it for more than thirty years. The prose alternated between grandiosity and self-abasement. "I have become a historic figure," he wrote. "I am the man that everyone knows about but no one knows."

After settling his lawsuit, Ray had moved to Scarsdale, New York, with Mauricette, but, after a few years, he felt that the relationship had "no content," and he got another divorce. In a draft of his memoir, Ray modified his definition of depression: "This is not an illness, it is not a sickness—it is a state of disconnection." He had started seeing a psychoanalyst again. He referred to this analyst as the "good father" (whereas Ross, he wrote, had been the bad one). Ray believed that if the Lodge had treated him with medications he might have never needed therapy, but now, he wrote, he had "lost the framework on which to build anything."

Following the collapse of his marriage with Mauricette, Ray moved to Cranford, New Jersey, to live with another former high school classmate, Paula, even though he found her tiresome and bland. He worked at a nephrology clinic near Cranford for a year, but, like the Lodge doctors, he felt constrained by the dictates of managed care: his supervisor reprimanded him when he spent more than twenty minutes with a patient. After a year, his contract wasn't renewed, and he "began to float around in entry-level positions," as he described it in a letter. "Can you imagine what it would be like to be ashamed to have your children see you this way—that you would want to run away from them?" he wrote.

Ray's oldest two sons, Joe and Sam, both became actors. When Ray visited them, he overwhelmed them with a repetitious account of how Chestnut Lodge had derailed his life. He also gave them new revisions of his memoir. "The book, the book," Joe said. "That's all he wanted to talk about." When Sam's first child was born, Ray showed up with a revised draft of his memoir and seemed more interested in discussing his writing than in meeting his granddaughter. Sam said that his father told him, "The memoir is going to blow people away. They're going to make a movie of this." He and Joe stopped returning their father's calls. Ray's youngest son was already estranged.

The memoir swelled to five hundred pages. The early

drafts had been textured and vibrant. But after three de-cades of revision, there was something oppressive and dis-honest about the writing, a tale of revenge. Perhaps the only improvement was Ray's portrait of his own father, who had been absent in early drafts. Now he revealed that his father may have abused him. His father's death became the primal scene. In their final encounter, Ray's dad berated him for not taking out the trash. "Suddenly, I'm aware of my anger to-wards him, and, no longer physically afraid of his rage, the thought of striking my father briefly enters my conscious-ness," Ray wrote. "The forbidden thought, though quickly suppressed, horrifies me." Ray ran out of the door without saying goodbye. Later that day, his father, who was forty-five, had a heart attack and died. Ray was responsible for identify-ing his body in the morgue.

"So what does this story add up to?" Ray asked. "How can I define myself? Who is Ray Osheroff now?" He had been taking psychiatric medications for three decades, but he still felt rootless and alone. "There is a painful gulf be-tween what is and what should have been," he wrote. He was an "unremedied man." Two different stories about his illness, the psychoanalytic and the neurobiological, had failed him. Now he was hopeful that he would be saved by a new story, the memoir he was writing. If he just framed the story right or found the right words, he felt he could "finally reach the shore of the land of healing," he wrote. "There will be a her-meneutic in your personal tragedy. You may be able to finally reconstruct a new legacy for yourself. Do it quickly! The hour draws near!"

IN THE EARLY 2000s, Ray got a job giving electrodiagnostic tests to patients who had been in car accidents. He analyzed electrical activity produced by people's muscles and nerves, to determine whether they had been injured. He may have started the work with good intentions, but soon he was working for clinics that exploited no-fault auto insurance policies that covered medical expenses. Some of the patients may not have been in accidents at all. In a conversation that he recorded with a new therapist, he complained, "I'm doing fake work. I am generating fake reports for fake accidents." He felt like "a hollow man, a simulacrum." After a day of work, he couldn't bear to spend time with Paula, whose idea of pleasure, he said, was going to a dinner party with Kosher Chinese food. "I can't go home to her. 'What's the matter, honey? You want to watch television with me?' I need to di-lute that experience."

When Paula and I spoke on the phone, she praised Ray's medical skills, telling me how impressed their friends were that he had two board certifications, in internal medicine and nephrology, and repeating a story four times about a man with cancer who had written Ray a letter, thanking him for sitting by his bed. But her description of his work was vague. "He did a certain kind of testing," she said. "Doc-tors that couldn't do it themselves, they'd call him and say, 'I heard you are very good with these tests—can you come to my office in the Bronx?'"

In early 2012, Ray told his friend Andy Seewald that his bank account had been frozen by federal investigators. The United States attorney's office was preparing racketeering charges against some three dozen people for a scheme to defraud medical insurance companies, and Ray suspected he would be indicted soon. He had recently been sued in a related case for billing automobile insurance companies for "illusory or medically-useless treatments," according to the complaint. Seewald said that Ray told him, "The shame is going to kill me."

Ray asked his middle son, Joe, whom he hadn't seen in more than ten years, to have dinner with him at an Italian restaurant in Manhattan's theater district. As Joe walked into the restaurant, he heard someone shout his name. "I looked over and saw my dad at a round table with at least eight or nine people, all of these Russian guys, taking pictures," Joe said. "They were like, 'We never thought we'd see the day when Dr. Osheroff reunited with his son!'" Ray stood up and made a speech. "Everybody got out their cell phones to record my dad," Joe said, "and at the end of the speech, my dad hands me this old tattered copy of this shitty book called *Finding Our Fathers*, and he's crying." Written by a Harvard psychologist, the book describes how a man's "unfinished business" with his father taints his relationships.

Everyone began eating. "And my dad sat down next to me and told me the story of Chestnut Lodge again, as if I'd never heard it," Joe said. "I froze. I just felt taken advantage of." Even when his father was trying to repair their relationship, his effort at emotional connection was swallowed up by the story he felt compelled to keep sharing.

Less than a month later, Seewald noticed that Ray, who was seventy-three, seemed unusually fatigued. "He kept saying, 'I have this awful feeling of deterioration. When I look in the mirror, I feel deteriorated.'" Two days later, Joe missed a call from his father while he was at a play in Manhattan. When the show was over, he listened to the voicemail: Ray's driver, who took him to clinics throughout the city so he could perform the electrodiagnostic tests, had left a message: Ray had died.

At the funeral, Sam and Joe noticed that the story of their

father's death kept evolving. Some people said he had fallen on his desk in his office and crushed his jaw. Others said he'd had a heart attack. The New Jersey *Star-Ledger* wrote that he had "passed away in his sleep." Paula told me that he had died in a bed in his office that he'd set up for snowy nights when he couldn't make it home. "Ray was supposed to come home that night, but he was very, very tired," she said.

After the funeral, Sam and Joe stayed up late, trying to sort through the different stories. They developed their own theory. They guessed that Ray was going to testify about his colleagues' criminal behavior. "I'm pretty sure my dad was murdered," Sam told me the first time we spoke. Joe said, "He was going to expose these dudes, and I think his handler took care of him. His legacy was that he became a disposable criminal."

No one else I spoke with believes Ray was killed, though Seewald briefly entertained the possibility of suicide. Ray's death certificate says "hypertensive cardiovascular disease." In the preceding month, he'd been hospitalized for fainting spells.

A psychoanalyst might say that Joe and Sam had killed off their father, just as Ray, in his memoir, had symbolically murdered his father by denying him the courtesy of saying goodbye. Not long before his death, Ray had read Freud's essays on Dostoevsky, one of Ray's favorite writers. In "Dostoevsky and Parricide," Freud writes that, when a son discovers that his father has been killed, "it is a matter of indifference who actually committed the crime; psychology is only concerned to know who desired it emotionally and who welcomed it when it was done."

Ray's memoir was left incomplete, the pages dispersed in the offices of different typists who had helped assemble the material. In the final drafts, he had searched for an overarching theory that explained why the life he'd wanted had ended forty years too early. One theory was that he was a man with a chemical imbalance. Another was that he was a boy deprived of a paternal model: "Underneath all of this," he wrote, "is there not the theme of the son in search of the father? Not the loss of a business. The loss of the father." A third was that he suffered from a kind of chronic loneliness—a condition that he characterized, quoting Fromm-Reichmann, as "such an intense and incommunicable experience that psychiatrists must describe it only in terms of people's defenses against it." But he also sensed that any story that resolved his problems too completely was untrue, an evasion of the unknown. "At the end of life, after having lost everything," he wrote, "I may be merely a crisp autumn leaf that blows away in a harsh October wind."

BAPU

"Is this difficulty I am facing the lesson
of total surrender?"

No astrologers were consulted before Bapu got married. Her family described the omission in hushed tones. Bapu's sisters had all exchanged horoscopes with their grooms, to determine their compatibility. But Bapu was a less appealing bride. She'd had polio as a child and walked with a limp. In a photograph circulated to suitors in 1960, Bapu wore her black hair in a braid to her waist and sat in a wooden chair, reading a book, her orthopedic shoe out of view. She was not in a position to be discriminating.

Her family was Brahmin, India's highest social caste, thought to be spiritually purer than the rest of the population. Bapu's father, a businessman and an eminent music critic, had bought her a stately colonial house in an upscale neighborhood in Chennai, South India, with the hope that the property would make her more desirable to suitors. The house had French windows, a red-tiled parapet, a long veranda, and a gated yard, and it sat on nearly an acre of land, surrounded by palm, mayflower, and mango trees. Before purchasing the house, her father consulted a priest versed in *vastu shastra* (the "science of architecture"), who warned that the property was not fit for a family. But her father ignored the advice. He named the house Amrita, nectar of immortality.

Bapu agreed to marry a suitor named Rajamani, a manager at an advertising company who was brawny with a chiseled jaw and dimpled chin. They moved into Amrita, but it was too large for one couple and quickly became a base for cousins, siblings, and friends who were studying or working in Chennai. Rajamani's brother moved in with his family and stayed for nearly a decade. In the new domestic hierarchy, Bapu was at the bottom. Every morning, she woke up by 5:00 a.m., took a cold bath, and put incense in the corners of the house. With rice flour, she drew a kolam, a geometrical diagram, outside the doorstep, to invite the sacred inside. While she menstruated, she was secluded in a corner of the house, prevented from cooking, worshipping, or touching men. On the other days of the month, she cooked what her husband and in-laws told her to. Her nephew Shyam, who lived there, said, "She never missed a heartbeat. She never missed a meal."

Bapu found her in-laws callous and judgmental. They mocked her for her weak leg, calling her *nondi*, a Tamil word for "lame." When she gave birth to her first child, a daughter named Bhargavi, her sister-in-law brought her a malted drink called Horlicks—marketed in India as "the Great Family Nourisher"—thought to be helpful for breastfeeding. But instead of making the drink with boiling water, her sister-in-law used water from the tap, a slight that Bapu dwelled on for years.

Bapu was turned off by her in-laws' preoccupation with money—a "scorpion" that was "always stinging me," she complained in her journal, written in Tamil. Her husband, Rajamani, came from a line of astrologer priests whose material needs had been met by the temple community where they worked, but his family had recently entered the urban middle class. Rajamani drew up detailed ledgers charting every domestic expense. "'What's the cost! What's the cost!' Ugh!" Bapu wrote. Rajamani built a smaller house on the property and moved his family there, renting out the original house to supplement his income. By then, Bapu had given birth to Bhargavi's brother, Karthik, after having had two miscarriages. As the wealthier member of the couple, Bapu was aware of the few realms in which she held power. "My husband considers me an enemy if he doesn't get my body or my money," she wrote.

In some wealthy Brahmin families in Chennai, it was customary, when the mango trees ripened each spring, for the most senior woman—the wife or mother-in-law—to distribute the fruit to relatives and friends, a complex social drama that gave rise to days of gossip. Bapu was disgusted that mangoes are "all my mother-in-law thinks of as salvation in this life," she wrote.

She began bringing her children to an ashram in Chennai to listen to lectures on the Bhagavad Gita, the Sanskrit scripture that unfolds as a dialogue between a prince and Lord Krishna, the Hindu god of tenderness and compassion. They sat on the floor as some sixty people gathered around a priest named Sri Anjam Madhavan Nambudiri, who led recitations of holy texts throughout India. Nambudiri wore saffron robes and a garland of flowers around his neck; his hair was black, and his beard, long and bushy, was white. He was a sannyasin, an ascetic who has given away his belongings and renounced the material world by holding his own funeral. Sannyasin are treated as the apogee of Hindu spirituality—they are said to have complete insight. They are not seeking insight into the workings of their own mind but into the nature of existence, their place in the cosmos.

Bapu began spending several hours a day in the prayer room, the one space in the house that she could claim as her own. It resembled a small closet, four by four feet. She bought new idols, flowers, bells, and incense for the room, even though in her family the prayer room was considered the man's domain. Bapu felt chosen—"The Lord's gracious hands have grabbed mine," she wrote in her journal—to lead a freer existence. She wanted to "immerse myself in the ocean of devotion, losing track of time." She didn't want to continue living what she called "a meaningless life." She was dismayed by the money spent at her wedding and by the idea that anything was her property. "This mind is yours!" she wrote to Krishna. "This speech is yours! This body is yours! Everything is yours!"

Bhargavi was jealous of the gods for consuming so much of her mother's attention. She and Karthik, who was two years younger than her, sometimes stood silently in the prayer room, just to be close to their mother. "She wouldn't mind—she would just ask us to sit down," Karthik said. "And then we'd get bored and run away. It was a dark room, and we couldn't figure it out."

BAPU BECAME ENAMORED of the sixteenth-century poet Mirabai, who wrote in the tradition of bhakti poetry, a genre of verse that began circulating in South India in the sixth century and remains popular today. According to legend, Mirabai had refused to consummate her marriage. She renounced her husband and his family, because she believed Krishna was her true husband. Like other female bhakti poets, she displayed a kind of madness known as "god intoxication." Eventually, she escaped her in-laws' house and wandered the country alone. "To me," Mirabai wrote, "even this shame seems sweet."

"Am I Mirabai?" Bapu asked in her journal.

She began composing songs for her children about Krishna, describing him as a handsome cowherd who bewitched anyone in his presence. Her lyrics were written in medieval Tamil, a form of the language that she hadn't previously studied. Her vocabulary was expansive, drawing on secondary meanings of words that her family couldn't understand without consulting a dictionary. "It was a mystery," Bapu's sister-in-law, Prema, said. "It was just flowing out of her without any training."

After she'd completed two books of verse, her family suggested that she send them to a specialist in medieval Tamil. The scholar invited her to his office. "He read about half of her poems and did some calculations," her nephew Shyam, who was at the meeting, told me. "He evaluated the meter and structure and said, 'It meets all the standards. It is a divine work.'" Bapu absorbed the news calmly. The writing, she explained, had been effortless.

Her books were published by a local press in 1970 and distributed to nearby temples. "Like the pure river Ganges, may the songs purify all hearts," Nambudiri, the sannyasin whose lectures she attended, wrote in a preface to one of the books. The news spread in Bapu's neighborhood that she had a divine gift. "A lot of ladies from the neighborhood would come to pray with her," Shyam said. "They assumed that she was a guide, a religious teacher, even though she did not assume the role herself."

Bapu began to wear simple cotton saris, and she stopped dressing her hair with flowers. "I will not spend money on things like powder, scent, and silk saris," she wrote. "One should let go of things that give one pleasure." Once, when a rickshaw driver said that his child was ill, she went into her house, opened her cupboard, and brought him a handful of her wedding jewels, most of them made of twenty-four-karat gold.

Bapu felt she had reached a new understanding of the "equality of all creatures," regardless of caste, and she found her in-laws' emphasis on rituals hollow. The people who read holy texts and "then waste their time baking cakes and biscuits can never find themselves," she wrote. They were "science students reading the books without doing any lab work."

In long, anguished letters written in 1970, Bapu asked Nambudiri, whom she now called her guru, for permission to pursue a spiritual path. She was willing to pay for a new wedding for her husband so he could find a more suitable wife. "Instead of ruining his happy life, I will live with less of a burden if he finds a good woman and gets married," she wrote.

Although Nambudiri approved of what he called her "noble undertakings," he counseled her not to abandon her family. If she prayed even five minutes a day, he told her, that was enough. "I cannot accept that that's all it takes," she responded. "Please forgive me for writing frankly like this." She told him that she wanted to follow the path of devotional poets like Mirabai. "If duty is more important than praising God's name," she wrote, then these poets "wouldn't have appeared on this earth."

ON JUNE 9, 1970, at eight in the morning, Bapu told her brother-in-law that she was leaving for Kanchi monastery, one of the most sacred sites in South India, fifty miles away.

She left fresh biscuits and chocolate for her children. "Be smart," she wrote them in a letter. "Many kisses."

She wore pearl earrings, a gold necklace, and two gold bangles, and took six hundred rupees. In her prayer room, she left a pile of letters. "The two of us cannot live even a minute in that house so long as there is doubt and disgust about me in your mind," she had written to Rajamani. In another letter, she observed that when a husband becomes angry "it is the wife who politely suffers." If the family asked about her disappearance, she wrote, "say that I ran off with an agitated mind."

Instead, Rajamani filed a report with the police: he was seeking a woman, five foot three, "limping on the right leg," who "is in the habit of visiting the holy places," he wrote.

The head of Kanchi monastery, Sri Chandrasekharendra Saraswati, was considered by many Tamil Brahmins to be Hinduism's highest spiritual leader. The Dalai Lama described him as "my Elder brother in religion." Saraswati, who had become an ascetic in 1907, at the age of thirteen, saw hundreds of devotees each week. When someone came to him with a problem, it was said that he could intuit their personal history and divine a remedy. Bapu had been to his monastery many times, and he had blessed her children when they were born.

Bapu spoke to him for twenty minutes. "I cannot perform my duty," she told him. "I cannot let go of my devotion. Because of me, everyone in my family has a troubled mind." She did not record his full response—only that he assured her that "all of your worry, doubt, devotion, and karma is an offering to the Lord."

About two weeks later, Bhargavi, who was then five, was sitting on the veranda when a police van pulled inside the gates of her house. In India, officers are permitted to detain a person who is "wandering at large" and who they have "reason to believe has mental illness," an order derived from British colonial law. It's unclear whether Bapu had attracted attention by behaving abnormally, or whether she was arrested simply because she had left home without her husband's permission and he wanted her home. The officers carried Bapu out of their van in a soft cloth wrapped around her body like a straitjacket. "I remember people yelling at her, calling her names," Bhargavi said. Bapu's hair was matted, and her sari was dirty and torn. When an officer finally unbound her, she walked silently into the house.

Bhargavi waited for her mother to return to her household duties, but instead Bapu seemed displaced, as if the house no longer belonged to her. She lingered in the hallways without entering rooms. She seemed to have crossed some sort of threshold, beyond which domestic duties, like packing her husband's lunch or tying Bhargavi's ponytail ribbons, no longer held any meaning. "She seemed to be on a different plane, a different level of existence," Shyam said. When people spoke to her, she wouldn't always respond.

Soon, she left home again. The night of her disappearance, her family was informed by telephone that Bapu had been in a train accident. Shyam drove to the site of the crash, an hour and fifteen minutes south of Chennai. The train had been in a rear-end collision. Families were shouting and wailing. Passengers were carried off on stretchers, bloody and unconscious. Shyam walked outside the train, from back to front, searching for Bapu. He found her in the second-to-last compartment, sitting still, surrounded by luggage that had fallen to the floor. She was reading the Bhagavad Gita. He described her as *sāttvika*, a Sanskrit word meaning balanced and harmonious. "She wasn't agitated," Shyam said. "She was totally unmindful of her surroundings." She had paid a boy ten rupees to notify her family that she'd been in a crash. Now, though, she seemed in no rush to leave.

TWO OF BAPU'S older sisters had married doctors, and they thought that Bapu should see a psychiatrist. "They were like, 'Hey, guys, get modern,'" Bhargavi told me years later. "'Psychiatry is a big science today. Go for it!'"

Bapu's husband took her to a psychiatric clinic in Chennai run by a psychiatrist named Peter Fernandez, who came from a Catholic family and was among the first generation of Indian psychiatrists to be educated and trained in India. "We read only the Western books—British and German and American," he told me. "We didn't have any Indian authors. No Indian psychiatrists were capable of writing a book at that time."

Fernandez said that all he had to do was look at Bapu to know she was schizophrenic. "The schizophrenic has no insight," he said. "She doesn't know who she is."

Some European psychiatrists used to say that they could diagnose schizophrenia intuitively; they sensed an aura of strangeness, as if the patient came from another world—a diagnostic principle that came to be known as the "doctrine of the abyss." "When faced with such people, we feel a gulf which defies description," the philosopher and psychiatrist Karl Jaspers wrote in 1913. "We find ourselves astounded and shaken in the presence of alien secrets."

The earliest phase of schizophrenia is often marked by what the German neurologist Klaus Conrad called "apophany"—a revelation that a new realm of existence has been unveiled. Patients feel that the world is pulsing with cosmic meaning; they are close to solving the riddle of life. The psychologist Louis Sass writes that patients in this state have the sense of "crystal-clear sight, of profound penetration into the essence of things."

Bhargavi was dimly aware that her mother had been diagnosed with schizophrenia, but no one in her family talked about it. The label made Bhargavi feel that her mother's experiences were foreign and impossible to comprehend. Psychiatric explanations, imported from the West, created in Bhargavi a sense of estrangement: she didn't know how to grieve her mother's absence. Her family, too, wasn't sure how to communicate about why Bapu seemed to inhabit a different reality from them. Whenever her mother went through one of her "states," as they were called, her family was silent. It was as if they had a "perceptual blackout," Bhargavi said.

In eight hundred pages of journals, Bapu never mentioned her diagnosis either. She described Krishna as a surrogate husband whose body at times seemed so close to hers that she could smell the sandalwood paste on his skin and feel the strength of his arms. He wrapped his soft hands around her neck, resting his head on her shoulder. He infused her with a sense of unconditional love. "Who in the 'scientific world'"—she wrote these words in English—"would believe all this!"

WHEN BHARGAVI WAS TEN, she learned that her mother had been taken to Chennai's government asylum, the Kilpauk Mental Hospital. The institution resembled a military barracks, with nearly two thousand beds and a concrete wall surrounding the grounds. Bhargavi visited and was struck first by the smell of urine and then the sting of bleach. Her mother was in a small cell with a door made of iron grilles.

She was chained to the bars. Bhargavi didn't know why her mother was there. "But I am certain she was in that position—in a cage, spread-eagled," she told me. "I have spent forty years fainting when I go inside hospitals because they have that same smell."

The superintendent of Kilpauk Mental Hospital at the time, Sarada Menon, told me that she did not remember Bapu, but her story—a patient who claims she is communicating directly with Krishna—was familiar. "In schizophrenia, too much religion is not good," she said. "I tell my patients, 'Don't go into philosophy. Study practical issues. It is better than letting your thoughts go astray.'"

Founded in 1794, Kilpauk Mental Hospital was one of many asylums established by the British colonial government—a project presented as proof of Britain's commitment to bringing science and reason to the continent. When foreign dignitaries visited India, the wives of British officers sometimes hosted concerts and dances in the asylums. Jal Dhunjibhoy, one of the first Indians to be appointed superintendent of a psychiatric hospital, in 1925, wrote that mental hygiene was part of a "nation-building programme" to secure the "onward march to civilization."

But doctors, both Western and Indian, worried that the onward march posed psychic risks: they proposed that people exposed to Western civilization were more likely to become mentally ill. In 1939, the anthropologist and psychoanalyst George Devereux claimed (with insufficient evidence) that the absence of schizophrenia in "primitive" societies is "a point on which all students of comparative society and of anthropology agree." Schizophrenia, he declared, could be brought on by a "rather brusquely imposed acculturation process." For this reason, it was claimed that the Parsis—a community of Zoroastrians in India who, in the first half of the twentieth century, emulated the British manner of living—had disproportionately high rates of schizophrenia. In a 1928 letter in the *British Medical Journal*, a Scottish doctor wrote, "If we are to advise the Parsees against anything, it is rather against their too wholesale acceptance of Western civilization," which was "breaking up these young people's minds." In a Bengali journal, another doctor warned that "in India, European civilization is the main reason behind this *citta vikriti*," a Sanskrit term for insanity.

India established a psychoanalytic society before France even had one—a source of pride for Sigmund Freud, who kept on his desk an ivory statue of the Hindu god Vishnu sent to him by the founder of India's society. "It will recall to my mind the progress of Psychoanalysis, the proud conquests it has made in foreign countries," he wrote in a letter. But Freud's psychoanalysis proved largely incompatible with a culture for which mysticism is often essential to people's lives. Bapu was not trying to arrive at an understanding of her own psyche; she wanted to transcend personal boundaries, because she felt that she was finally grasping the folly and loneliness of her prior view of the world.

Freud's friend Romain Rolland, who wrote biographies of two Hindu mystics, urged Freud to examine what he called the "oceanic sentiment," the "simple and direct fact of the feeling of the 'eternal'"—a concept Rolland took from his study of Eastern religions. Freud replied, "I shall now try with your guidance to penetrate into the Indian jungle from which until now an uncertain blending of Hellenic love of proportion, Jewish sobriety, and Philistine timidity have kept me away." But he described mysticism in cursory and belittling ways, as an infantile regression. The Indian psychoanalyst Sudhir Kakar writes that Western psychological sciences have failed to understand that the "mystical quest is not apart from the dailiness of life but pervades and informs life in its deepest layers," expressing the "depressive core at the base of human life which lies beyond language." In mystical states, Kakar writes, the "reality of being utterly and agonizingly alone is transiently denied."

N. C. Surya, who directed Bangalore's All India Institute of Mental Health in the 1960s, warned his colleagues that they were adopting Western theories as if they were universal truths. "We will end up as ineffectual caricatures of Western psychiatric theory and practice, or reduce our living patients into a set of prestige-loaded foreign jargon," he wrote. He did not accept the Western view of mental health as the "statistical norm." A healthy person, according to this view, is "like every other John or Jean in the neighbourhood." But Indian healing cultures were meant to raise the self to a higher ideal—detached, spontaneous, free of ego—rather than simply to restore the person to a baseline called normal.

Surya felt like a stranger in his profession, "completely out of tune, as I was applying totally different value systems, alien both to myself as well as to the patient," he wrote. He held perhaps the most prestigious psychiatric position in India, but he became disillusioned. When he was fifty-two, at the height of his career, he quit the field and entered an ashram. The ashram was devoted to the mystic Sri Aurobindo, who said, referring to Freud, "One cannot discover the meaning of the lotus by analyzing the secrets of the mud in which it grows."

AN INDIAN DRUG gave rise to the discovery that transformed psychiatry, a fact that is generally written out of the history

of the field. The psychiatrist Nathan Kline, the author of
From Sad to Glad, who helped introduce antidepressants to
the American public, had read an article in *The New York
Times* in 1953 about the Indian snakeroot plant, *Rauwolfia
serpentina*, used by Indigenous healers in India for hundreds
of years. "Ayurvedic drugs, easily available in India, may be
worth a thorough investigation in some Western institutions
for the mentally afflicted," the *Times* reported. The next year,
Kline and his colleagues decided to give an extract from
the *Rauwolfia serpentina* plant, called reserpine, to patients
at Rockland State Hospital, in New York. Describing reserpine's calming effect on one patient, Kline wrote, "She was
not suddenly cured of her delusion, but the terror had gone
out of it." On the ward where patients took reserpine, Kline
said, the hospital's glazier noticed that there were fewer broken windows to replace. New York's commissioner of mental
health eventually recommended that reserpine be given to
nearly all hospitalized patients in the state. "It was my peculiar distinction to 'discover' a drug that was 2,000 years
old," Kline wrote, adding that reserpine had been dismissed
by British doctors as "just another curious aspect of the ex-
otic East."

   After seeing how reserpine could "swing the emotional
pendulum down," Kline thought there had to be another
drug that could "swing it up"—the hypothesis that inspired
his experiments with iproniazid, the tuberculosis drug. Kline
was awarded a Lasker Award, one of the most prestigious
prizes in medicine, for his early work with reserpine, which
"greatly reinforced the case for drugs as a treatment for mental disorders," the citation for the award said. The American
neuroscientist Solomon Snyder described reserpine as the
"keystone of psychopharmacology." But in India, reserpine

was not widely studied. Dhunjibhoy, the superintendent who thought psychiatry could advance the nation, had run experiments on reserpine at his own hospital, but he apparently considered the homegrown drug unworthy of scientific study. He seemed more enamored of new Western techniques.

By the time Bapu arrived at Kilpauk Mental Hospital, most schizophrenic patients there were prescribed the antipsychotic chlorpromazine (the generic name for Thorazine). Advertisements at the time presented the drug as a civilizing force that would tame a patient's wildness. To dramatize the premedicated state, there were images of war staffs, walking sticks, and fertility statues. Another early antipsychotic, Eskazine, was advertised in the *India Medical Journal*, in 1969, with the sentence, "It makes them cooperative and communicative." The ad featured a woman holding her palms out and screaming, her eyes and mouth glowing ghostly white.

As soon as Bapu was discharged from the hospital, she refused to take the chlorpromazine that she'd been prescribed. She understood her devotion through a story that was celebrated by fellow worshippers and by the literature she read, and, when it was forcibly replaced by a new one about mental illness, she felt diminished. The new explanation felt like an affront, which isn't to say that her previous reputation was free of stigma either. Psychiatry isn't the only framework that has a kind of double-edged quality, offering a story that can save a person but that also, under different conditions, feels lonely and intractable. I wonder about the character of Bapu's distress before it was classified as either mysticism or mental illness, just as I question whatever basic feelings existed in me before they were called anorexia. In each case, the original experience couldn't be captured or understood on its own terms and gradually became something that wasn't entirely of our own making.

IN THE MONTHS following her hospitalization, Bapu was so detached from her domestic duties that her mother-in-law moved into the house to manage the tasks that Bapu was neglecting. She "scolds me in front of everyone," Bapu complained. "Worry takes hold of me before the rise of dawn. How many accusations will come up today?" Her in-laws routinely called her crazy, the insults uttered so loudly that Bapu was nervous that the rickshaw drivers at the stand outside their house would hear. She wrote to Krishna, "You are driving me mad before the eyes of the world!"

Bapu wasn't the only woman in her family to defy expectations of how a Brahmin wife should behave. Her mother, Chellammal, had also pursued an independent existence. When Chellammal's husband died of a heart attack, not long after purchasing Bapu's house, Chellammal embraced her freedom. She took over her husband's business, a thriving cosmetics company. "At a time when only men made the moves in business, here was a lady who put her business on the map," reported the national daily *The Hindu*. Chellammal traveled widely through Asia, promoting her signature hair product. A feature about Chellammal in the Indian women's magazine *Femina* observed, "A woman of her age and background, one would automatically presume, would be spending all her time in pooja, fondling grandchildren." But instead, "she is all alone in that many-roomed house with only her footfalls and the whispering of the trees for company."

Bapu worried that others would "see me in light of my mother." The neighborhood gossip was that the women in

her family couldn't settle down. But Chellammal did not relate to her daughter's form of escape. She begged Bapu's guru,
Nambudiri, to persuade her to stay home. "I know that my
daughter is a simple girl whose one ambition in life is to realize herself," she wrote him in a letter. "But the method she is
following is not correct."

THE FAMILY TRIED a new arrangement: Bapu could live
independently—but at home. She moved back into Amrita,
the house that her father had bought for her. The rest of her
family remained in the smaller house, a short walk away. The
first floor was now occupied by tenants, so Bapu confined herself to the second floor. It was unfurnished, except for a steel
table, a stove, and two chairs. Bapu slept on the floor without
a mattress or sheets. Her husband and in-laws instructed her
children not to visit her. They weren't even supposed to say
her name.

The children split their alliances in the family. Karthik
sided with his mother. "I was the troublemaker, the irksome
boy who supported the wrong adult in the house," he told me.
"The longing to be with her was what kept me going. When
will she be back? That was my million-dollar question, all the
time."

Bhargavi was loyal to her father and handled the household chores. She seemed to have a different relationship with
gravity than other children; she was so light on her feet that
her presence in a room made no noise. She spent her free
time alone, drawing pictures of ghoulish creatures with broken limbs and misplaced eyes. When family friends came
over, she was ashamed of being a "motherless child." Sometimes she hid behind the wall. "The fact that my mom left
me made me think I had no right to exist," she said. She

projected an aura of "I'm not here, so why would you look at me?"

Bapu cooked a small dinner every evening, hoping that her children would join her. Karthik was told that his mother's cooking could be poisonous, but he still snuck over to eat. One night, after Bapu had been living in the house for less than three months, Karthik came to visit. The front door was open. Bapu wasn't inside. "We knew," he said. "Yes, the bird has flown." In a letter to her mother, Bapu wrote, "The Lord suddenly gave me a turning point and called me on a lonely road."

BAPU'S ESCAPES BECAME ROUTINE. "There would be a flurry whenever she left," Bhargavi said. Her family interrogated the drivers at the rickshaw stand outside their house to determine which way she'd fled. Karthik wondered if their concern was even sincere. "If she came back and reclaimed her rightful place in the home, some of her in-laws might have had to find a new place to live," he said. "The house was in her name, and a lot of people wanted the property."

Bapu's destination, it soon became clear, was almost always Chennai Central, the main train station. Her nephew Shyam studied the train schedule to determine which trains were headed toward temples devoted to deities that Bapu had described in stories to her children. Then he traveled to the temples, wandering their halls and the encampments outside. He showed Bapu's photograph to worshippers. "I was fascinated by Perry Mason detective stories, and I assumed the role of detective," Shyam told me. "I tried to remain objective, and I was always looking for clues."

In 1973, Karthik learned through a friend of the family

that his mother had been spotted at Kanchi monastery, the temple she'd visited before the police had detained her. Karthik, who was ten, convinced Chellammal, his grandmother, to send him there. He traveled in a car driven by a worker from her cosmetics factory. When they arrived, Karthik searched for his mother, walking through a grassy courtyard with water taps for devotees to wash their legs before praying.

When he didn't see her, he walked through a residential area with small thatched hermitages where sannyasin live and meet with worshippers. A person with a shaved head, sitting under a tree, called out his name. Karthik came closer and realized the sannyasin was his mother. Instead of a sari, she wore a saffron robe wrapped around one shoulder and her waist. She had taken off all her jewelry. Karthik was shocked by her appearance. But, he said, "the only thing I cared about was that I had found her. That was the prize. I was just desperate to sit on her lap."

Saraswati, the pontiff at Kanchi monastery, taught that women do not need gurus, because they have their husbands as their guiding lights: "She is to look upon him as her God, and in that attitude she has to surrender herself to him, body and soul." He praised wives who, according to tradition, threw themselves on their husband's funeral pyre.

Bapu had been waiting three days to speak with the pontiff. Karthik watched the conversation from twenty feet away. "She was quite intense in her own soft-spoken way," Karthik said. "She had a vociferous argument with him. She asked, 'Why is it that in your tradition men can run away from home and drop their families and live like beggars, and women cannot?'"

Karthik said that the pontiff "tried to reassure and pacify

her. He told her that her family misses her, and she should do these things in balance, and that she can achieve whatever state she seeks—God will certainly bless her—but there's no need to be extreme about it." At the end of the conversation, following custom, Bapu drew her palms together and kneeled at his feet.

But she was dissatisfied by the encounter. "For the soul that has found god there is no gender," she wrote in her journal.

When she returned home, her family was appalled by her shaved head. Bhargavi said, "I still remember my aunt shouting, 'Paithiyam!'"—the Tamil word for "insane."

BHARGAVI AND KARTHIK felt that their house was teeming with apparitions. Uncanny phenomena became routine: a large catlike creature was spotted climbing down a tree with its head cocked up. Karthik saw sparks of light enter the house and bounce off the walls, leaving soot in their wake. Bhargavi avoided the tamarind tree behind the house, because if people walked under its branches, it was said, they could be caught by a ghost. She saw women in red saris flit through the house's back rooms.

The family wondered if Bapu's father should have listened to the priest who had warned him against buying the house. Now the priest's admonition more than two decades earlier seemed prescient. Rajamani decided to invite three priests from Kerala, a lush, green state on the southwest coast of India, to visit his house. They were experts in a form of divining unique to Kerala: They gathered information from the family, noting positive and negative omens as people spoke—a bell ringing was good; the sound of an owl or a crow was bad. They tossed small conch shells on a board marked with signs and, based on where the shells fell, advanced theories about the house's misfortunes.

After three days, the priests concluded that the house was haunted by a Brahma Rakshasa, the spirit of a Brahmin scholar who had nearly reached a state of enlightenment before dying—by suicide, the priests proposed. His spirit was now hovering near the place of his death and had taken over Bapu's mind.

Bapu rejected this story, just as she had dismissed the one that psychiatrists had imposed on her life. "Saying that it is because of a Brahma Rakshasa is stupid," she wrote. "Only with the blessings of god do songs and prayers flow out of me like water."

But her in-laws found this explanation compelling. Her brother-in-law, N. Balakrishnan, told me that Bapu "was a little lady, a weak lady, and that must have been a strong man who had entered her." His wife, Prema, said, "We think he might have come into her soul and made her write these poems. It was his unfinished work."

BAPU BECAME MORE strategic about covering her tracks. Rather than immediately heading to the train station, she'd linger a few days in Chennai, sleeping at local temples or on railway platforms. "I do not ask for a bed," she wrote. "I do not ask for a home. I do not ask for loving children. I do not desire a home or a country!"

Her favorite place to go was Guruvayur, one of the most famous temples in Kerala. The temple's inner sanctum was surrounded by tiers of brass cups holding candles that were lit every evening. Outside, there were tethered elephants and several red-roofed halls. The temple offered a safe space for vulnerable, isolated people to find company, even a sense of fellowship. On the temple grounds, they were free from judgment about the ferocity of their devotion. When they prayed in bizarre or erratic ways, writhing on the temple's main walkway, people would quietly step around them. Every day, priests offered freshly cooked food to the gods and then brought the leftovers, rice and occasionally sweet pudding, to devotees in a cup made of dry leaves. The food was called *prasadam*, a Sanksrit word for "grace."

Bapu slept on a platform, a kind of elevated sidewalk, directly outside the temple. She spent her days chanting "heart melting" songs with other devotees and praying. "It is very apparent that the distance between the Lord and this individual is steadily decreasing," she wrote. Chatting with a fellow devotee one day, she felt Krishna embrace her. "If I mention all this," she wrote, "you all will think to send me straight to Kilpauk Hospital," the psychiatric institution established by the British. "But it truly happened. It's not a lie!"

In her journal, Bapu chastised herself for desiring food; her hunger was proof that her ego could not be fully controlled. Like the anorexic who becomes addicted to the high of starvation, Bapu felt she had become more discerning—an achievement expressed as both superiority and self-abnegation. In her next life, she wrote, she wished to be a dog that wandered around Guruvayur Temple, or a cow that pulled carriages there.

The Upanishads, a collection of texts foundational to Hinduism, describe a person who has achieved transcendence as one who has lost all individuality: she is like a lump of salt in water, dissolving. Bapu felt she might achieve a similar state if only she could rid herself of her longing for her children. "The love of a child does not spare anyone," she wrote. "Only a mother will know." "My sweet ones!" she went on. "Is it my mistake to have left you? I did not leave your playground and come of my own volition!" It was the work of the gods, she said. "But the blame is on me."

WHEN CHELLAMMAL LEARNED how her daughter was living—Bapu occasionally sent letters—she arranged for Bapu to live in a small room at Elite Lodge, a hotel for pilgrims a short walk from Guruvayur Temple. Bapu's room was on the first floor, under a stairwell. There was just enough space for her to lie on the floor.

Bapu wrote on any scrap of paper she could find: calendars, the backs of newspapers and old photographs, and several notebooks, each nearly four hundred pages. When she reflected on her misgivings, her handwriting was symmetrical, but it became sloppy and wild as she wrote about Krishna. She titled one of her notebooks "Mohana Ramayana," a reference to the Sanskrit epic *Ramayana*. *Mohanam* means "enchanting" in Tamil; in Sanskrit it means "mentally confusing." Perhaps Bapu was aware of how another person might see her project: the chronicle of an unsettled mind.

Bapu refers to herself as a madwoman or a lunatic more than a dozen times in her journals, but only sometimes with despair. She saw her alienation from society as proof of her insight. Her inner world had come to feel more substantial than the reality to which her family was bound. The saints she admired had also ruptured ties with family and devoted their lives to phenomena that others could neither see nor touch. Ramakrishna, a nineteenth-century mystic, told his devotees that madness was a mark of devotion and should never be mocked. "A perfect knower of God and a perfect idiot have the same outer signs," he wrote. The eighteenth-century Hindu poet and saint Ramprasad promised, "In heaven there is a fair of lunatics."

~~~~~~~~~

A man with schizophrenia named Thomas, whom I corresponded with for several years, once told me that he had tried to cultivate a kind of "genius for homelessness." He lived on the streets in Chicago in the early 2000s. "I was able to survive even in the cold with an almost feral sense of what to do," he wrote me. He assumed that, if he was thoughtful enough, he could find a way to make homelessness empowering. "Like what the Buddhists do," he said. "Walk around meditating—without a house, or possessions. They are able to invest their lives with meaning outside of the normal conventions of ownership." But he couldn't fully divert his attention from the reality that he was suffering. "The fact that I was not able to do that for myself was one of the things that showed me I had an illness," he wrote.

The metrics by which Bapu assessed her own state of mind were murkier, because she drew from a rich tradition that gave her anguish purpose and structure. She studied the lives of mystics, and understood that their stories were not about seeking God and then victoriously finding him. Their conviction often flagged. They lamented that they had given everything away for a vision, an experience of oneness with the divine, that they could never attain. Bapu's favorite saint, Mirabai, had dramatized this state of mind: Mirabai wrote that she was "deprived of the sight of the beloved, a lonely and lost soul," who is "sad every moment of the day."

Bapu had rejected the idea that her path could be explained by mental illness, but the stories that defined Mirabai and other saints could feel self-fulfilling and chronic, too. Bapu said that her legs were sore from running behind Krishna, constantly chasing him. She felt like a "fruit that will not ripen," a "hollow sack," a "dead tree," a "misfortunate worm," an "abandoned house." But she also wondered, "Is this difficulty I am facing the lesson of total surrender?"

At some point in the midseventies—Bapu did not date these journal entries—she was forbidden from participating in a religious festival that her guru, Nambudiri, was holding, a seven-day recitation of the Bhagavata Purana, a holy text. She assumed that her guru was "disgusted with me because I am poor." When they had first met, she was a handsome, wealthy woman who wore silk saris and was driven to temples in Western cars. Eight years later, she was scavenging for food in the compost pile behind the temple.

"The promises you made to me—have they become a delusion?" she wrote to Krishna. "Why did I leave all my loving relatives behind and come to you?"

The complexity of Bapu's early poems gave way to a plain, lamenting style. At times, it is difficult to tell whether she is directing her questions toward Krishna, her husband, or her guru—her attention shifts between the three men around whom she had structured her life. "Did you think I was an ugly old woman?" she asked. "Is this why you forgot and abandoned me?"

ONE NIGHT IN 1978, Peter Fernandez, the psychiatrist who had treated Bapu at his clinic in Chennai, drove four hundred miles to Guruvayur. Acting at Bapu's mother's request, he and two attendants showed up at the Elite Lodge and opened the door of Bapu's room. "She was ugly," Fernandez told me. "She was living like a witch, and looking like a witch." Fernandez gave Bapu an injection of Valium and lifted her into his car.

"Was she scared?" I asked him.

"We never bother with schizophrenics being scared," he replied. "I was scared." He told me, "She could not even reason. Her thinking was illogical. She cannot be a normal person." He drove her to a private hospital in Chennai, and she was admitted there against her will. "In the fifty years of my service, it was one of the worst cases of schizophrenia I've seen," he said.

The philosopher Miranda Fricker describes a species of inequality called "epistemic injustice," which is a "wrong done to someone specifically in their capacity as a knower." At the hospital, Bapu was not treated as a credible witness to her own experiences, not only because of her status as a patient but also because of colonial notions about the irrationality of Indian religions. When patients come to see Fernandez, who now runs a different hospital where fifty patients with schizophrenia live, they often wear amulets around their wrists or necks. But Fernandez, a devout Catholic, told me, "I take the amulets off them when they come here," a practice he has maintained for decades. In his desk drawer, he keeps a plastic bag full of his patients' talismans, mostly silver tubes in which a small piece of paper or palm leaf has been inscribed with verses meant to protect them. The fact that his patients are still sick, he told me, is the proof that these charms have not worked.

Bapu stayed at Fernandez's hospital for several weeks. She would linger near the windows and sing devotional songs loudly. Trained in Indian Carnatic music, a genre developed around the fifteenth century, Bapu had a lovely, melodious voice. When the staff told her to be quiet—she was disturbing other patients, they said—she sang louder. Fernandez described Bapu as "a very insistent woman, a very sticky woman."

Karthik, who was then fourteen, visited frequently. Once, he arrived as his mother was being wheeled out of her room on a stretcher. Karthik followed as she was pushed into a small room with a machine that delivered electroconvulsive shocks. He watched his mother through a small window on the door.

At the time, electroconvulsive therapy, or ECT, was the standard treatment for Indian psychiatric patients, regardless of their diagnosis. (In America and Europe, it was more often limited to those with severe depression.) The procedure, which causes a brief seizure, appears to stimulate the release of hormones by the hypothalamus and pituitary gland, but the precise action in the brain has never been fully understood. India at that time had fewer than two thousand psychiatrists for half a billion people, and ECT could be administered to dozens of patients in an hour, often without anesthesia or muscle relaxants. Fernandez said that in the late sixties he gave electroconvulsive therapy to about fifty patients each day. "I was thirty-five, full of energy," he told me. "The boys would hold down the patients' arms." He clenched his teeth and then imitated the sound of the machine. "*Zick, zick,*" he said cheerfully.

Karthik watched as two attendants put a piece of wood in his mother's mouth, to prevent her from biting her tongue. An electrical current was applied to her head. Karthik heard a dull buzzing noise. His mother's body spasmed. Karthik immediately began sobbing.

Once Bapu was wheeled back to her own room, she opened her eyes and saw that her son was distraught. Karthik said that she told him, "Don't worry. These things will only make me stronger." Karthik concluded that the procedure was "just a very faint echo—not a sound she was paying attention to. She had already surrendered and nothing was touching her physically."

AFTER BAPU WAS discharged from the clinic, she "skipped town," Karthik said. "No one knew her whereabouts." He called the Elite Lodge to see if she had returned to Guruvayur. Her belongings were still in her room, but no one had seen her and she'd provided no forwarding address. Karthik said that for a long time his mother "was torn between these two forces—the pull of the family and the pull of the divine—but from then on it was a straight path."

Karthik had become accustomed to people reporting sightings of his mother at her favorite temples, but months passed with no news. He blamed his grandmother for essentially arranging his mother's abduction. "That's what hastened everything," he said. "She lost the little faith she had in her people. If there had been one arm of support, her life would have been different." (Dr. Fernandez, who is now eighty-nine, disagreed, saying that after he treated Bapu "she became perfectly normal. When she left, she was very happy, the family was very happy, the family thanked me," but he also acknowledged that he never followed up.)

After she had been gone for a year, Bapu's family stopped mentioning her at all. By then, Bhargavi and Karthik were in high school. "I don't think any of us had the words to talk about it," Bhargavi said. "There was the guilt that we were living in her house while she could be living on the streets. Who fed her? Who gave her clothes? Did someone rape her? Those questions have never left me." In her spare time, Bhargavi wrote melancholy poems: "It seems / eternity is finite / it waits / upon a rotten memory."

Karthik said that eventually, "it was almost as if she didn't exist." Once, he eavesdropped on his father and uncles saying that Bapu was dead.

Karthik began using his dad's camera to take photos of his cousins as well as birds, rare plants, and snakes. To save money, he rarely printed the photos; instead, he paid a man one rupee to process the film and then projected the images on the wall at night. Sometimes he took shots when there wasn't any film in his camera. "I don't think he had many thoughts except that he had to compulsively take pictures," Bhargavi said. "It was the fact of his life." She guessed that photography was her brother's way of keeping himself at a remove—of "living on the balcony, just watching."

Bhargavi had her own form of detachment. After graduating from high school, she studied philosophy at a college in Chennai. She was drawn to the discipline because it "insulated me from my inner emotions and self," she said. She rejected her "haunted childhood," as she described it, by becoming an atheist. "It was raining gods in my house—in every nook and corner—and I hated them." She gravitated toward European philosophers like Habermas, Sartre, and Camus. "I dealt with my problems by being a total rationalist," she told me. "What I hear, what I smell, what I touch—these are the only things that are true."

~~~~~~~~~

Srirangam, a temple town with some fifty shrines, rests on an islet formed by two rivers in southeast India. The temple is believed to be the birthplace of the ninth-century female mystic and poet Andal, about whom Bapu had once written a book. Most of the pages of the book, which was never published, have been lost. Only a few lines remain: "If we think of our Andal," Bapu wrote, "will not all the illnesses that bother the body simply melt like snow?"

Andal is famous not only for her devotion to Krishna but for her determination to actually marry him. "So great is my desire / To unite with the lord," she wrote, "that emotion chokes my breath." One day, Andal dressed like a bride, walked into the Srirangam temple, and embraced the feet of the idol, Ranganatha—an incarnation of the god Vishnu, of whom Krishna is an avatar. Then she disappeared. She was never seen again. The union was celebrated as the ultimate merging of a devotee with God.

"Am I Andal?" Bapu wrote in her journal. "Oh Lord, reply straight away."

In 1982, one of Bapu's old friends, a former classmate, saw a woman who resembled Bapu on the thoroughfare leading to the main temple of Srirangam. It had been more than five years since her family had any news about her. The classmate stared at the woman, who was among a group of people begging for food. The woman wore a torn sari and looked emaciated. The classmate kept walking, but later she called Bapu's mother. When Karthik learned of the sighting, he took a cab two hundred miles to Srirangam. "I spotted my mother instantly," Karthik told me. Bapu was sitting on the curb of a street lined with tourist vans, taxis, food vendors, and hundreds of people streaming toward the temple.

She was with a group of women who lived in a choultry, a hall for pilgrims with no bedding or running water, near the temple. Her hair was greasy and knotted, and she had sores on her body. Karthik explained who he was, and a few of the women urged Bapu to go home with him. When Karthik approached her, he said, "she seemed gone. The past was gone."

Karthik's heart pounded as he led his mother to his cab. "It was the same tension from childhood," he said. "How am I going to take her back? Will my dad let her in?" Bapu was so weak she could barely talk. He lay her across the back seat of the car. "She seemed to somewhat recollect me—somewhat," he said. "Then something stirred in her, and she told me, 'You've grown so tall.'"

IN AN AUTOBIOGRAPHICAL play titled "The Fugitive," Bhargavi dramatized her mother's homecoming. "Her blouse is badly stitched, loose and hanging immodestly on her," she wrote. "She is preoccupied, smiling to herself, sometimes giggling in an inhibited way, closing her mouth with her hand and looking at the others to see if they noticed." Her husband finds her intolerable. "Why don't you do something about that wife of mine?" he tells a psychiatrist. "Increase the dosage or something." At other times, though, he doubts whether she's even ill. "Her madness is just a facade behind which she hides," he says, "so that she can do what she wants, and live as she wills."

Karthik and Bhargavi, who were both living at home while going to college in Chennai, found their mother a new psychiatrist, one who was willing to visit Bapu at home and talk with the whole family. "He was a wave of fresh air," Bhargavi said. "He didn't just look at her and say, 'Schizophrenia—here's some pills,' and then walk away." He prescribed antipsychotic medications, but he also told the family that Bapu felt isolated and encouraged them to talk with her about her experiences at healing temples. Bhargavi struggled to fulfill her end of the conversation. "I don't think I was prepared to listen," she told me. When her mother spoke about her relationship with gods, Bhargavi said, "I felt like I was being choked, like someone was strangling me."

After four years living with her mother, Bhargavi moved away. She went to Mumbai to get a PhD in philosophy at the Indian Institute of Technology, where she focused on the problem of how we know what we claim to know about human behavior—where to draw the line between knowledge and belief. In her dissertation, she wrote, "One wants to know whether synthetic knowledge pertaining to the human mind . . . is possible," given its status as "science and culture, as truth and metaphor." She asked "whether the search for a scientific rationality, particularly in terms of causal laws, is a threat to autonomy," and how to make "such a science respond to a society's needs."

In another paper, she called for a revival of the phenomenological tradition to which Roland Kuhn had belonged. "A 'depressive' does not just enact the symptoms," she wrote. "She experiences the world differently. She uses language differently. She experiences emotions differently." By ignoring these sorts of experiences—the "unclassified residuum," as William James called it—doctors risk misunderstanding why mental illness can be so isolating, altering people's lives in ways that cannot be captured only by symptoms. "These experiences of ill-health determine the way we look at the world, and at ourselves," Bhargavi wrote. The lives of the mentally ill had been erased from the public record, she went on, but "in the writing of history and personal stories, we make ourselves present."

WHILE BHARGAVI WAS away studying, a willowy twenty-year-old woman named Nandini was introduced to Karthik as a potential bride. Nandini knew that Karthik, who was working as an industrial photographer, had a tainted family history, but her marketability was complicated, too. She had never learned to cook or to wash clothes, her brother was chronically ill, and her family could not afford a dowry. When Nandini visited Karthik's house the first time, Bapu was sitting on the stone parapet of her veranda. "Her face was so baby-like, approachable, easy," Nandini said. "She asked me, 'Do you like me? Do you want to come and live with us? Do you like my son?' I was so moved. Nobody will ask these questions. Even Karthik never asked."

They got married in Karthik's photography studio. Nandini moved into Bapu's house and became a kind of de facto nurse, watching over Bapu without judgment. The antipsychotic medications that Bapu had rejected in a hospital setting she now accepted when Nandini handed them to her. The pills seemed to make Bapu less restless and inflexible. Although she continued to write devotional songs and poems, she no longer addressed them to Krishna. "She knew that her devotion to Krishna pulls her out of the family, and she did not want to do that," Nandini told me. Instead, she wrote to Murugan, the Hindu god of war. She had arthritis in her hands, so Nandini transcribed her words. At Bapu's direction, Nandini sent the poetry to the governing bodies of temples where Bapu had once lived. "Sometimes her letters bounced back, but I respected her feelings, and I kept writing, writing, writing," Nandini said.

After years of feeling shunned by her in-laws, Bapu seemed to feel lifted by the steady presence of her daughter-in-law, her new caretaker—her "eyes, hands, and legs," as Karthik put it. They began describing each other as best friends. "Karthik went away to work, and my life was with her," Nandini said. Karthik sometimes asked his mother if she wanted to return to Guruvayur, but she told him, "I don't have a wish to be anywhere else." In devoting herself to a new god, one whom she described as less seductive than Krishna, Bapu seemed to have found a way to maintain her spiritual identity without being alone.

Word circulated among their neighbors that Bapu possessed healing powers. If she touched the forehead of a sick baby, it was said, the baby's fever would dissipate. Mothers in the neighborhood came to her for counsel if their sons were struggling in school. Fishermen who worked on the Bay of Bengal a mile away asked her to pray for their children when they were ill. Bapu sat on a chair on her veranda with one leg hanging down and the other folded, the bottom of her foot touching her inner thigh—a posture adopted by Hindu goddesses. "The neighborhood ladies thought she was a saint, just like Mirabai," her nephew Shyam said.

Bapu's husband, Rajamani, did not object to his wife's new role in the community. He had a congenital eye condition and was going blind. "I think his disability might have brought some sensitivities to him," Bhargavi said. "At the end, my father really did bow down to her way of being."

Twelve years after Bapu came home, Rajamani died of malaria, at the age of sixty-two. When Karthik told his mother that her husband had died, she said, "He had a good end," and nothing more.

AFTER HER FATHER'S DEATH, Bhargavi returned home to give birth to her first child. She had married a classmate, and their baby, a girl, was born with a spinal disability. The baby spent most of her waking hours crying. After half a year, she died in Bhargavi's arms. "My child brought me the entire drama of human suffering in about six months," she said.

Karthik blamed the tragedy on their house. Two different priests, two decades apart, had said it wasn't fit for a family. At night, Karthik often heard strange noises; sometimes he went outside with a flashlight looking for the source. He had dreaded the idea of Bhargavi giving birth in their childhood home, but, he said, "Who am I to tell her, 'Please don't come into your house'?" But Bhargavi didn't disagree: "The havoc we faced in that house—nothing short of an evil spirit can explain what happened to us."

On either side of the property, there were two heavy iron lamps. Karthik went outside with his German shepherd one morning and discovered the lamps were twisted, as if by a great force. He asked an electrician to install new lamps. The next morning, they were destroyed again. He had the lamps fixed, and a few weeks later the same thing happened. Shortly after, he found his German shepherd dead in a pool of blood.

Karthik said, "I went out and bought myself a sledge-hammer—a really huge sledgehammer." He walked to the northeast corner of the property—the area where, according to the priests from Kerala, the ghost of the scholar who'd died by suicide was said to reside. He stood near a shed full of construction tools and junk. "All these stories about our haunted house were floating around my head," he said. "I destroyed almost a thousand square feet of the shed." Smashing the wood with his sledgehammer, he shouted, "Come out! Show yourself!"

But the shadow over their house did not pass. A few months later, Bapu told Karthik, "My end is coming." Soon, she had a stroke and fell into a coma. Bapu's in-laws came to see her at the hospital, but Bhargavi refused to let them into her mother's room. She told them they'd already done enough harm. "I never realized I was that angry," Bhargavi said. "I'm not known for anger. But I just stood there, saying, 'No, you're not going in.' I physically prohibited them from seeing her." There was little the doctors could do for Bapu, so Karthik took her home. A day later, he carried her onto the veranda of their house, so she could feel the breeze from the ocean. "I put her head on my lap, and, as I was touching her hair, she stopped breathing," he said. "That was it. It was very quiet."

On the day of Bapu's cremation, construction workers, local gardeners, and fishermen gathered outside her house. They had seen her as a kind of informal guru and had come to say goodbye. As she was carried to the cremation ground on a stretcher made of bamboo and palm fronds, the people she'd blessed trailed behind. In her journal, she had left instructions for her funeral rites along with a note to her children. "The garment that we call 'this body' has come to one person as a child, to another as a wife, to another as a mother, to another as an enemy, and to some as a friend, and it perishes entirely," she wrote. "Why be sad about it! It's the fate of the world."

AFTER THE DEATHS of her daughter and parents, Bhargavi said, "I went to another plane and another orbit." She was living in Hyderabad, where her husband worked, and she almost never left her house. Her time was spent in the "all-consuming universe of nothingness," she said. She often envisioned her own death. A few times, she felt so violent that she took dishes from her cabinet and shattered them on the floor. Her marriage deteriorated. She realized, she later wrote, that in mental illness "there is a sense of loosely hanging together, not hanging together at all, of not owning your body or thoughts. You lose a sense of being able to predict what you are about."

She joined a Buddhist meditation group, to try to overcome her anger. Biographical accounts describe the Buddha enduring a period of depression, an experience that he turned into a cornerstone of his teaching: *sabbam dukkham*, the pain of being alive. In one story, a mother has gone mad after the death of her baby and begs the Buddha for medicine to revive her child. The Buddha agrees, with one condition: she must procure a mustard seed, a cheap Indian spice, from a family in which no one has died. Elated, the mother begins knocking on doors. By the end of the day, though, she realizes that no houses are free of death. The mother comes to see her grief as part of a universal problem of existence. She finds solace in generalizing her hopelessness from herself to the world.

In her proximity to death, Bhargavi began to feel a kind of freedom. She made a series of decisions. She joined a feminist reading group. She cut her hair. She changed her stride when she walked. Eventually, after having a second daughter, she got a divorce. "I lost my gentleness," she said. "I became more candid and sharp." She realized that hidden agendas and emotions had been "popping out of me every time I speak." Even her dissertation, an examination of the difference between what she called a "'human' science and a 'good' science," she now saw as being fundamentally about her mother. She said, "I've carried my mom on my back for decades, like a chant." She worried that if she didn't change her way of living, her second daughter would become estranged. "History is going to repeat itself," she said.

She began going every day to a library in Hyderabad, where she read about women's rights and the history of psychiatry. She came to believe that the feminist movement in India understood the sources of women's distress better than much of psychiatry did. The traditional upheavals in a woman's life—the adjustments required of a young bride, adapting to new sexual and social expectations, or the isolation and shame of being widowed—often led to a fractured sense of self. When Bhargavi's baby had died, she said that her in-laws had told her, "Don't mourn a child who has gone to God." She said, "I was not even supposed to cry—I was just supposed to wait for the next one." She realized, "I had individualized everything. It was, 'My father is bad, my in-laws are bad, the house is bad.' When I moved into feminism, I saw that my dad shouldn't have done the things he did, but it was part of a larger picture of all the things he had imbibed growing up."

IN 2001, a shelter for the mentally ill in Erwadi, a village in South India, caught fire. The shelter was near a Sufi healing shrine reputed to cure mental afflictions. At night, the people living at the shelter were tied to poles and trees while they slept. The blaze spread quickly, and twenty-five people died. "Some were sitting up, their arms locked in place like plastic dolls," *The New York Times* reported. "The bodies defied identification."

The fire led to unprecedented prohibitions on Indigenous methods of healing. India's Supreme Court ordered that mentally ill patients be "sent to doctors and not to religious places." Fifteen homes for the mentally ill near Erwadi were shut down, and more than 150 people who had found shelter there were sent to Kilpauk Mental Hospital, where Bapu had once been. Newspaper reporters followed the relocated patients and discovered that the hospital was rundown and filthy; patients were isolated and neglected, checked on only once every fifteen days, and there seemed to be no protocol for prescribing medications. The Indian magazine *Frontline* concluded that for these patients "there seems to be no real deliverance."

A year after the fire, psychiatrists from the National Institute of Mental Health and Neurosciences published an article in the *British Medical Journal* that found that people with psychotic disorders improved significantly after staying at a Hindu healing temple where residents spent their days praying and doing light chores. The psychiatrists endorsed the benefits of a "culturally valued refuge for people with severe mental illness," as long as there was no coercion or restraint. "We should welcome—rather than fear misuse of—evidence that psychopharmacological and neurophysiological frameworks are not the only ones pertinent to effective psychiatric practice," they wrote.

Though the researchers cautioned that their findings should not be generalized to all healing temples, the study was met with outrage by some psychiatrists. In a letter to the journal, a doctor at a hospital in Kerala wrote, "I am appalled that a team of eminent psychiatrists in this era of evidence-based medicine could even think of designing such a study." He warned, "Now the faith healers can quote BMJ!"

Bhargavi followed the debate closely. In 1999, she and her daughter had moved to Pune, a city in West India with one of the largest mental asylums in Asia. Eager to broaden her work beyond academia, Bhargavi had started a non-profit mental-health organization called Bapu Trust. She felt she had spent her life passively observing. "It wasn't right," she said. "I should not be a bystander to everything. I should have some moral stance."

Bapu Trust offered the kind of counseling that Bhargavi imagined might have helped her own family. The counselors there helped families find an explanation—or multiple explanations—that resonated with their own experiences of illness, rather than using languages that seemed to have been designed for a different model of the self. Often, this meant acknowledging not only a malfunctioning brain but a break in a person's sense of spiritual identity.

In slums throughout Pune, Bhargavi and the counselors she hired knocked on doors, searching for people who might be in psychological anguish. They spoke not only with the person struggling but with their family and their neighbors, holding conversations in informal settings, at people's homes or on the streets, using their dialect. "The much talked about 'stigma' surrounding the mentally ill is at some fundamental level a problem about not having an ordinary, existential language for talking about mental distress," Bhargavi wrote.

The counselors referred those who might need medication to doctors, but they also held meditation, drumming, and art-therapy groups. They avoided diagnostic categories or rigid treatment models that might diminish people's sense of autonomy, their belief that they could control their own story. Vikram Patel, an Indian psychiatrist and a professor of global health at Harvard, has raised similar concerns about the risks of imposing Western ways of describing and explaining illness on people with different backgrounds and histories. He warns of a "credibility gap between the way that modern psychiatry has divvied up the symptoms of mental distress and the way these conditions are experienced by ordinary people in ordinary communities."

Bhargavi and her staff collected the stories of hundreds of people who had spent time in healing shrines. She wrote that the healers described themselves as "doctors of the soul," offering "maternal love" to their devotees. Healing rituals created a sense of catharsis, purpose, and spiritual connection. "Psychiatry and psychology have described only a small part of human consciousness," she wrote.

Bhargavi has been intrigued by a series of studies conducted over three decades by the World Health Organization that examined the course of mental illness in different cultures. The studies found that people were more likely to recover from schizophrenia in developing nations than in developed ones. Some of the best outcomes for schizophrenia were in India. "If I become psychotic, I'd rather be in India than in Switzerland," Shekhar Saxena, the former director of the WHO's Department of Mental Health and Substance Abuse, said in 2006.

There have been disparate explanations for the WHO findings, none fully supported by evidence. One theory is that India has a plurality of healing practices, so people may seek out different forms of mental-health care, sometimes several at once, and be given latitude in how they interpret mental crises. Another theory is that large Indian families may be more supportive of relatives whose productivity has been impeded by mental disorder. But Patel, the Harvard professor of global health, believes that the WHO studies do not sufficiently account for the high mortality rates of people with mental illness in developing countries, as well as the abuse and discrimination they face. He worries that this omission promotes a naive and "extremely Northern perspective about the enlightened native"—a modern reprise of the colonial myth that those who haven't been exposed to civilization are innocent and happy.

Bhargavi is conflicted about the meaning of the studies, but she does know that her mother would have felt less alone had her family welcomed her devotion rather than trying to make it disappear. "In a modernizing world, devotion is not an acceptable emotion," Bhargavi told me. "Devotion takes you to the bottommost pit, to the fact that I am sitting here today but tomorrow I may not wake up. That is terrifying, and it is close to madness. But devotion can also help you feel a deep connection to this fact: that I didn't ask for this life, so whatever I have is a bonus."

KARTHIK BUILT A career taking photographs of industrial sites, like gas terminal plants, cooling towers, and water dams. He ran his own photography lab, where he developed a novel technique for reproducing photos from old negatives. In 1988, he was approached by two disciples of Ramana Maharshi, one of the most influential religious figures in modern India. The disciples had collected nearly two thousand photographs of their guru, who died in 1950. They were looking for help restoring images marred by water damage, fungus stains, and scratches.

Karthik agreed to take on the project. He consulted with leading chemists in India and began studying the photographs of Ramana. His presence alone—"his benign look and gentle touch" and "eloquent silence," a disciple wrote—was said to bring worshippers peace. "There is something in this man which holds my attention as steel filings are held by a magnet," another disciple wrote.

Karthik began paging through Ramana's works. Ramana teaches that there is no need to mourn our parents, because when a person reaches enlightenment he sees that he is not a distinct and bounded self—the people he loves are actually within him. The "desire to regain one's mother is in reality

the desire to regain the self," Ramana has said. "This is surrender unto the mother, so she may live eternally."

Karthik, who had a young son, became so devoted to Ramana that just speaking about him brought him to tears. He
was given his own office at the ashram, where about fifty
devotees lived. He was supposed to be working on the photos there. But some days he would sit in his office without
moving.

Karthik felt that he was fated to move away from his family. When his son was three—the age that Karthik had been
when Bapu first disappeared—Karthik told the president of
the ashram, "I don't think I'm built for this life." He decided
to make the ashram his new home. "My heart is here," he
said. The president of the ashram called Nandini to see if she
consented to the plan, and then told Karthik, "Your wife is
more or less in agreement." (Nandini told me she didn't grasp
that Karthik wanted to live there permanently.)

On Karthik's first night at the ashram, he spoke with a
former fighter pilot in the French navy who had been at the
ashram for years and who was reputed to have lost the need
to regularly eat or sleep. Karthik told the man his plans.
"The ashram agreed with my point of view," Karthik said.
"Nandini had accepted my point of view. My son was too
small to know anything. It looked like I could pull it off."
The man told him, "Now is not the time for you. Please
go back to your family. Now is not the time for you." They
talked until late at night. When Karthik said he was sleepy,
the man laughed. "He was basically taunting me. He said,
'You're not ready for anything, young man. What are you
doing here?'"

At the ashram, Karthik found himself unable to medi-
tate. He kept standing up and walking outside of the tem-

ple, before forcing himself to turn around and try again to be still. But the same thoughts kept surfacing. He imagined what Nandini and his son were doing in their house at that moment. He wondered if his son was asking for him just as Karthik had done three decades before. On Karthik's third day away from home, he walked out the gates of the ashram. This time he didn't force himself to turn around. He took a bus back to Chennai.

Later, he was reading written conversations with Ramana Maharshi and came across several passages in which Ramana discouraged devotees from renouncing their families. "That was like a slap in my face," he said. "Ramana didn't say, 'Go into the forest and live alone.' He didn't say, 'Go live forever in this temple.' What he said was, 'If you go to those places, beware: the same mind is going to follow you wherever you go.'"

~~~~~~~~~

Bhargavi lives in a seventh-floor apartment in Pune with a roof garden. On cloudless mornings, when she is gardening, she is sometimes seized by the desire to "leave everything and go away," she told me. She doesn't want to see a computer or stove. She feels she has too many clothes and wants to give them to others. One morning, she was on her terrace and felt herself melting. "I had an immense urge to jump off and mingle with the sky," she said. "It is a very expansive, loving feeling. In that space, you can allow anything to come in and occupy you. The only thought that finally drew me back was: I have a daughter. And I am not going to do to her what my mom did."

Bhargavi's daughter, Netra, who is now in college, had started asking her mother questions about Bapu and surreptitiously recording the answers on her phone. "What I always heard growing up was that my grandmother was able to talk to God and to connect deeply to other people's suffering," Netra told me. "She could see them for who they really are and what they'd been through. It's been a pattern for three generations: it's something my mother does, and I'm that way, too."

When Bhargavi was younger, she would have been appalled had someone pointed out similarities between her and Bapu. She was her father's child, she told herself: practical, loyal, responsible. But now, she said, "I enact her life, sometimes consciously and, at other times, not so consciously." Bhargavi, too, had chosen a path that gave her freedom from a circumscribed role in society, but in the process she felt she had abandoned her mother, leaving the caretaking to her sister-in-law. "I cleanse my guilt by posturing as her ally," she said, referring to Bapu Trust.

Bhargavi and I began corresponding in 2015, when I was interested in writing a story about the work of Bapu Trust. Then, while gardening one morning on her terrace, Bhargavi said she had an epiphany: I should write about her mother instead of her. "I feel the 'real thing' is my mom's story," she emailed me. "I would love to leave that behind as a legacy for my daughter and for the world."

A few days after proposing the idea, Bhargavi started reading her mother's journals. For twelve years, ever since Nandini discovered the journals in a cabinet of Bapu's house, Bhargavi had kept her mother's writing in her apartment, without reading the words. She had flipped through the pages a few times, but even looking at her mother's handwriting felt "volcanic," she said. Her mother's penmanship shifted over several hundred pages, becoming looser and less coherent, the sentences running off the page. Bhargavi had worked on

cultivating what she called a "personal lightness," and she
worried her achievement would be undone if she read her
mother's words. "I couldn't withstand that level of intensity,"
she said.

Bhargavi had always assumed that her mother, fulfilled by
her love for Krishna, had given little thought to her while she
was away. Now she was amazed by the number of times her
mother had written that she longed for her children. Bhargavi emailed me, "All my fears of knowing my mom through
her writings came true."

IN THE WINTER OF 2019, Bhargavi traveled from Pune to
Chennai for her aunt's ninetieth birthday. She brought her
mother's journals with her, and I met her there. She stayed
with Karthik and Nandini, who had just moved into a two-
story house with French windows overlooking a garden of
which Nandini posted pictures on Facebook nearly every day:
there were pomegranates, roses, betel leaves, jasmine, pepper-
mint, and plumeria. Every day, she and Karthik fed the neighborhood crows, which are said to link the world of the living
with the dead. They also gave rice to more than a dozen stray
dogs, doting especially on a dog named Guard Man, whom
they had recently nursed back to health after he was hit by a
car. When I met Karthik the first time, Nandini was putting
ointment on his finger. One of the stray dogs had bitten it.

Thomas, the man with schizophrenia who had been
homeless in Chicago, once complained to me that all stories about mental illness follow the same arc. They are, essentially, stories of haunted houses. There's an idyllic setting
and a happy family, and, eventually, the dawning recognition
of an intrusive force or unwanted inheritance. Shortly after
I arrived at his house, Karthik drew a picture of his mother's

home, Amrita, on a page of my notebook. He marked the upper-right corner of the house with an X, surrounded by a circle, which represented the space haunted by the Brahma Rakshasa, the spirit of the scholar said to have killed himself. Under his drawing, he listed five bullet points. The first one said, "Warning to Grandpa"—the priest had told him not to buy the house. The last one said, "Life becomes really hard." In Karthik's telling, Bapu's illness wasn't located in her mind so much as in the space that she shared with three generations, the problems of one generation morphing into the conditions of the next. Her illness didn't have one etiology, or one cure, or even some essence that could explain why she had failed to be the mother and wife that her family had wished her to be.

Karthik and Nandini spent several days reading Bapu's journals, which they had never read closely. Nandini sat on a low green sofa that resembled an analyst's daybed, and Karthik sat in a reclining chair below a photograph he had taken: a bleached landscape of geese on a muddy coast. Nandini read out loud in Tamil, and Karthik said "mm-hmm" after nearly every line. Several pages of one journal described a journey Bapu had taken to Ramana Maharshi's ashram, where Karthik had once planned to spend his life. Karthik hadn't realized his mother had been a devotee of Ramana, too.

He translated a passage for me: "When Karthik grows up, he may want to go down the path of philosophy. No one should force him into a family life." He told me, "See, she's saying, 'The son you gave me—I'm giving him back to you right now.'"

His eyes were wet, but the tears didn't spill over. He continued translating his mother's words: "Please take him. Make him listen to your greatness. Make him live by your grace."

"That's what she wrote," Nandini said.

Karthik laughed. "And I have been living on grace for the last twenty years. Her prayer was heard."

ALTHOUGH BHARGAVI AND KARTHIK had always had a close bond, deriving in part from a shared sense of neglect, they almost never talked about their childhood. During Bhargavi's visit, she and Karthik compared their memories of their mother's disappearances for the first time. Bhargavi felt little ownership over her memories. When she said she remembered priests performing an exorcism on their mother, Karthik said, "There was no exorcism. No exorcism." Bhargavi accepted his word.

She also told Karthik, referring to their father, "I have a very strong memory of Appa beating you."

"Nah," Karthik said.

"After my mom left, I think he turned his wrath on you," she said. Karthik insisted that it hadn't happened, so Bhargavi abandoned that memory, too. "I would like some of these memories to leave me anyway," she told me later. "Just let me go."

There was only one contested memory that she wasn't willing to relinquish. She remembered visiting her mother at the Elite Lodge at Guruvayur Temple, though Karthik doesn't recall her ever going there. The walls of Bapu's room were covered in tiny script, from floor to ceiling. "It was incomprehensible—we could not read what she had written," Bhargavi said. "That's where my doubts begin, because the person I saw—that was not a spiritual person. That was a person who was quite lost. It could be that she was hungry and malnourished, that she was all alone. But it has stayed with me. I am not able to reconcile the amazing monk who lived with us, the radiant being who sang and filled our house with sacred things, with the woman she had become."

After Bapu died, one of her brothers-in-law apologized to Karthik. "He just came close to me and held my hands and said, 'I wronged your mother,'" Karthik said. "'I didn't know what kind of person she was. She was a saint—I did not realize.'" Other family members had also begun to describe Bapu as if she had been a figure like Mirabai. In a few temples in Chennai, Bapu's two books of published poetry are sought after by devotees.

Bhargavi resisted the way that relatives rewrote her mother's life. "When they tell us she was a saint, I think they are overdoing it," she said. "This kind of sentiment helps us overlook the moral questions that we disregarded when we shared our lives with my mom."

Bhargavi was haunted by the number of references to hunger in her mother's journals. "For me, that is deep personal suffering," she told me. Yet, she added, "in her moments of ecstasy or whatever, she was with God. And that story is true, too." Bhargavi feels closest to understanding her mother's life when she reads the poetry of Mirabai. "I am mad with love, and no one sees," Mirabai wrote. "Anguish takes me from door to door, but no doctor answers."

NAOMI

"You're not listening to me"

Naomi Gaines was looking for someone who would smile at her. It was the Fourth of July, 2003, and she was at the Taste of Minnesota, an annual celebration with live music in downtown Saint Paul. Vendors sold hot dogs, grilled pork chops, onion blossoms, and funnel cakes; children carried small American flags. Naomi was twenty-four and the mother of four young children. She pushed her youngest two children, twin boys who were fourteen months old, in a stroller. (Her older children were spending the afternoon with her sister.) When she passed people, she smiled, but in return all she got was "glowers," she said.

A few weeks earlier, she had applied for welfare benefits, and her caseworker told her, "You shouldn't be living off the taxpayers' money." Naomi, who was Black, assumed each person she passed at the Taste of Minnesota was having the same thought. She searched the crowd, which was almost entirely white, for a face that would tell her, "I care—I am here." But, instead, she sensed that people were asking themselves, "What is she doing here? She doesn't belong here. This is our place." She thought she heard someone say, "There's another mophead," referring to her hair, which she wore in dreadlocks.

She had recently read *Behold a Pale Horse*, by Milton William Cooper, a former navy sergeant, who claimed to know government secrets withheld from the public. The book describes a government program designed to "target the 'undesirable' elements of society." Naomi was alarmed to read that the name of that program was MKNAOMI—an acronym, she assumed, for "Must Kill Naomi." She read the passage over and over. She believed that the "ruling elite," as Cooper called them, were occupying the new building across the street from her apartment and watching her from behind tinted glass—a sign, she thought, that time was running out for "undesirables" like her and her children.

She stepped onto the sidewalk of the Wabasha Street Bridge, which overlooks the Mississippi River. On both sides, the bridge has pedestrian walkways, eleven feet wide. She accidentally bumped her stroller into a girl not much younger than her. "Excuse me, you need to watch what you're doing," the girl said. Naomi felt as if the encounter proved that "all the love had been taken out of the world."

She longed for proof that the annihilation of "undesirables" hadn't already begun. She continued walking on the bridge, scanning the crowd for another single Black mother. But all she saw were white couples and families, preoccupied by their own lives. "We're all the same really," she thought. "We are all mothers of children. How could they walk by and not say a word?" She silently recited a line from the New Testament: "For men will be lovers of themselves, lovers of money, boasters, proud, blasphemers."

It was a muggy day, but the air felt suddenly chilly. There was a crescent moon, which Naomi interpreted as a sign of coming destruction. The water, more than fifty feet below, smelled sour. She walked to the southwest corner of the bridge, where an American flag was posted on one of the bridge's pillars. Lyrics often came to Naomi unbidden, and she thought of a line from a poem by Saul Williams: "Our stars and stripes / Using blood-splattered banners as nationalist kites."

She was afraid to go back to her car, where she thought she would be killed in private, without witnesses. She wondered if she was the only Black mother on the bridge because the others had already been murdered. She looked down at the water, which seemed to offer her only escape. She and her children had two choices, she felt: a merciful death or a torturous one. She lifted her boys one at a time, kissed them, and dropped them over the railing of the bridge. Then she climbed over the railing and fell backward with her arms open. On her way down, she shouted, "Freedom!"

A MAN ON the riverbank below heard the splash. Like hundreds of others, he had been standing near the bridge waiting for fireworks. "At first I thought it was the splash of an animal—a dolphin or something, and I continued walking," he said. "But then I saw a child in the water rotating from belly to back." The man dove into the water. As he swam toward the child, he noticed that an adult was in the river, too. "I saw a young beautiful woman, far removed from reality," he told me. "She was there, but she wasn't there. She kept singing or yelling, 'Freedom. Freedom. Freedom.'"

Naomi was taken to Regions Hospital, in Saint Paul, and shackled to her bed. "Do you hurt anywhere?" a doctor asked her.

"My back and my heart hurt," Naomi replied.

Physically, Naomi was largely unscathed. But she told a young white police officer, Sheila Lambie, who stood beside her bed, "I'm hurting inside." She explained that "people want to turn away. Sweep women and children, poor brown kids. Keep them under the rug, just forget about them."

Naomi was wheeled into an examination room to get X-rays, and Lambie followed her. She asked if Naomi had been frustrated by her responsibilities as a mother: it must be hard, she offered, to do all the childcare, with little help from the twins' father. "No one to maybe give you a night out," she said.

"You're not listening to me," Naomi replied.

Lambie left the room to consult with medical staff. When she returned, she told Naomi that only one of her boys had been rescued from the water. The other had died. "It's okay that you are crying," Lambie told Naomi. "It's a lot of emotions. Say something to me. You are just staring at me."

"I didn't mean to hurt my babies," Naomi said. Then she began muttering, "Oh God, they were watching me. He's not important to them."

"Who's 'them'?" Lambie said. "Help me. Who's them?"

"The powers that be," Naomi responded. She wouldn't elaborate. Then she recited a poem by Julia Dinsmore, a Minnesota poet who writes about poverty. "My name is not 'Those People,'" she said, quoting Dinsmore. "The wind will stop before I let my children become a statistic."

"So get me back to the bridge," Lambie interrupted. "You're walking, looking for a friendly face, and you're not finding one at all."

"It felt like they were all like oh, a—a rat," Naomi said.

"A rat?"

"Like a dirty rat from my home."

~~~~~~~~

Once, when Naomi asked her mother, Florida, to tell the story of her birth, Florida responded, "Why do you want to know about that? Don't talk about that." Naomi told me, "I never asked her again. But one thing I know for sure: she was alone when she had me, and she was depressed." Florida didn't disagree with Naomi's interpretation, but she also found depression irrelevant. "Who wouldn't be depressed when you don't have enough money to take care of your children?" she told me. "Oppressed/depressed—either way, you can't feel good about yourself," she said.

Florida raised Naomi and her three siblings in the Robert Taylor Homes in Chicago, with minimal help from their fathers. (Naomi didn't know who her dad was until she was three.) When the Homes were built, in 1962, they were among the largest public-housing complexes in the world. Twenty-eight identical concrete buildings, wedged between railroad tracks and an interstate highway, covered ninety-two acres on the South Side, and housed twenty-seven thousand people. "The world looks on all of us as project rats, living on a reservation like untouchables," one early resident told the Chicago Daily News.

Originally trees and gardens had surrounded each building, but, to reduce maintenance costs, the vegetation had been paved over. Naomi grew up in a building that did not have a view of anything green. According to the magazine Black World, "Anyone who has seen huge, treeless, towering, regimented public housing projects like Robert Taylor Homes in Chicago will understand that many white architects do not seem to be psychologically equipped to design for poor or culturally-different people." A study in Environment and Behavior found that residents who lived in parts of the Robert Taylor Homes overlooking trees and grass rated the challenges in their lives as less severe and intractable than did those living in barren surroundings. "A modest dose of nature," the study concluded, "could enhance an individual's capacity to manage the most important issues in her life."

Naomi lived on the fifteenth floor of a building that was part of what residents called the Hole—three buildings, arranged in a U-shape, controlled by the Mickey Cobras gang and known as the most violent in the complex. (In 1998, when a journalist asked about the name, an official with the Chicago Housing Authority smiled and said, "It's a hell hole.") Basic services in the building were so depleted that, when a fire erupted on the fourth floor of Naomi's building, firefighters had to fill hand pumps from kitchen and bathroom sinks—the building's standpipes were broken—before giving up and jumping out the window. The elevators almost never worked. The lightbulbs in the stairwell were usually burned out. Holding her breath in the stairwell, to avoid the smell of urine and vomit, Naomi found her way home by counting the number of landings she passed and peeking through the doors until she recognized her hallway. She rarely left the building, except to go to school. By the nineties, 99 percent of residents at the Robert Taylor Homes were Black and 96 percent were unemployed. It was a "Goddamn public aid penitentiary," one resident told *The New York Times*; another said, "A long time ago, I decided that to survive here, you had to be crazy, chemically saturated, Christian, or some kind of character."

Each month was divided in two: the weeks before and after Florida's welfare money ran out. During the second half of the month, Naomi sometimes carried written requests from her mother to her neighbors for bread. For lunch, Naomi and her siblings went to the recreation room on the first floor of the building to get what the children called their "chokes": free bologna sandwiches so dry that the children joked they couldn't swallow their food without coughing. For dinner, they made what they called "wish sandwiches": two slices of bread with syrup in between. Naomi's aunt and uncle, who lived in the same building, ran a snack shop out of their apartment, selling candy bars, chips, and frozen Kool-Aid in Styrofoam cups, to save children the risk of walking to a store. A 1993 article in the *Chicago Tribune*, titled "Living in a War Zone Called Taylor Homes," said that violence was so integral to daily life that "gunfire might just as well be snowfall."

Naomi's sister Toma, who was two years older than her, taught her to read. It was from books that Naomi began to understand that other children didn't have a "bricked sky," as she put it. She also discovered grassy lawns, brightly colored playgrounds, and large windows with potted flowers. "Toma told me to pretend these things were happening to me," Naomi said. "She told me to imagine how I'd feel if I were the main character in the story. What would I do? How would I act?"

Naomi played the game with her younger sister and brother, too. "She always wanted us to listen to her read," her sister Natalie, the youngest in the family, said. "She'd be like, 'Are you paying attention? Pay attention!' If we weren't, she'd kick us off the bed." Florida avoided these scenes, because she didn't want her children to discover that she had never learned to read confidently. She was functionally illiterate. "Naomi was so smart that I was sure she was going to find out," she told me. "My weakness was her strength."

NAOMI HAD THE sense that she was growing up in the wrong home. The house where she really belonged was six miles south, a three-bedroom brick house with white trim and a manicured garden in Washington Heights, then a middle-class neighborhood in Chicago. The house was owned by Florida's foster mother, Ms. Jackson, a statuesque Black woman who wore pearls. Florida had moved in with Ms. Jackson when she was two, after the Department of Children and Family Services (DCFS) removed her and six siblings from their mother's apartment, and she was still living there when she gave birth to her first child, Toma, at the age of sixteen. Toma and Ms. Jackson maintained a special bond, and Toma slept over at Ms. Jackson's house nearly every weekend. Naomi longed to join—Ms. Jackson brewed fresh coffee every morning, and her refrigerator was stocked with containers of strawberry Yoplait—but she and her younger siblings were only occasionally invited. "Grandma Jackson wasn't feeling us," Naomi said. "She didn't want us. She wanted my sister."

One afternoon, when Toma was seven, she sat on the floor of the bedroom she shared with her siblings and whined that she wanted to live with Ms. Jackson. She kept demanding to move out. Florida had occasionally hit her children, but never more than any other mother Naomi knew. This time, though, she seemed to become unhinged. She hit Toma with an extension cord. Naomi sensed that the real reason her mother had lost control was that she shared Toma's desire to leave.

The next day, Naomi waited for Toma after school, which was at the center of the Robert Taylor Homes. Instead, Naomi's older cousin appeared. "She's gone," he said quietly.

When Naomi returned home, Florida was sitting on the floor, sobbing. A teacher had seen Toma's bruises, and DCFS had intervened, placing Toma with Ms. Jackson. Florida was convinced that Ms. Jackson had plotted Toma's disappearance in advance. "She knew the system," she told me. "My foster mother wanted my baby, and she finally got her."

Florida repeatedly asked DCFS for visits with her daughter, but she was told that all contact was at Ms. Jackson's discretion. In the nineties, Illinois had the nation's highest rate of children in foster care, and nearly 80 percent of the children were Black. Florida said, "I didn't have the education, the lawyer, the nothing to fight back for her—I didn't even know how to start the process."

Florida was so ashamed to have her daughter taken away that she never mentioned the subject. "Nobody ever explained it to me," Naomi said. "I somehow knew my sister wasn't dead, but that's all I knew." Naomi had a reputation in her family for feeling too much—little slights set her off, while the other children moved on. Once, she wrote a poem called "Crying" on a scrap of paper and placed it on her mother's bed: "My eyes are red and sunk, but / nothing is wrong / I've just been / crying." At the time, Florida laughed at her overwrought poem. Years later, however, she told me, "Girl, it was the truth!"

The family didn't reunite until Toma's eighth-grade graduation, six years after her sudden departure. Toma was wearing a cap and gown, surrounded by friends from her comparatively prosperous neighborhood. Florida said, "Naomi cried so hard when she saw her. She said, 'I had thought you were a dream I had! I thought you were a dream where I had a big sister.'"

WHEN NAOMI WAS NINE, Florida woke her in the middle of the night and ordered her and her two younger siblings to get dressed without making noise. Then they walked down fifteen flights of stairs and hailed a taxi to the bus station. Florida stared out the back window of the cab. She was dating a man who routinely beat her, and she needed to escape. At the station, Florida's boyfriend showed up. A security guard allowed them to hide in the garage, inside a parked bus.

In the early hours of the morning, they took a Greyhound bus to Milwaukee, the closest large city, and went to a church operating as a homeless shelter. At 5:00 a.m. each morning, they were woken by an administrator shouting, "Get your feet on the floor, get your bodies out the door!" They weren't allowed back into the shelter until dinnertime, so they spent up to eight hours a day at the public library. "I was in book heaven," Naomi wrote in an unpublished memoir. "Shelves appeared higher than the buildings in Robert Taylor projects." While their mother tried to find a job and an apartment, Naomi read to her younger siblings—usually Dr. Seuss or Shel Silverstein—and pretended she was their teacher. Sometimes, when schoolchildren visited the library, Naomi trailed behind them, imagining she was part of their class.

Florida eventually found a rental apartment, and Naomi and her siblings enrolled in school, but Naomi felt uneasy there. Her classmates teased her, calling her Black Midnight. Although nearly everyone at the school was Black, Naomi said she had the darkest skin in the class. Once, a few kids ran in circles around her, holding sticks and wrapping garments around their waists like loincloths. "Do you see someone there?" they said. "Or is that just black spots?" Florida felt a sense of kinship in her daughter's shame; she had been mocked for the same reason. In middle school, Florida had tried to defend herself, telling a classmate, "Black is beautiful." The classmate responded, "Yeah, but on you it's ridiculous."

They had been in Milwaukee for less than a year when Florida abruptly decided to return to Chicago, to live with the boyfriend who abused her. "I thought to myself, 'She's doing this because she's stupid,'" Naomi said. Naomi's brother was so opposed to returning to Chicago that he stayed in Milwaukee with a foster family. Natalie had more compassion for their mother's decision: "She didn't know she was beautiful," she told me. "She didn't know she was smart. She didn't know she could raise kids by herself. She took the first thing that showed her some interest and ran with it." She added, "Think about her history. Your upbringing will trickle down."

Florida got a new apartment in the Robert Taylor Homes, where she began drinking more frequently. With her boyfriend, she also did cocaine. She sensed that when Naomi looked at her, she was thinking, "Every mother is better than mine." Alcohol increasingly became a form of self-medication, but at the time Florida didn't think of it in those terms. She felt hopeless and self-loathing, but psychological treatment seemed like a fanciful luxury. "As far as we knew, white people were the only ones who got help for stuff like that," Florida said. Her aunt had washed imaginary dishes in an alley, but no one had ever labeled her mentally ill. Other relatives seemed a little too angry. "I understood that," Florida said. "But mentally ill? No." Florida told me, "In our family, if you feel a little down you just take a nap. That's the solution: take a nap."

Mental-health institutions were not designed to address the kinds of ailments that arise from being marginalized or oppressed for generations. Psychotherapy has rarely been considered "a useful place of healing for African Americans," wrote the scholar bell hooks. For a Black patient to reveal her fears and fantasies to a therapist, trained in a field that has been dominated by middle-class white people, requires a level of trust that hasn't typically been earned. "Many black folks worry that speaking of our traumas using the language of mental illness," hooks writes, "will lead to biased interpretation and to the pathologizing of black experience in ways that might support and sustain our continued subordination."

Black Americans are systematically undertreated for pain, as compared to white patients, a disparity that holds true even for children. A study in the *Proceedings of the National Academy of Sciences* found that more than 40 percent of second-year medical students agreed with the statement, "Black people's skin has more collagen (i.e., it's thicker) than white people's skin." Fourteen percent of them agreed with the idea that "Black people's nerve-endings are less sensitive than white people's nerve-endings." Their suffering is naturalized, as if they were built for it, a myth with a long history in this country. The antebellum physician Samuel Cartwright, a professor of "Diseases of the Negro" at the University of Louisiana (now Tulane University), once proposed that the reason enslaved people defied their masters was because they suffered from "Dysaesthesia Aethiopica," a disease that caused them to be "indifferent to punishment or even to life" and produced "partial insensibility of the skin."

Similar myths about suffering shape the field of psychiatry, where depression in Black patients is often undertreated and misdiagnosed. Helena Hansen, a psychiatrist and an anthropologist at UCLA who studies racial stereotypes in medicine, told me, "It is woven into the fabric of this country that Black women's role is to do the work, to do the suffering, so why would we—the mainstream mental-health field—be chasing them down and asking, 'Can I treat you for your sadness?'"

IN 1996, Florida decided that she had no more patience for the indignities of Chicago. She and Natalie, Naomi's younger sister, packed their belongings and moved to Minnesota, which Florida had heard was "a women and children's state." At the time, more Black Americans were migrating to Minneapolis–Saint Paul, where the social services were comparatively robust, than to any other place in the North. Naomi didn't want to leave Chicago, so she stayed with the family of a boy named Nate whom she was dating.

At a homeless shelter in downtown Saint Paul, Florida and Natalie were given a private room with their own bathroom and a key. Breakfast, lunch, and dinner were provided. At previous shelters, Florida had slept on a mat, on a concrete floor, holding her purse. This felt like a hotel. "I'd never seen anything like that in my life," Florida told me. "This was all I needed to get my head together. Your child was not patting you all the time because she's hungry. You could think. You could save money for an apartment."

She got a job as a chambermaid at a luxury hotel in downtown Saint Paul and rented an apartment overlooking the Wabasha Street Bridge. The building had a doorman. "That was so huge for a woman who has been in the projects," Naomi said. "My mom was just so proud. She had never had that good feeling about herself."

In 1997, after finishing high school, Naomi decided to join her mother in Minnesota. By then, she and Nate had had a baby son together, but Naomi was disillusioned by the relationship. She followed her mother's path: after staying at a homeless shelter, she eventually got her own apartment in Saint Paul. She was amazed that in Minnesota "even the ghettos have lawns," she said. She became a teacher's assistant at her son's preschool, and at night she took classes at the Minnesota State Community and Technical College. "I fought with everything in me to keep from becoming another casualty of circumstances," she later wrote. "I figured if I was a good mom, a good person, a good worker, everything would be fine."

She joined a group called the Vibin' Collective that met every week in the back of an Applebee's in Saint Paul. The group composed poetry and songs about poverty, police brutality, and the failure to educate Black children. Naomi began writing hip-hop songs about women with upbringings like hers. "I feel that someone needs to tell the story of single, urban mothers in this country," she said at the time. She performed at local clubs, adopting the stage name Pleasant. But she didn't get as many bookings as she'd hoped. Natalie suggested that her music had "too many metaphors." Naomi wondered if her lyrics were "too controversial—too strong."

Naomi searched for literature about the history of Black women. "I was looking for—I don't know—some continuity: to get rid of the loneliness," she told me. "I wanted to know there are people feeling what I'm feeling." She read *In Praise of Black Women*, a four-volume series that pieces together songs, poems, travelers' tales, and folk legends to reconstruct the lives of Black women through history. "Black women have either been completely written out of history or have had their roles so trivialized as to make them appear to be insignificant," the book's foreword explains. Then she bought the coffee-table book *Without Sanctuary*, a collection of photographs and postcards—originally part of an exhibition at the New York Historical Society—of lynchings. In many of the photos, white people watch serenely as Black adolescents hang from trees. Naomi looked at the pictures for clues, an explanation of what the dead person had done wrong. "What was the story?" she said. "What was the justification for killing? I wanted to know why, and then eventually I started thinking, 'What makes my children any different?'"

For the first time in her life, Naomi found it difficult to get out of bed in the morning. "Naomi had always been up with the birds eating cereal," Natalie said. But some days she couldn't stop crying. If what she suffered from was a kind of melancholia, a grief that cannot be articulated, she was starting to name the thing she had lost. She felt debilitated by the historical resonances of her own story. She suddenly had language to describe the kind of pain that had haunted her family for generations.

In *Hope Draped in Black*, the scholar Joseph R. Winters revisits Freud's "Mourning and Melancholia" to describe what happens when Black people realize that an ideal, like freedom or equality, has been withheld from them. The loss becomes internalized, undermining "any notion of self-coherence," Winters writes. "Melancholy registers the experience of being rendered invisible, of being both assimilated into and excluded from the social order." Barred from full recognition, the grief never resolves. "That's what makes it all so hysterical, so unwieldy and so completely irretrievable," James Baldwin said, using a similar image to evoke this unnamed loss. "It is as though some great, great, great wound is in the whole body, and no one dares to operate: to close it, to examine it, to stitch it."

Florida was pleased that Naomi, after years of hating her skin color, was "getting involved in the Struggle," she said. Although Florida's great-grandmother, who lived to be 102, had been an enslaved person in Tennessee, she said, "we were just never interested in it." Florida worried that Naomi had read too much about her history, too quickly. "Kids her age grow up not knowing the history," she told me. "And when they find out, that's traumatizing itself—to think that's how you were done."

THREE YEARS AFTER moving to Minnesota, Naomi slit her wrist. She didn't really want to die, she said, but "the pain I was experiencing was so great that I just wanted to hurt myself, so I could have something else at the forefront of my mind."

Her family took her to the hospital, where she was diagnosed with "adjustment disorder," a label in the *DSM* that describes a disproportionate emotional response to an identifiable source of stress. Next to the diagnosis, her psychiatrist wrote, "Single mother working two jobs." A social worker wrote, "She believes her depression is due to 'all the hate in the world' and being discouraged about discrimination."

Naomi was discharged with a prescription for the antidepressant Zoloft, but she stopped taking it after a few weeks, because it made her tired and she didn't believe it would work. Drugs will not "change the heartache in the world," she had told her psychiatrist. To be her true self, Naomi felt, required suffering in the face of a racist and violent reality.

Her family didn't dwell on her suicide attempt. They prayed that she would get better. "We trust an invisible force more than we trust doctors who, in our opinion, haven't proven that they have our best interests at heart," Naomi said. Naomi took pride in being the anchor of her family—the person everyone expected to be there when a cousin had an emergency and needed a couch to sleep on and a comforting meal. "People would say, 'Girl you ain't got time to be sad,'" she said. "'You're a strong Black woman, pick yourself up, pray about it, and it's going to be all right.'"

ONE OF THIS country's founding myths is that Black people don't go crazy. The 1844 issue of *The American Journal of Insanity* reported that, according to survivors of the *Amistad* slave revolt, "insanity was very rare in their native country. Most had never seen an instance." Just as there was a myth that people in India were insulated from madness until the British brought them civilization, Black people were thought to be unreflective and sunny. "Where there is no civilization there is no nervousness," declared the neurologist George Miller Beard in his 1881 book *American Nervousness.* The superintendent of the Missouri State Lunatic Asylum once told his colleagues that "prior to the war between the States, a crazed negro was the rarest bird on earth."

In the history of insanity, the United States' sixth national census, in 1840, represented a kind of landmark. State agents attempted to record the number of "insane and idiots" in every house in the country. The results seemed to be a revelation: insanity was eleven times more common in free Black people in the North than among those enslaved in the South. "Here is proof of the necessity of slavery," John C. Calhoun, the secretary of state, told Congress. "The African is incapable of self-care and sinks into lunacy under the burden of freedom." The *Southern Literary Messenger*, a journal once edited by Edgar Allan Poe, declared that Black people "are not only far happier in a state of slavery than of freedom, but we believe the happiest class on this continent." Given the results of the census, the *Mes-*

senger said, abolition was impractical: freed slaves would "furnish little else but materials for jails, penitentiaries and madhouses."

Within a few years, it became clear that the census was riddled with mistakes. In some Northern towns, state agents had labeled nearly every Black person insane. The social historian Albert Deutsch described the 1840 census as "one of the most amazing tissues of statistical falsehood and error ever woven together under government imprint." Nevertheless, the idea that emancipation damaged the Black psyche remained deeply ingrained in American psychiatry. In 1913, Arrah B. Evarts, a psychiatrist at the Government Hospital for the Insane, in Washington, D.C.—the country's largest federal mental institution—warned that "civilization is not to be donned like a garment." Insanity rates were rising among Black patients—those "strangers within our gates," he called them—because they "demanded an adjustment much harder to make . . . than any other race has yet been called upon to attempt." Like the Parsis, the group of Indians thought to have assimilated to British colonialism too abruptly, their minds, it was said, were buckling under the shock of transition.

Black people's troubles were seen in sociological and collective terms. They were denied the singularity of their psychological experiences and dismissed as deficient patients. Mary O'Malley, another doctor at the Government Hospital for the Insane, complained that Black patients couldn't tell a linear narrative. "They never reproduce that general intellectual effect which is termed experience," she wrote. "Their sorrows and anxieties are not staying in quality and do not make a sufficient lasting impression on them to create a desire to end their life." Even their impulse to work through their problems was seen as a failing, as if they weren't introspective enough to want to die.

For much of the last hundred years, the suicide rate for African American adults has been roughly half that of white people, a finding that may be complicated by stigma and neglect. (Suicides may end up classified as other forms of death, like overdoses or accidents.) Nevertheless, suicide has historically been so closely associated with whiteness that a 1962 article in the *International Journal of Social Psychiatry* explained that "some veteran southern psychiatrists who have had extensive experience treating Negroes consider a serious suicidal attempt to be prima facie evidence of white ancestry." In his 1992 book on African American beliefs about suicide, the sociologist Kevin Early said that his interview subjects chided him for even asking about suicide. "As a rule blacks don't kill themselves," one pastor told him. "You should know this already." Early observed that suicide was seen as "almost a complete denial of black identity and culture," because it represented the opposite of enduring. Black people should "bold up, brace our shoulders back, and stand firm," one of his sources told him. "In a sense, allow the bullets to bounce off."

Some therapists felt there was no point in addressing sickness in a Black patient without first accounting for the sickness in his society. "Negro self-esteem cannot be retrieved, nor Negro self-hatred destroyed, as long as the status is quo," wrote two white psychoanalysts in a widely cited book, *The Mark of Oppression*, from 1951. "There is only one way that the products of oppression can be dissolved, and that is to stop the oppression." But this approach also risked becoming another iteration of dismissing individual accounts of Black people's pain.

To declare preemptive defeat in the face of intractable social forces made it seem as if there was no point in exploring a Black person's innermost thoughts—an approach resonant with the indifference of more explicitly racist psychiatrists. "Modern psychiatry got on its feet through the lush fees demanded of rich patients," wrote the novelist Richard Wright, and it has long ignored a "chronic human need, glaring and scandalous." In 1946, Wright helped found a psychiatric center, the Lafargue Mental Health Clinic, in the basement of a church in Harlem. The clinic gave free treatment to impoverished Black patients, who typically had access to psychiatric care, Wright wrote in an essay about the clinic, like "the Negroes of Mississippi, in theory, have access to the vote!" Wright hoped that the Lafargue Clinic would instill in patients "the will to survive in a hostile world." But the clinic shut down after thirteen years; both the city and the state rejected its applications for funding.

The Martinique-born psychiatrist and philosopher Frantz Fanon set a similar goal—psychiatry had to be practiced with a "brutal awareness of the social and economic realities," he wrote. But most of Fanon's analysis was focused on men. Some "may ask what we have to say about the woman of color," he acknowledged in his 1952 book, *Black Skin, White Masks*, about how racism and colonialism affect the male psyche. Whether because of a lack of studies or because the literature was marred by stereotypes, his answer was straightforward: "I know nothing about her."

NOT LONG AFTER her hospitalization, Naomi got back together with Nate, her boyfriend from Chicago. He followed her to Minnesota, and they had a second child, a daughter named Kaylah, but their reunion was brief. Soon, Naomi began dating a musician, Khalid, who said he admired her "colorful way of describing the world." Khalid, who is biracial, was part of the Five Percent Nation, a revisionist movement that had split from the Nation of Islam. Founded by a student of Malcolm X, the Five Percent Nation taught that Black people are the mothers and fathers of civilization, and that Black men are gods. Naomi let Khalid hold weekly Nation meetings in her apartment, and she began to study the teachings, which transformed her sense of what was possible in the world. Natalie remembered Naomi saying, "We've been asleep—we need to wake up. Our history is not in these books."

Having been raised in a different socioeconomic environment, Naomi's oldest sister, Toma, who had graduated from college, didn't relate. "All that stuff about the white man keeping us down—it bothered me," she told me. "I was raised that no one stops you from getting an education but you. Even if that's what you believe: that I can't become the CEO of a *Fortune* 500 company, because they're going to give it to a white man—and that may be reality—we should not focus on that all day, every day."

Sometimes Naomi would look at Khalid and say, "I'm smarter than you." "Looking back, maybe she was starting to get sick," he said, "but it registered as 'She's being an asshole.'" He broke off the relationship. A few weeks later, Naomi discovered that she was pregnant, with twins. She showed up at a club where Khalid was performing and shared her ultrasound photo. He promised he would be there for the birth, but he did not want to get back together. Naomi felt she would never find someone who could match what she called her "love ethic," a willingness to devote herself to another without limit.

In May 2002, Naomi had a scheduled cesarean section. The hospital room she'd been assigned felt metallic and industrial. She sensed that she should not be giving birth there, and not so abruptly. The room was frigid. One staff member injected chemicals into her hand; another, into her back. Khalid, who showed up as promised, observed that all the doctors and nurses were white. "We're in Babylon's heart," he said.

The anesthesia didn't seem to fully work. "I felt their tugging, pushing, moving, cutting, and poking of my flesh and organs," Naomi wrote in her memoir. "Something was wrong. Bile rose up from my throat. There was nothing in my stomach to regurgitate except emptiness."

In mental illness, the boundary between self and other often seems to erode, but pregnancy gives that confusion physical form. The philosopher Iris Marion Young describes pregnancy as the "most extreme suspension of bodily distinction between inner and outer." Describing the growing fetus, she writes, "It feels somewhat like a gas bubble, but it is not: it is different, in another place, belonging to another, another that is nevertheless my body."

Naomi wondered if the twins had been implanted into her womb by some sinister, external force. "This is unnatural," Naomi wrote. "Babies shouldn't be born in this fashion, so far removed from anything human." When Khalid held the twins up for Naomi to see, she looked away. She was reminded of a friend's dog who had to be put under during labor. When the dog woke up after a C-section, she appeared not to understand why these foreign puppies were sniffing her body as if they were entitled to it.

Khalid named the babies Supreme and Sincere. Naomi overheard one nurse ask another, "Did you hear what the names are?" Khalid told me, "I'm positive the nurses and doctors disapproved. The way we named the children put up a barrier. We made them uncomfortable. They couldn't wait for us to leave the hospital. We didn't feel wanted."

———

NAOMI TOOK HER babies home to the largest public-housing complex in Saint Paul, the McDonough Homes. More than six hundred people lived in beige- and cream-colored two-story town houses near the expressway. Four years earlier, in 1998, a twenty-four-year-old Hmong woman named Khoua Her, who lived in the McDonough Homes, had killed her six children in her apartment. "I don't know why. I don't know why," she had told the police. "I can't figure it out." Naomi watched the news coverage on TV with her mom and her sister. "I'll never forget standing up and saying, 'That dumb bitch,'" Natalie said. "When they brought up mental health and things of that nature, I was like, 'Whatever. She was tired of all those kids—that's what it was. She could have at least left them on the doorsteps somewhere.'"

I had first gotten in touch with Naomi in part because I was struck by the uncanny convergence of two young women living in the same building complex, who at the same age had committed the same unthinkable act. I was reminded of Karthik's picture of his mother's house, which had mapped out the historical events that haunted the property.

The McDonough Homes housed many people of color, particularly South Asian refugees who had relocated to Saint Paul, a city that is among the most segregated in the country. A large body of studies has found a greater incidence of psychosis in communities with less "ethnic density"—the proportion of people from the same ethnic group. For people of color, the risk of psychosis rises the whiter their community is. They are more likely to feel alienated and alone and to be targets of discrimination. Naomi bristled at what she called "Minnesota nice"—the courteous but passive-aggressive, even secretly terrified, tone that she felt her presence inspired.

As soon as Naomi came home with her twins, she said, "I

had this sense that I just had to get out of the house. I didn't trust the house."

Her family began doing shifts at her apartment, because they saw that Naomi was too distracted to attend to her children. She listened to an album called *Spiritual Minded* by KRS-One on a loop. On the cover of the album was an image of KRS-One trapped inside a small cell, his hands pressed against either wall. "What if Malcolm X returned?" he sang. "Or Dr. King returned, tell me what have we learned?" Naomi was too mesmerized by the music to eat; all she drank was orange juice. "I felt like someone hit me with a hammer and opened my mind to things I wasn't privy to," she told me. "It could be called a moment of clarity, but it was much more psychologically violent than that."

Naomi felt as if she'd acquired a new kind of literacy, the ability to extract symbolic meaning from whatever she read or heard. She struggled to articulate her revelations, except that she was responsible for the fate of the world. With her music, she believed, she could cure racism. "Naomi, you're only one person," Florida told her. But Naomi responded, "Well, we've got to start somewhere!"

A few weeks after the twins were born, Florida's cousin, who had been helping Naomi with childcare, fell asleep on Naomi's couch. She woke up abruptly from a nightmare. "They are in here—demons," she told Florida. "They are here. We need to get in every corner of her house and pray." They prayed for Naomi, but her behavior didn't change.

A month after giving birth, Naomi took her twins outside, sat in a puddle, and wouldn't get up. Florida called 911, asking for help. During the phone call, Naomi could be heard shouting in the background, "No Mama, no Mama— they'll take my babies!" One of Naomi's cousins reassured her: "I'll kill them before they take your babies." Interpreting the overheard comment as a threat, a crisis outreach team showed up with two officers from the Saint Paul Police Department. By the time they arrived, Naomi was in bed, her face partly covered by blankets. When asked how it felt to have four children, she replied, "It is the stench of injustice."

Florida persuaded Naomi to get into an ambulance, which took her to Abbott Northwestern Hospital, in Minneapolis. At first, she refused to talk. Then she began to scream and rock in place. "Why do you hate me?" she asked a social worker. Hospital staff tied Naomi's ankles and wrists to the corners of her bed so they could give her a sedative. "The nurses gathered around me and stuck a needle in my butt—I was just terrified," Naomi said. She felt she was being punished for a crime but she wasn't sure what it was.

After five days, Naomi was discharged with a prescription for an antipsychotic, Zyprexa, and a diagnosis of "possible onset of bipolar symptoms." She was told that bipolar disorder was caused by imbalanced brain chemistry. With the medication, a psychiatrist wrote, Naomi "became much less guarded and (per mother) generally suspicious of Caucasians." But Naomi didn't take the medication. Khalid, who sometimes visited her and the twins, told her he was skeptical of any answers psychiatry could provide. He had spent periods of his childhood in foster care and in juvenile detention, and he said, "It was a bunch of urban kids, and we were all getting dealt with and chastised by a bunch of suburbanite psychiatrists who don't see what we see. It was all about these problem labels, like 'let's revisit your authority problem'—and that label is the only thing they are going to work on the whole time, instead of digging a little deeper and figuring out what kind of individual this is."

Two weeks after Naomi was discharged, she couldn't stop crying. When Florida brought her back to the hospital, Naomi stripped naked and ran through the halls of the psychiatric ward. She was terrified that she was about to be arrested. "I felt like I needed to take off my clothes to show them: I don't have any weapons," Naomi said. "I don't have anything that would be a threat to you. Why are you so scared of little old me?" Later, she watched a documentary about the Kenyan activist Wangarĩ Muta Maathai, who had led a demonstration where mothers stripped naked to protest the wrongful incarceration of their sons. Naomi identified with these mothers and interpreted her impulse to expose her naked body in a new light: "It's like we were saying, 'Look, we have nothing. We have nothing. You've taken everything from us.'"

This time, Naomi was diagnosed with "psychosis not otherwise specified," even though she showed clear signs of postpartum psychosis, an illness that affects one in a thousand mothers. After four days, she left the hospital. She was on Medicaid, and the insurance wouldn't cover a longer stay. Her treatment was dominated by the principles of managed care, the philosophy that had led to the downfall of Chestnut Lodge. In an ethnography of an emergency psychiatric unit, the anthropologist Lorna Rhodes describes how hospital work has been reshaped by the dictates of managed care: patients must be diagnosed, prescribed medication, and discharged within a few days. Rhodes observes that the hospital staff rarely "speculate directly about economic or political causes of the patients' problems. They were able to tune out the larger social background." Their work, she writes, "can be described in terms of an implicit expectation: they had to produce empty beds." She characterized the emergency psychiatric unit—a place that, unlike much of psychiatry, treats people of all ethnic and economic backgrounds—as "the 'unconscious' of psychiatry."

A month after her discharge, Naomi went outside with

all four of her children in the middle of the night. A police officer stopped her and asked her what she was doing. When Naomi did not acknowledge the officer's presence, instead "singing at a very high pitch," an officer wrote, she was taken back to the hospital. This time she was diagnosed as bipolar and discharged within a week. "She keeps relapsing, cycling," a doctor wrote. "Patient has no insight into her disease."

At Chestnut Lodge, psychoanalytic insight was often achieved by upending a person's story: the therapist uncovered the unconscious conflict or fantasy around which the patient's life had always secretly revolved. A biochemical framework for suffering can operate as a similar jolt, prompting a person to let go of an interpretation of the world that has made him or her hopeless. But to have a new explanatory framework foisted onto one's life is not always healing or generative. It can also feel diminishing, a blow to one's identity and worldview. "Where is the sensitive side of psychiatry?" Naomi said. "They missed the mark. The doctors' lack of knowledge about who I am and where I come from pushed me farther and farther away." She didn't accept that she had a mental illness, she said, "because I felt I was being shown things that were being hidden from me all my life about the reality of me as a Black woman in America raising children."

Helena Hansen, the psychiatrist and anthropologist at UCLA, said she's found that Black patients tend to be less responsive to the idea that "your biology is deficient and you can fix that with technology," a framework that was designed in part to reduce stigma. "When it comes to affluent white patients you can take care of moral blame using a biological explanation," she said. These families often feel freed by the idea that an illness is no one's fault. "But when it comes to Black and brown and poor patients, that same biological explanation is used to deflect blame away from the societal forces that brought them where they are. Because there *is* moral blame: the blame of having disinvested in people's communities by doing things like taking away affordable housing or protection for workers." She said that her patients have found it therapeutic and empowering when she acknowledges the societal structures that have contributed to their state of mind.

Naomi tried to get her doctors to recognize the reality of these social forces, too, but when she complained that "white people are out to get me," the sentiment was described in her medical records as one of her "bizarre statements." When Naomi sang "let my people go," a doctor observed only that she was "singing at the top of her lungs" and noted, approvingly, that she "did soften the volume when staff asked her to."

Eight months after the police stopped her—and four months before jumping off the Wabasha Street Bridge with her twins—Naomi was back in the emergency room again, with the same set of complaints. "She says that she can change people's minds from their typical beliefs to better ones," a psychiatrist wrote. "She wants to convert people into not being racist and accepting her people."

~~~~~~~~~

After being rescued from the Mississippi River, it took Naomi several weeks to grasp the reality of what she had done. She spent three days in the hospital recovering from her fall before being sent to the Ramsey County Jail, which overlooked the Mississippi River. Naomi was placed in a cell that happened to have a view of the bridge. She interpreted her cell number, which was 316, as a sign that she was God. The New Testament verse John 3:16 reads, "For God so loved the world, that he gave his only begotten son."

She asked a guard for a pencil and drafted a letter. "To

whom it may concern," she wrote. "If we looked at our communities as a tree, where would the 'root' be, or better yet, who would the 'root' be? Mothers would be the beginning." She went on, "But the surface cannot maintain, it cannot be strong and stand if the 'foundation' is damaged."

A few days later, she stripped naked and ran through the halls of the jail. She wanted people to "see my scars," she told a doctor. "The pain of motherhood." A social worker wrote that she was "vacillating between total catatonic behavior to a primal scream." Her behavior seemed to embody the principle that Karl Jaspers applied to people who had fallen out of the realm of shared human understanding—the "doctrine of the abyss."

After a month, Naomi was transferred to the Minnesota Security Hospital, the state's largest psychiatric institute, where she was civilly committed as "mentally ill and dangerous." A doctor wrote, "Her insight is nonexistent." A judge ordered that she be forcibly medicated.

Naomi took the antipsychotic Geodon, along with the mood stabilizer Depakote. After a few weeks, she told her mom on the phone, "When I take these medications, I'm not scared that people are worming their way into my life so they can hurt me." The drugs gave her clarity about why she was in the hospital. She spent days in bed weeping. When a nurse asked Naomi how she was doing, she responded, crying, "I don't know how spiritual you are, but I hope my baby don't hate me." She told the nurse, "The person here today would never have harmed her children."

NAOMI WAS CHARGED with second-degree murder. She wanted to plead not guilty by reason of insanity, but her public defender told her that after reviewing twenty years of cases in

Ramsey County, which surrounds Saint Paul, he could not find a single case in which a jury had accepted a defendant's insanity plea. He warned her that, unless she thought her babies were sacks of potatoes, it was unlikely that a jury would find that she met the legal requirements. Like more than half of U.S. states, Minnesota determines whether a defendant qualifies as insane by using the M'Naghten Rule, a standard, established in the United Kingdom in 1843, that requires that "the accused was laboring under such a defect of reason, from disease of the mind, as not to know the nature and quality of the act he was doing or, if he did know it, that he did not know what he was doing was wrong."

One of the first American uses of the M'Naghten Rule was in 1846, in the case of William Freeman, a Black and Indigenous man in New York who had been imprisoned for five years after being falsely accused of stealing a white man's horse. While in jail, a guard struck him on the head with a board, and he suffered a brain injury that altered his personality and destroyed his intelligence. He became consumed by the injustice of his incarceration. "Remuneration with him was the one idea," a doctor wrote. Not long after his release, he killed a white family for reasons he could never explain. He was sentenced to be hanged.

"You have been tried for killing . . . do you understand that?" the judge asked him.

"Don't know," Freeman replied.

"We are now going to sentence you—the jury say you killed him. Do you know what I mean?"

"I don't know," Freeman said.

"Did you hear what I said? Do you know what I mean? You've been tried for killing him—do you understand that?—do you know that?—the jury say you're guilty; that you did kill him—do you understand that?"

"I don't know," Freeman said.

"Do you know who the jury are?—those men who sit along there. Well, they say you did kill him, and now we are going to sentence you to be hanged. Do you understand that?"

"Yes."

"Have you any thing to say against it? Any thing to tell me about it?"

"I don't know."

Freeman's defense attorney, William Seward, who later became Abraham Lincoln's secretary of state, told the judge that he was "shocked beyond the power of expression, at the scene I have witnessed here of trying a maniac as a malefactor." The state admits "in the abstract that Insanity excuses crime," Seward said, "but they insist on rules for the regulation of Insanity, to which that disease can never conform itself." While Freeman's lawyers were appealing his case, he died in jail. His brain was removed from his skull. "I have never seen greater or stronger evidence of chronic disease of the brain and its membranes," a medical examiner wrote.

Knowledge of the brain has evolved, but the legal definition of insanity has not. When Naomi was evaluated at the Minnesota Security Hospital, two doctors concluded that she did not meet the requirements for a M'Naghten defense. Her delusions, they noted, stemmed from astute observations about the society in which she lived. She told the doctors, "When the framers of the Constitution were signing the document, they told a Black person, 'Hey nigger, go get a pen.'" On the bridge she said she had felt terrified for her children, because she knew "their life would be filled with inferiority, indifference, and ridicule." She explained that "I did not want them to die. I just wanted them to live better."

She also said that she felt the world was ending, that

everyone she loved had already been killed, and that she had "tipped into another dimension," but the evaluators seemed distracted by the truth of her sociological insights. Delusions are not spun from pure fantasy. It would be impossible to separate Bapu's desire to wed Krishna from her dismay over the way that wives in traditional Indian households were treated; or Ray's obsession with avenging his failed life and career, his fall from grace, from his expectation that white educated men should not have to contend with such a fate.

Naomi's psychosis drew from reality, too, but her doctors seemed to expect that delusions couldn't on some level make sense. They concluded that her crime was not "based upon psychotic delusion or distortion," because it was "meaningful within her religious and philosophical belief system, and suggests a young woman who was in the midst of an emotional and spiritual crisis." Jumping off a bridge was "a choice she made in order to act out her defiance to society which she perceived as 'oppressive and unjust,'" they wrote. Until her crime, psychiatrists had seemed unwilling to engage with her remarks about race except as "bizarre" pathology. These doctors recognized the validity of her insights about society— it was the first time her perspective had been validated at an institutional level—but only to use them against her, as evidence that she deserved to be punished.

Naomi and her family wanted to go to trial and argue that she had not truly understood what she was doing on the bridge. "The truth should be presented," her sister Natalie said. But when the prosecution offered Naomi a plea deal of eighteen years—fourteen years in prison and four on supervised release—her lawyer encouraged her to accept.

Naomi agreed, because she didn't want to risk being separated from her children for the rest of her life. "I needed to give the state my pound of flesh," she said. The twins' father, Khalid, also felt she should be punished. "The severity of the situation deserved some accountability," he told me. "And maybe that's not only on her: Does the county or state need to be held accountable? Did they neglect her issues? Did they need to pay more attention?"

At her sentencing hearing, the county attorney asked Naomi if she had known that her sons would die if she threw them into the river. She hesitated and then answered, quietly, "Yes."

"You know that's not true," Natalie said. She got up and left the courtroom.

NAOMI WAS SENT to the Shakopee Correctional Facility, the only women's prison in Minnesota, twenty-five miles from Saint Paul. When she arrived, a psychologist described her as "hesitant, quiet," and "fearful that she can't make it in prison and shouldn't be here." The psychologist added that Naomi believed a hospital was "the only place for her to get what she needs." Her civil commitment as "mentally ill and dangerous" was still in place, and, after completing her criminal sentence, she would still have to prove that she was mentally fit to rejoin society. But first she'd be punished.

Minnesota was once a leader in reforming mental-health care. In the late 1940s, Minnesota's state governor Luther Youngdahl toured the state's mental asylums and saw men and women shackled to benches and chairs in filthy and overcrowded facilities. A quarter of them had been confined in state institutions for an average of three decades. The state was guilty of "particeps criminis," he said. "We have all participated in a social crime against these sick people." In

1949, Youngdahl championed a new mental-health law that enabled more patients to be discharged and treated in their communities. On Halloween, he went to a mental asylum north of Minneapolis and lit a pyre of 359 straitjackets. "The roots of demonology are deep," he said. "We have burned one evidence of this tonight. We must be on our guard that it does not creep up in other forms." The next year, at an American Psychiatric Association convention, Youngdahl announced: "There is no such thing as a rich patient or a poor patient . . . There is no such thing as a black patient or a white patient. There is only one type of patient—and that is a sick patient."

His approach helped to universalize mental illness, but it also reflected a lack of curiosity about the ways that race and economics shape the experience. In 1963, John F. Kennedy passed the Community Mental Health Act, legislation designed to replace the "cold mercy of custodial isolation" with a network of behavioral-health centers and halfway homes, a shift that psychopharmacology had helped make possible. But the centers, which were poorly funded, ended up catering to the easiest patients, those with few social and financial needs. Donald G. Langsley, the president of the American Psychiatric Association in the early eighties, complained that the clinics were merely offering counseling for "predictable problems of living." A 1978 report by Jimmy Carter's Commission on Mental Health found that few of the centers served people with schizophrenia. Instead, they provided treatment to people who were "socially maladjusted" or had no mental disorder at all.

Vulnerable people were released from mental hospitals back into their communities, with little attempt to integrate them. "For the most massive movement of medical care in

twentieth-century America," the psychiatrist E. Fuller Torrey has written, "there was no master plan, no coordination,
no corrective mechanism, no authority." Instead of spending
their days in hospitals, patients found themselves in other
forms of confinement: homeless shelters, group homes, jails.
Then, in the eighties and nineties, in an effort to appear
tough on crime, politicians began passing legislation that
penalized more types of behavior. People who in the previous era may have been committed to asylums ended up behind bars, because they struggled to adapt to social norms
or to defend themselves once accused. According to a study
by the U.S. Department of Justice, more than two-thirds of
women incarcerated in jails and prisons have a history
of mental illness. In the past four decades, the number of
women incarcerated in Minnesota has increased by more
than 1,000 percent.

Shakopee was called a "cupcake prison" by some of the
staff there. It had carpeted hallways, cushioned chairs, and
an outdoor dining area with a garden. Until 2016, there was
no fence or wall around the perimeter of Shakopee—just a
knee-high hedge. "Freedom is the test of a penal institution,"
Isabel Higbee Hall, who helped found the prison, had said in
1915. As Naomi understood it, there was no need to worry
about women escaping. "They'd know where to look for us,"
she said. "The first thing we'd do is find our kids."

Naomi's youngest child, Supreme, the twin who had survived, lived with Khalid, but he also spent time with Naomi's
sister Natalie, who took care of Naomi's two oldest kids. Natalie had given up the chance to attend Spelman College,
the country's oldest Black liberal arts college for women, so
she could stay in Minnesota and raise Naomi's children. "I
had my own anger," she told me. "Some days I didn't want

to talk with her. But I kept her kids together—that's all that mattered to me."

Supreme longed to join his siblings when they visited Naomi in prison, but he was not allowed, because the Department of Corrections forbids offenders from having contact with their victims. All that Supreme remembered about his mom was that she had dreadlocks. When his brother and sister returned from visits to the prison, he told me, "I'd ask them, 'What does she look like? What is her personality?'" His older sister, Kaylah, told me, "I could tell him things—how she smells, how she would act." She said, "I felt like he was close to me because I looked like her."

NAOMI HAD ASSUMED that she'd become friends with other mothers of color at the prison—roughly 16 percent of the women at Shakopee are Black, more than double the percentage of Black people in the state—but, she said, "they completely shunned me. They looked at me like, 'How dare you break down and do that to your kid?'" She sensed that the correctional officers took a similar view. In a note to one, she wrote, "When you spoke to me I felt like a small ant who had just been stepped on but did not die." She began keeping a journal. "Dear Paper," she wrote. "I feel obsolete." She continued, "I need help and not the help that dry judgmental therapy sessions with PhDs give."

She had been at the prison for a few months when she met Khoua Her, the Hmong woman who had lived down the street from her at the McDonough Homes. Khoua, who had been sentenced to fifty years in prison, now lived in the educational unit, a small block for people with model behavior. Naomi said, "She just came up to me and said, 'Hey,

I don't know if you know me, but if you ever need someone to talk to, I'm here. I know what you are going through. I understand.'"

Khoua had spent much of her childhood at a refugee camp in Thailand and said she'd been raped, at twelve years old, by the man who would become her husband. "If I thought my experience was bad, as far as the patriarchy, it paled in comparison," Naomi said. "When she told me her story, it was like a spiritual awakening." They had both been young mothers crushed by the idea of their children growing up in a society that lacked imagination about their potential. "To think I'd once judged her," Naomi said.

In a four-part essay published in the *Hmong Times*, in 2000, Khoua described how, at the height of her depression, when "the burdens in the world were heavy and a crushing thing," the boundary between her own suffering and that of her children dissolved. "The more I felt their pain the more I became weaker," she wrote. "It reminded me, back to when I was little and how I suffered like them." She urged readers, "Please listen to your inner self and ask some questions like, 'How am I going to get help for my problems?' Nobody will know about your problems if you don't speak up."

In the Hmong community, some believe that after death a person's soul returns in different form, and that an individual has many souls, only one of which resides in the physical body. Naomi was also drawn to these ideas. "I started to ponder whether Khoua and I were part of something that was beyond my or her comprehension," she told me. A local paper had noted "concerns among some in the Hmong community that the spirits of the six children remained in the house."

Naomi watched the movie *Beloved* in prison and began

to think more about the role of ghosts in her own history. In the movie, based on Toni Morrison's novel, the protagonist has run away from her slave master and, as she and her family are about to be captured, she kills one of her daughters to prevent her from growing up under his rule. Years later, the dead daughter returns to her mother's house as a ghost, an intrusion that the family comes to see as part of life's order. "Not a house in the country ain't packed to its rafters with some dead Negro's grief," the dead baby's grandmother explains.

Florida was also shaken by the movie *Beloved*. "I saw how the mother thought she was protecting her kid," she told me. "Just like Naomi." Naomi wanted to talk with her mother about how trauma is passed between generations, but she also felt ashamed that her mom might think she was making excuses. Once, when Naomi complained about the unfairness of the legal process, her mother reminded her that, after prison, she would have a life. Her son would not. Naomi told me, "I will never forget the pain in her voice when she said that."

Naomi drafted a letter to her dead son, Sincere. "Forgive me," she wrote. "I thought I was doing the right thing . . . Everything I ever learned got mixed up inside my head like a psychological gumbo." She apologized for each life event she had caused him to miss. "We'll meet again," she promised. "I feel you when you're near. The bond between mother and child is the strongest there is."

NAOMI SPENT AS much time as she could in the prison's library, one of the few places in prison where it was socially acceptable to have conversations about ideas. The prison's librarian, Andrea Smith, told me, "From the beginning, Naomi self-identified as a curious person, and I think she saw me as a kindred spirit. She came to the library to test out ideas about spirituality and philosophy; about how to live in the world; about how to be seen, and how to see others."

Naomi began reading two to three books a week. She crafted her own bookmarks herself. "They were really colorful and personalized and large," Smith said. "You'd see speckles of glitter." In Naomi's cell, she kept a collection of pink slips of paper used for sick calls, on which she scrawled the names of the books she intended to request from the library: *All God's Children*, by Fox Butterfield; *The Resurrection of Nat Turner*, by Sharon Ewell Foster; *We Real Cool: Black Men and Masculinity*, by bell hooks; *The Silent Cry: Mysticism and Resistance*, by Dorothee Soelle.

Smith gave Naomi the job of library clerk, one of the most desirable positions at the prison. (Other women were assigned to fold balloons, make state-police clothing, or craft rubber dog toys.) On the whiteboard behind her desk, Naomi copied quotes from her reading. For a long time, she featured the line, "Prisons don't disappear problems, they disappear human beings." Another woman incarcerated there told Naomi, "You don't read for you—you read for other people." Naomi said, "I loved that comment. It is not everybody's passion to read books, but I damn sure can disperse the information to whoever is listening."

Naomi had always felt that experiencing depression was incompatible with being a Black woman, but in reading (and in music, too) she found lives with which she could identify. "I thought, 'Oh my God, there is a group of people somewhere who understands my outlook,'" she said. "I was breathing the same air as them. It was a form of invisible fellowship."

Smith said that it was not uncommon for Black or Indigenous women to come to the prison library, read about their history, and discover for the first time the way that history had shaped them. "The lightbulb clicks on for them," she said. For Naomi, though, "these ideas were already playing in her mind: that she came from a history of enslavement, from a family whose roots were not recognized, and there's a reason why her own family has been broken and estranged." She said that Naomi often described people "not only as individuals but as pawns in a larger play." When Black women showed up at the prison with longer sentences than white women who'd committed the same crimes, Smith said, "Naomi would make comments about the orchestra that is playing out in front of us."

Smith and Naomi had long conversations about how "the pain has to go somewhere—it can't disappear," Smith said. "It doesn't simply dissipate. You pass it on."

Naomi wanted to re-create the experience of fellowship for other readers who felt alone. She started writing a novel about a dystopia where hip-hop is illegal. Then she began a memoir in which she tried to capture the experience of carrying her mother's trauma. "I have survived the darker aspects of myself," she wrote in the book. "What I've done and where I've been is not who I am."

TO RESEARCH HER MEMOIR, Naomi interviewed Florida. She'd always been afraid to ask questions about her mother's past, but now, she said, "I had the perfect excuse." Naomi learned that Florida's own mother, Velma, had had a nervous breakdown. "Her mental illness was the dirty little secret in my family that nobody wanted to explore," Naomi said.

Velma had drunk heavily and left home for days at a time, leaving Florida and her six siblings alone. They lived in the Ida B. Wells Homes—public housing in Chicago built exclusively for Black tenants. Velma's seven children were so hungry that they ate dry oatmeal from the box. When Florida was two years old, police officers came to the apartment after someone had reported that children inside were crying. At first, Florida's older sisters refused to let the officers in. Then the officers came back with doughnuts. Florida's sisters relented, opening the door.

Florida never saw her home again. A social worker with the Department of Children and Family Services took her to Ms. Jackson's front door and told her it would be her new home. Her six siblings were placed in different foster homes throughout Chicago. "I was scared to even move," Florida said. For two years, she didn't speak.

At school, Florida was assigned to a class that her teacher told her was for students who would become factory workers or maids. She stared out the window or put her head on her desk and slept. "I wasn't learning anything—I was just traumatized," she said. "But I didn't know why I felt the way I did—I didn't even have a recollection that I had sisters and brothers. Ms. Jackson had to tell me about all of it." Ms. Jackson had a biological daughter who was one year younger than Florida and excelled in school. Florida said, "I would comfort myself by repeating: you can't expect her to treat someone else's daughter like her own. I forgive her, I forgive her." In ninth grade, she walked through the school's entrance and out the back door. She never returned.

A witty, steely woman with a husky voice, Florida spoke casually with me about the experience of hunger, poverty, and domestic abuse. When she recalled her education, though, she began weeping. "I'm sixty, and I still can't do basic math," she told me. Periodically, she purchased phonics books, but she hasn't pushed past a fifth-grade reading level.

"It is very emotional—to raise kids and not be able to read to them," she said. "Maybe the teachers just put up their hands and said, 'Hey, we can't teach her,' but I don't know. It seems like they didn't try."

She eventually took classes through Job Corps, and it was only then that she gathered the courage to ask a question she had wanted to pose for years: When you are multiplying two numbers, like nineteen times two, and you need to carry the one, where do you put the one? "You could put the one anywhere on top," the teacher replied. Florida began crying. "It was amazing—it was amazing—to hear someone give me the information," she said.

After she became pregnant with Toma, Florida decided to search for her own family. She'd had no contact with them for more than a decade. "I got on the L train and went to a part of the North Side of Chicago where I'd been told two sisters lived," Florida said. "I knocked on doors. I asked people on the street: Do you know my sister?"

She eventually found all her sisters, including one who, it turned out, had lived two blocks from her all along. "None of us understood how they could have done what they did—snatching all these kids," Florida said. She also reunited with her mother, whom she hadn't seen for fourteen years. But the shock and humiliation of losing seven children seemed to have exacerbated Velma's condition—an experience Florida came to understand when, a few years later, her firstborn, Toma, was taken away, too. "If you think you are not a good enough mother, then you carry yourself different," she said.

ON JULY 4 every year, the anniversary of her son's death, Naomi would break down. She tried to distract herself by reading, but if she saw the number eleven—the total of seven plus four, the date of her crime—or the words "falling" or "freedom," she felt paralyzed. She stopped eating. She didn't want to leave her room.

Naomi was assigned a therapist at the prison, Karley Jorgensen, a petite woman who had grown up in a small, homogeneous town in Minnesota. Jorgensen worried that Naomi thought, "Here comes this young white girl who doesn't have any experiences like mine." There was only one Black therapist at the prison. There were no Indigenous therapists, and Indigenous Americans made up nearly a quarter of the prison's population. Jorgensen observed that the women of color were less likely than white women to have had access to mental-health care before prison, and, once they were incarcerated, their struggles were more likely to be considered acts of defiance than signs of illness.

Nearly all of Jorgensen's patients had experiences of trauma: physical or sexual abuse, incest, domestic violence, rape, abandonment. Arthur Blank, one of the first psychiatrists to recognize the struggles of Vietnam veterans who returned from the war, characterized trauma as an experience that a person doesn't have "the capacity to integrate, digest, narrate . . . a foreign body in the psyche." But the inability to assimilate trauma, he warned, can afflict a therapist as well. "As a clinician, I've seen a lot of denial that's based on an inability to shoulder the burden of treating," he said in an interview. "I've had many, many therapists talk to me about this: 'I don't know what to do, how can I treat these people? Should I try to treat them when I don't know how?'" The inability to connect may be especially acute when a white doctor is faced with a Black patient whose experiences are unfamiliar. In the 1968 book *Black Rage*, one of the first books about Black mental health to reach a wide audience, the psychiatrists William Grier and Price Cobbs warned, "White clinicians may unconsciously withdraw from an intimate knowledge of a black man's life because placing themselves in the position of the patient, even mentally, is too painful."

It is rare for people in prison to have weekly therapy sessions, but for a period of time Jorgensen saw Naomi for an hour each week. Naomi could access mental-health services more readily than others, because of her dual commitment, criminal and civil. Jorgensen hoped that, within the confines of her tiny, windowless office, "there was this atmosphere of acceptance. I wanted Naomi to know: 'I have hope and belief in you as a person; I don't look down on you; I see you as an incredible woman who is doing everything she can to move herself forward.'" Jorgensen listened to Naomi without judgment, trying to make her feel respected, not feared. As Fromm-Reichmann, the so-called queen of the Lodge, once wrote, "The patient needs an experience, not an explanation."

But their progress in therapy was undermined by triggers that were part of the texture of daily life. Tom Vavra, a lieutenant who became close with Naomi, told me that when women at Shakopee lashed out at him, "I analyze that: What happened to them when they were younger? If there is sexual trauma and they're here facing unclothed body searches, I can see why they're struggling." He went on, "Honestly, there are a lot of women here incarcerated because of their mental state. Do I think they'd benefit more from a hospital-type setting? Yes, in a heartbeat."

Naomi hated the med line, where she waited every day to be given her pills. It wasn't the act of taking the pills so much as the ritual itself: standing in an hour-long line with women whom she didn't like; being watched, like a child, to see if she'd swallowed the pills. Sometimes people passed and shouted, "Look at the crazy-people line!" Naomi was tempted to just step out of line and walk away. "They say, 'Take your meds, just take your meds,' as though everything will be okay," she complained, according to her prison records. "It is not okay and it doesn't 'just go away.'"

IN 2010, Naomi was taken off her antipsychotic, Geodon, "due to cost," according to a nursing note. Within a few days, she stopped sleeping. She was afraid that, as soon as she drifted off, she would be raped by prison guards. "She does not want to go to sleep when feeling 'unsafe,'" a psychologist wrote. She had been taking Tegretol, a medication that treats mania and insomnia, but she decided to stop the Tegretol, too. She also refused to eat, because she thought her food might be poisoned. One night, when a guard rejected her request to call her family, she picked up a metal chair and threw it against a wall, breaking a window. She was ordered to immediately return to her room. When she didn't obey, officers sprayed her with a chemical irritant.

She was escorted to the prison's segregation unit, which has thirty-three cells. Two guards stood at the door of the cell and instructed her to take off her clothes, run her fingers through her hair, open her mouth, squat, show the skin behind her ears and the bottoms of her feet, and cough three times. She was given a heavy, tear-proof quilt, like a baby's sleep sack, to wear around her body.

She remained in solitary confinement for sixty days. She was alone for twenty-three hours a day, in a ten-by-twelve-foot cell. She told a psychologist that she felt "insane, unwanted, and unproductive." She had no access to pens, paper, or books. Bagged meals were slid through a small window on her door. To go to the bathroom, she had to ask a guard for a few squares of toilet paper. When she met with mental-health staff, she was handcuffed to a table. "She spoke in another language and informed me that 'We do not speak the same language,'" one therapist wrote.

Another woman incarcerated at Shakopee, Elizabeth Hawes, recently interviewed fifty-one women about their experiences in segregation—a project she sent to state policymakers. She concluded that, "regardless of age, race, or sexual orientation, the common denominator was not a tendency for violence, but a history of trauma." Hawes spoke with women who had been placed in solitary confinement for a range of infractions, including singing at the wrong time, eating someone else's piece of cake, or violating the prison's no-touch policy. The women at Shakopee were not allowed to hug, give one another high fives, link feet below a table, or braid one another's hair. Naomi said that in the courtyard, on sunny days, she and other women would manipulate their shadows so that they could have the illusion of hugging without breaking the rules.

Several women whom Hawes interviewed had been placed in segregation for suicide attempts. Often, they had been punished for breaking apart a razor, a violation of prison rules, in order to cut themselves. The women told Hawes that segregation only amplified their thoughts of death. "Putting someone in seg makes mental illness," one woman told Hawes. "Walls breathe," another said. A woman with anorexia told her, "I was suicidal as soon as my seg door shut. After fifteen days, I'd hallucinate. I'd hear operas and marching bands."

Tom Vavra, the lieutenant, said that when he visited Naomi in segregation, he was shocked by her deterioration. "She was talking in almost like a tribal language," he told me. "She kept referring to her ancestors."

Andrea Smith, the librarian, had never visited a prisoner in segregation, but she received special permission to see Naomi. Smith stood outside her cell and tried to have a conversation with her. "I couldn't understand what she was saying, but the language she was using was familiar to me," Smith told me. "It reflected the discussions we'd had about her beliefs, about the greater forces at work in the world. Naomi feels very deeply the dichotomy of good and evil." Without her medications, Naomi's symbolic thinking had ratcheted up to a new level. "I think it was inevitable, especially with the amount of CNN that she consumed," Smith said, "that sometimes her mind would take her to the place of: Evil is winning. Injustice is winning." Smith told Naomi, "This is scary for me. I'm trying to understand you right now, but I don't fully recognize you."

Smith wasn't sure if Naomi even registered her presence. But Naomi said that the visit was a turning point. "Ms. Smith wasn't treating me like a problem to be fixed only with medication. She understood the language I was speaking. She knew me intellectually, philosophically, and even on some level spiritually. She was a huge barometer to judge my wellness and nonwellness." After the visit, Naomi began taking Tegretol again. Perhaps if Naomi had encountered this kind of understanding years earlier—someone who grasped the different frameworks necessary to describe her pain—she would have had a different "career." Her delusions might not have taken hold so firmly if she hadn't felt so alone.

As Naomi began to feel better, she passed time in segregation by closing her eyes and imagining the lyrics to her favorite songs. "I heard these songs as clear as if I had a radio in the room with me," she told me. Eventually, she began singing out loud. She discovered that the segregation unit was the only part of the prison where "the acoustics were fabulous." The women in neighboring cells nicknamed her "the Radio" and put in song requests. She said, "The music made me feel like I still had a life."

IN APRIL 2014, after a decade in prison, Naomi received a typed letter from a stranger. "Hello Naomi, I was never able to properly introduce myself," the man, whom I'll call Carl, wrote. "I was there with you in the river that July evening when both our lives became entwined."

Carl said that he had been writing the letter for ten years. Every Christmas, he sat down at his computer to complete the note, before getting stuck. "Many thoughts come to-gether too fast and it seems the words and their meaning tend to wanna jam up right at my finger tips," he wrote. He told Naomi that when he dove into the Mississippi River he had been depressed. "I, too, have faced this destroyer of hope and love," he wrote. "The fear of failure, the darkness and sorrow, that hides in all human hearts."

Naomi asked Carl to visit her in prison. A few months later, he drove from his house, in a suburb of Saint Paul, to the visiting room at Shakopee. He was a burly white man, a grandfather of six. The son of a chief petty officer in the navy, he had spent his early childhood in foster care, after his mother had a nervous breakdown and vanished. "That's what childhood was—being on the move, never having friends, really," he told me. He remembers hiding under his blanket and wondering, "Why am I here?"

In the months before July 4, 2003, he had been in a kind of free fall. He was a vibration analyst at an oil refinery. As the economy contracted and the work became streamlined—his company hired outside consultants to increase efficiency—he felt marginalized and demeaned. "People would tell me,

'Change is good, change is better,' but for some people change is a death sentence," he said. He lashed out when new procedures were introduced at work and became so paranoid and angry that he had to take a leave of absence. "You can put all the experts together to talk about depression, but until you've lived it—the whole spectrum of depression—you don't know what they're talking about," he said. At night, lying in bed with his wife, he couldn't sleep. "I would go downstairs and pray and pray and pray," he said. "I needed to cry out, to confess, 'You're a big bag of hot wind. You're a failure, admit it. That big fancy personality you think you have—it's air.'"

In the visiting room at Shakopee, Naomi was startled by Carl's warmth. "In walks this man with salt-and-pepper hair, his arms wide open," she said. They hugged—physical contact is briefly allowed at the start of visits—and then sat two feet apart, as required, facing the officer on duty. Carl explained to Naomi that he saw their time together in the river as a rebirth, a "renewed Baptism." Until that moment, he had been in the kind of mental state in which every bridge or balcony was an invitation to jump. "You saved me and no one can say different to that fact," he told her. He thanked her profusely.

Smith remembers Naomi leaving the visit with "a real sense of wonder and gratitude—I think she felt loved, and I think she really felt she could love him. They were both such sad, hurt people in that moment, and I think their kinship came from knowing the world is much bigger than them."

Years later, when I sent a letter to Carl, he called me immediately. He said that he had wanted to share his story for years, but his pastor had told him to keep waiting; the time would come. Now, at sixty-eight years old, he had stage-four lung cancer. He knew he would die soon, though his family didn't like him to acknowledge it. He began recounting what had happened the day he rescued Naomi as if he had been rehearsing the details for years. "It was a beautiful, beautiful evening," he told me, in a raspy voice. "We were going to watch the fireworks. You could smell food and hear music, and for some reason I heard a splash." He saw a young child, floating on the water, his eyes open.

Carl handed his wallet to his wife, climbed over a fence on a bank below the bridge, and ran down a rocky bluff. He shouted to God, "I need your help!" Then he dove off the rocks. He swam toward the area in the water where he'd last seen a child "slowly tumbling, like he was in a washing machine, as he went down the river." But when he got there, the boy was no longer floating. "I stuck my hand deep in the water and the first thing I felt was a leg," Carl said. He wanted to give the child mouth-to-mouth resuscitation, but he was too exhausted to tread water. Then another man tapped him on his shoulder. He had followed Carl into the water. He lifted the child from Carl's arms and swam with him back to shore.

Naomi was farther down the river, in a section where the water was darker, the current rapid. It was the kind of water that Carl said he wouldn't feel comfortable even going into with a boat. Nevertheless, he found himself swimming toward Naomi. He thought of Psalm 69: "Save me, Oh God / For the waters have come up to my neck. I sink in the miry depths." When he reached Naomi, she seemed barely aware of his presence. He thought, "Wherever you're going, young lady, I am going with you. I am not going to let you go."

Throughout our conversation, Carl frequently used the word "sandbox." He defined the sandbox as the space where the pressures of society bear down on a person. "My issues were coming from needing to stay in that sandbox," he told me. "I was so afraid of losing control. You could see it at work, with my body posture, with the way I dealt with my family." He had been shocked to find himself in the water—he was overweight, and not a good swimmer—and surprised to be holding a Black woman's hand. "It sparked something in me—I became less prejudiced," he told me. "How can you love someone that you don't even know?"

Carl told me that he didn't want to use his real name, because saving Naomi and her son was the Lord's work, not his. "If you want to call it being born again, I don't know, but it's a wonderful, wonderful feeling," he told me. "When I dove off the rock, I stepped out of that sandbox and into nothingness, into infinite space. I gave up my place in the world."

I remarked that the symbolism of the baptism in the river was profound.

"It's not symbolism," he told me. "It's the truth. It's the truth for me."

Although he had taken psychiatric medications for years—"I know how pills help," he told me—he said he had recovered from depression because of his time in the water with Naomi. "I found a place where I can go at night when the lights are out, when I am lying in bed in a panic, wondering what I will do about tomorrow," he said. "I needed a rock. The experience with Naomi helped me gather myself, to find that rock."

During chemotherapy sessions, he had been reading her novel, the one about hip-hop, which a company called Page Publishing had helped her to publish. He asked me to give Naomi his phone number. "Tell her I want to hear about the great author she turned out to be," he said. They had fallen out of touch after a few visits, when Naomi sensed that her role in Carl's life was making his wife uncomfortable. Carl recognized that Naomi meant more to him perhaps than he did to her, and he didn't mind. "I just wanted to be someone who could give her courage and redemption—I'm not saying that I can offer all that, but there were so many layers of human doubt that people were throwing at her, and I wanted her to know that I didn't judge her," he told me. "I didn't want to be the law. I just wanted to be someone who wasn't going to let go of her in the river."

NAOMI'S CORRESPONDENCE WITH Carl made her feel, even in moments when she wanted to give up, that "I have a responsibility to keep breathing," she said. It also felt to her like a sign that she was ready to be accepted into society. But in 2016, as she was nearing her release date, she learned that the state was not ready to let her go free. Her civil commitment as "mentally ill and dangerous" was still in place. A psychiatrist interviewed her for three hours, and concluded that "Ms. Gaines is not currently capable of making an acceptable adjustment to open society. She has not achieved adequate stability." The psychiatrist wrote, "There is nothing more Ms. Gaines could have done than she has done but she needs time to transition back into the community." Thirteen years earlier, she couldn't meet the legal bar for insanity, but now she was deemed ill enough to be indefinitely detained.

At a hearing before a Special Review Board tasked with determining her custody status, Naomi challenged the findings of the assessment. "The report lacks sympathy with African American life and culture," she told the board. The evaluation described her preoccupation with her ancestors as evidence of psychosis. "Native Americans get to report about hearing from dead relatives but African Americans do not get the same liberty," she said. She also objected to the fact that the psychiatrist had cited her fear of being gassed as evidence that she was delusional. In fact, as her psychologist noted in her records, right before Naomi was placed in segregation, "the officers did gas her."

On Naomi's release date, she was transported back to the Minnesota Security Hospital. "All these years Naomi had been asking for help—she was willing to do whatever the psychologist told her to do to get well, and that didn't seem to mean anything," Smith said. "It was really hard not to say, 'Yeah, it's because you're Black.' That was in the back of my mind, because I follow the news. I see white women commit crimes, and I notice that they're not coming to meet me in prison—they're going other places."

AT THE MINNESOTA SECURITY HOSPITAL, Naomi told the staff, "This is the final step, to see if I am ready to live in a wide-open space." She joined the hospital's band, the Therapeutics. There were fifteen members, including patients, psychiatrists, and the hospital's recreational and security staff. "By having doctors and staff in the band as my equals, I had one of the rare opportunities to critique them, to say things like, 'That's not the right chord. Can you try going up?'" she said.

Naomi attended therapy groups called Beyond Violence, Self-Care, Healthy Relationships, Rejoicing Readers, and Insight. In the Insight class, she was told that being mentally ill was not her fault. In a worksheet, she defined it as "a clinical disease of the brain that disrupts the normal reasoning." Naomi shared what she had learned with Florida, who said the definition made her feel lighter. "I had been thinking I'm the only person that this ever happened to, who goes through this mental-illness stuff," she said. "It put the icing on the cake: to know I wasn't alone."

But sometimes Naomi resented the idea that all biologies

are universal. She wanted to tell her doctors, "Your mental break could never be my mental break. We have different fears than white people, so you're going to miss the mark." She said it felt like, "I'm coming to the doctor for a headache, but you're looking at my knee?"

Psychiatric insight can save a life—a person about to leap off a building, convinced she can fly, needs to know that her brain is not properly functioning. But a constricted view of insight may also blind doctors and family members to certain beliefs—a relationship to God, a new understanding of society and one's place in it—that are essential to a person's identity and self-worth. Naomi felt nostalgic for the sense that she had access to truths withheld from others. When she was psychotic and unmedicated, she said, "I feel like I am on a higher plane, on top of a very tall building, and I can see the whole expanse." But taking her medications didn't eliminate her awareness of social context, as she had once feared. It wasn't a zero-sum game. She planned to take medications for the rest of her life—"unless someone cures mental illness," she said. Florida wasn't optimistic that day would come. "God left that to himself," she told me. "God left the brain to himself."

When Naomi could get Supreme on the phone— whenever he was at Natalie's house—she tried to teach him about mental illness. Once, he asked her, "What does it mean when they say you were sick? Sick how? Like a headache?" She told the story from the beginning, when she met his father, to the end, when she was convinced that her family would be killed by the government. Then she told him, "Supreme, sweetheart, now I want you to tell me what I just told you. Tell it to me again in your own words."

Supreme told me, "I was never angry at her, because she

explained to me that when you are sick you do things you would not normally do—you are not you."

NAOMI WAS TERRIFIED that she'd have to stay indefinitely at the Minnesota Security Hospital. Some people are held there for their entire lives, but she moved through the program in less than a year. Sixteen years after her crime, in the fall of 2019, Naomi moved into her own place, a one-bedroom apartment. She decorated it with framed expressions like "Free Hugs" and "Love Makes a House a Home," as well as reminders to others, as if she were still living in an institution, like "Please dry hands with paper towels under sink."

I met Naomi and her daughter Kaylah at the new apartment, and at first Kaylah, who was nineteen, rarely looked up from her homework. She was a sophomore at the University of St. Thomas, in Minneapolis, and she was writing a paper about the Haitian revolution in a notebook perched on the arm of her mom's couch. She wore her hair in a high bun and looked strikingly like Naomi. Her personality resembled her mother's, too, a fact about which her family often remarked. Kaylah said, "Sometimes they compared us when I was being creative or being an introvert, but I felt like other times they said it in the wrong tone. It didn't feel like they were saying it as—"

"A compliment," Naomi offered.

Kaylah nodded.

When Kaylah took a health class in high school and learned about the genetics of mental illness—studies with twins suggest that the heritability of some mental illnesses is between 50 and 80 percent—she panicked. "She started terrifying herself," Natalie told me later. "She said, 'I learned today that mental illness is hereditary and I might lose my mind!'"

Naomi's oldest child had been briefly hospitalized for a mental breakdown a few years earlier, but he had recovered and was now doing well. His family was present for him in a way that they wished they had been for Naomi: they sat by his bed at the hospital from 6:00 a.m. to 10:00 p.m., working on jigsaw puzzles with him, making sure he was never alone. "With what my brother went through, I've also been thinking that maybe I'm not the one who is going to get sick," Kaylah told me. "Maybe my role is to help somebody else—to be the one close to it, who understands—instead of the person going through it." Like Carl, she would be the one who would not let go.

SUPREME'S EIGHTEENTH BIRTHDAY was in May 2020. Naomi received permission from her probation officer to see him, since he would be a legal adult. On his birthday, they gathered in Florida's apartment, in a low-income housing complex where Natalie also lived. The last time Naomi had seen Supreme he was a toddler, with short curly hair, just learning to walk. Now he was taller than her and lanky. He was about to graduate from high school. Naomi wrapped her arms around him and cried. She had not held him in seventeen years. "Supreme wasn't shy—he fell right into her arms," Florida said. "He just lay there, like, 'This is what I've been waiting for.'"

His father, Khalid, who is now a chef, has not spoken with Naomi since she was arrested. "I don't hate her," he told me, "but at the same time it just needs to be known that I can't take away the loss that I feel for my child." He said that when Supreme reunited with Naomi, "I think he was expecting, like, rainbows. He was expecting that right away he would find all the answers—everything would get tightened up. He wanted to be babied and cradled and fixed, and it doesn't work like that. The reality hit him that he's part of *her* healing process, too." Still, Khalid described the reunion as "the best thing in the world for Supreme. You could see it right away: he was more full, some of those empty spots were no longer there."

SHORTLY AFTER GETTING her own apartment, Naomi took a two-week training course offered by the Minnesota Department of Human Services to become a peer specialist: the job involved visiting people with mental illness in their homes and offering them companionship and support. A week before her new job was set to begin, in July 2020, she was told that she was ineligible because of the nature of her crime. "I'll be paying the debt to my family and son for the rest of my life," she told me. "But I thought I'd already paid my debt to society." She got a job at Dollar Tree instead. After a few months, she was promoted to management. But, when she submitted her paperwork for the new position, she learned that, because of her criminal record, she wasn't eligible for that job, either.

Whenever Naomi has a destabilizing thought—that it is her job to save the world from racism, for instance—she asks herself what would happen if she interviewed a hundred people: Would they label the thought a delusion? If the answer is yes, she tries to put less stock in the idea. She told me, "I still have certain things I believe about who I am and my destiny—there are still some mysteries, some questions in my mind—but I am able to put those thoughts on the back burner, so that I can be a good sister and daughter and mother; so that I can take a shower, have normal conversations; so that I can go to work. But meds don't take it all away—there are certain ideas I carry with me."

On her bookshelf, Naomi kept some of her favorite books from prison, as well as a few new ones, including *A Guide to Starting a Business in Minnesota* and *Music Marketing for the DIY Musician*. She was working on an album of songs, many of which she had composed when she was in prison. She had recently emailed the link to her YouTube channel to Andrea Smith, the librarian. "As I look back on my time at Shakopee," she wrote, "I wonder if there is a woman like me there now. Not who has my crime, or even time length, but someone who no one expects to be greater than her past and can't necessarily prove that now, not even to herself."

One song, dedicated to all the families separated by prison, describes her dream at Shakopee of holding someone else's hands. Another song is about John 3:16, the Bible verse that haunted her when she was arrested. A third song is dedicated to Khoua Her, the Hmong mother who had lived in the McDonough Homes at the same time as Naomi. In the song, Naomi recalls how in 1998 she watched the coverage of Her's crime and cursed her.

> *When I came to prison, guess who held out her hand?*
> *Guess who said, "If you need someone, I'm a friend?"*
> *Guess who understands what no perfect mom will?*
> *The same mom back in '98*
> *I condemned Her*
> *My friend*

LAURA

"He could read my mind, as though I didn't
need to explain anything"

Laura Delano thought she was "excellent at everything, but it didn't mean anything." She grew up in Greenwich, Connecticut, one of the wealthiest communities in America. Her father descended from Franklin Delano Roosevelt, and her mother was introduced to society at a debutante ball at the Waldorf Astoria, one of the oldest hotels in Manhattan. By eighth grade, in 1996, she was the class president at her private school—she ran on a platform of planting daffodils—and one of the best squash players her age in the country. Still, she worried that she hadn't met people's expectations. "There was the best, and there was everything else," she said.

The oldest of three sisters, Laura felt as if she were living two separate lives, one onstage and the other in the audience, reacting to the performance. She felt exhausted by the effort, which made her feel as if she had an "empty core." She didn't want to pursue what she called the "good-girl model of life," fulfilling the prim ideals of Greenwich society. She snapped at her mother and locked herself in her room. She had two friends who cut themselves with razors, and she was intrigued by what seemed to be marks of individuality and defiance. She tried cutting herself, too. "The pain felt so real and raw and mine," she said.

Her parents took her to a family therapist, who, after several months, referred her to a psychiatrist, to whom she confessed that she had thoughts of killing herself. The psychiatrist gave her a diagnosis of bipolar disorder, which had only recently begun to be diagnosed in children. A few years earlier, an influential researcher at Harvard had proposed that irritability in youth—"affective storms," as he put it—could be a sign of mania. Between 1995 and 2003, the number of children and adolescents given the diagnosis rose by nearly 4,000 percent. Laura was prescribed Depakote, a mood stabilizer that had just been approved for the treatment of bipolar disorder, but she hid the pills in a jewelry box in her closet. Then she washed them down the sink.

Laura gave little thought to her diagnosis, focusing instead on her social life. A classmate described her as "a big figure in our class, a social butterfly, a woman about town who was extroverted and a kind of shape-shifter," merging seamlessly with any clique at school. But Laura said that she doubted whether she had a "real self underneath."

She was hopeful that she might find it at Harvard, where she arrived as a freshman in 2001. Her roommate, Bree Tse, said, "Laura just blew me away—she was this golden girl, so vibrant and attentive and in tune with people." On her first night at Harvard, Laura wandered the campus and thought, "This is everything I've been working for. I'm finally here."

She tried out new identities. Sometimes she drank until early morning and was praised by boys for being chill. Other times, she was a nihilist, disillusioned that her peers were all competing for an ultimately meaningless goal. "I remember talking with her a lot about surfaces," a classmate, Patrick Bensen, said. "That was a recurring theme: whether the surface of people can ever harmonize with what's inside their minds."

There were also nights when she couldn't carry on a conversation. "Why do I have these extra layers of thought that others don't have and that pull me farther and farther away from being human?" she wrote in her journal. Each day felt like a new performance. "In the morning, I had to get myself motivated enough to shower and change and go be Laura Delano," she said.

During her winter break, she spent a week in Manhattan preparing for two debutante balls, at the Waldorf Astoria and at the Plaza Hotel. The balls were once the occasion for girls to make their first appearance among potential mates—Eleanor Roosevelt, to whom Laura was distantly related by marriage, had described her own debutante ball as "utter agony"—and, though the parties are no longer explicitly about marriage, the pageantry surrounding them has remained largely unchanged. Laura went to a bridal store and chose a floor-length strapless white gown, designed by Vera Wang, and white satin gloves that reached above her elbows. She and her fellow debutantes spent the days before the ball being trained to spin, bow, and walk gracefully in heels, to prepare for their formal entry into society.

At the first ball, Laura and the other girls were introduced in alphabetical order on a loudspeaker; when it was Laura's turn, she walked onto the ballroom stage, and her escort, a friend from school, spun her around and she curtsied. "I remember thinking Laura was so much a part of it—she was going with the flow," her sister Nina said. "We were all trying to abide by the expectation to be beautiful, well-dressed, fun, and in the mix."

Yet, in pictures before the second party, Laura is slightly hunched over, as if she were working to minimize her muscular shoulders. She wears a pearl necklace and her hair is slicked back in an ornate bun. Her smile is pinched and dutiful. She performed the required motions, walking to the stage and curtsying again. But by the end of the night, drunk on champagne, she was sobbing so hard that her escort had to put her in a cab. She felt "pure and unadulterated loneliness," she said. In the morning, she told her family that she didn't want to be alive. She took literally the symbolism of the parties, meant to mark her entry into adulthood. But she didn't believe in the adult she was supposed to become. She told me, "I was trapped in the life of a stranger."

WHEN LAURA RETURNED to Harvard for her next semester, her parents helped her make an appointment at McLean Hospital, the oldest mental hospital in New England, built on the grounds of a former estate. Less utopian than Chestnut Lodge, McLean has been an emblem of the medical establishment for more than a century, treating a succession of celebrity patients, including Robert Lowell, James Taylor, and Sylvia Plath, who described it as the "best mental hospital in the US." The socialite Marian Hooper Adams once remarked that McLean "seems to be the goal of every good and conscientious Bostonian." As Laura walked through a double-leaf iron gate and up the hill to her appointment, the institution felt to her like a "pulsating, living being of mythic strength."

Her psychiatrist had multiple Ivy League degrees, and Laura felt grateful to have his attention. In his notes, he described Laura as an "engaging, outgoing, and intelligent young woman," who "grew up with high expectations for social conformity" and was "repressed by the values of her upbringing." In his waiting room, Laura was chatting so easily with other patients that he wrote, "At first I did not think it was her, as she looked like she had been in the place many times before."

The psychiatrist confirmed her early diagnosis, calling it Bipolar II, a less severe form of the disorder. The diagnosis is given to patients who have had at least one episode of depression and one episode of hypomania, a state in which a person may have a reduced need for sleep, inflated self-esteem, and unremitting energy. Unlike mania, hypomania (meaning "less than mania") doesn't necessarily impair a person's functioning—sometimes it even temporarily improves it.

This time Laura was relieved to hear that she had a disease. "It was like being told: It's not your fault. You are not lazy. You are not irresponsible." After she left the hospital, she felt nearly giddy. "The psychiatrist told me who I was in a way that felt more concrete than I'd ever conceptualized before," she said. "It was as though he could read my mind, as though I didn't need to explain anything to him because he already knew what I was going to say. I had bipolar disorder. I'd had it all along." She called her father, crying. "I have good news," she said. "He's figured out the problem."

She began taking 20 milligrams of Prozac. But the pills didn't make her feel better, so she was prescribed 40 milligrams, and when that didn't work, 60 milligrams. When Laura complained that she felt alienated at Harvard, the pinnacle of achievement, it may have been hard for her doctors, steeped in the same cultural expectations, to imagine how this setting could be deeply uncomfortable and dissonant. Her life appeared so free of obstacles that any sort of distress was ascribed to pathology.

Laura saw each prescription as a sign that her pain was being taken seriously. She wasn't even sure whether Prozac actually lifted her mood—roughly a third of patients who take antidepressants do not respond to them—but her emotions did feel less urgent and overwhelming, and she was more productive. She directed all her attention to her coursework, to her treatment, and to squash. She stopped socializing, deeming it frivolous, and considered it a victory when she got through a day having spoken to fewer than five people. Her friends now seemed to her "emotionally greedy"—like insects, they buzzed around, having fun, a concept that struck her as showy.

Occasionally, Laura drank enough that the idea of socializing and even romance became appealing again. But up to 65 percent of people who take antidepressants report that it dampens their sexuality, a side effect that Laura experienced but felt ashamed to raise with her pharmacologist. "I assumed he'd see sexuality as a luxury," she told me. "He'd be like, 'Really? You have this serious illness, and you're worried about *that*?'" At parties she enjoyed flirting, but by the time she and a partner were naked in bed, she said, "I'd kind of get hit with this realization that I was physically disconnected. And then I'd feel taken advantage of, and I would kind of flip out and start crying, and the guy would be like, 'What the heck is going on?'"

Her psychiatrist raised her Prozac prescription to 80 milligrams, the maximum dose. The Prozac made her drowsy, so he prescribed her 400 milligrams of Provigil, a drug for narcolepsy often taken by soldiers and truck drivers to stay alert for long shifts. The Provigil gave her so much energy that, she said, "I was just a machine." She played the best squash of her life. She was so alert that she felt as if she could "figure people out," unpacking their body language and guessing what kind of childhoods they'd had. She liked to stay up late sitting on the steps of the Pit, an area surrounding the Harvard Square T station, where teens who were homeless congregated. Laura's freshman roommate, Bree, who became her best friend, said, "She'd come home at two in the morning and we'd be like, 'Were you talking about life with strangers again?' She found the conversations really interesting, so I was like, 'Hey, power to her.'"

When the Provigil made it hard for Laura to sleep, her pharmacologist prescribed Ambien, which she took every night. In the course of a year, her doctors had created what's known as a "prescription cascade": the side effects of one medication are diagnosed as symptoms of another condition, leading to a succession of new prescriptions. Often, prescription cascades are a feature of neglect, a way for overburdened psychiatrists to quickly manage their caseloads. But in Laura's case, her psychiatrists seemed to feel a duty to preserve her capacity to function at the highest levels, almost treating subpar performance as a symptom of its own. They kept tinkering with her drugs, as if they could eventually bring her to an emotional state that corresponded with all the advantages she'd been given. In her writing about injustice, Miranda Fricker reflects on the ways that "epistemic goods" (like education or access to expert guidance) are unfairly distributed. Some, like Naomi, receive too little, whereas others, like Laura, perhaps receive too much.

Laura spent $121 on her own copy of the DSM. She could recognize when her impulses were "textbook"—for instance, buying three dresses from Nordstrom at once—but the insight didn't prevent the behavior. Her father, Lyman, a money manager, recommended that she try something new: take off a semester and spend three months in the wilderness. Laura liked the idea of re-creating Henry David Thoreau's experiment on Walden Pond, to live simply in nature, which she had read about in high school. She signed up for an Outward Bound trip along the Rio Grande, leaving her medications at home.

On the flight to Texas, she listed her goals for the trip in a notebook: "Overanalysis must go"; "connect with people gradually; let's get over this intense addiction to the intense passion of pouring out one's soul"; "find some faith in something, in anything."

Her journal alternated between lyrical descriptions of vast expanses of earth (she longed to be like "the wind, strong and overwhelming in its nothingness") and fear that she wasn't actually changing. She scolded herself for eating too much trail mix and dreaded the moment when her family would see her new figure and realize that their hopes ("she'll be trim and fit," "she'll be happy," "she'll be fixed") hadn't been realized. Lying under a blue tarp, resting her head on her sack of clothes, she drafted a letter to her future self: "Can you relate to the fact that right now, March 15th, some time in the late afternoon, you feel so ashamed of your body and your thoughts that you don't really even know what to do?"

By the time Laura returned from her trip, the thought of returning to Harvard induced such panic that she felt suicidal. At her request, her parents took her to a hospital in Westchester County, New York, and she stayed for two weeks. In her medical records, she was described as "pleasant and sociable," "cooperative and motivated"—a patient with good insight. It was easy for her to assimilate the perspective of her doctors. But Laura stopped trusting her own view of herself and the world. She required confirmation from experts to make her unhappiness feel real. Her psychiatrist at the hospital put her on a new combination of pills: Lamictal, a mood stabilizer; Lexapro, an antidepressant; and Seroquel, an antipsychotic that she was told to use as a sleep aid. But her father, Lyman, said, "I had no conviction that the drugs were helping. Or that they weren't helping."

LAURA RETURNED TO Harvard and managed to graduate, an achievement she chalked up to muscle memory. She considered herself the kind of student who could regurgitate information without absorbing it. After her graduation, she bounced between jobs, like working for a state agency that issued building permits, that she didn't believe would lead to a career. She drank almost every night and sometimes got sexually involved with men in ways that made her feel used. She interpreted each disappointment as the start of a black mood that would never end. She seemed to be caught in a loop, depressed over the fact that she was entering a phase of depression. The diagnosis reflected her state of mind, but it also influenced her expectations for herself.

A friend from squash tournaments, Justin Cambria, was surprised when Laura informed him that she would be on medications for the rest of her life. "We had connected about the fact that we were both from these socially pretentious cultures, and I hadn't realized the severity," he said. "I just thought she was struggling to figure out who she wanted to be."

For a few months, Laura saw a psychiatrist who was also a psychoanalyst, and he challenged the way she told her story. In a letter, he told her that he wasn't sure what to make of her early bipolar diagnosis, since "many depressions are given a 'medical' name by a psychiatrist, ascribing the problem to 'chemistry' and neglecting the context and specificity of why someone is having those particular life problems at that particular time." He reminded her, "You described hating becoming a woman." Laura stopped going to her appointments.

His explanation didn't match hers, and she decided "he wasn't legit."

She began seeing a new psychiatrist, whom I'll call Dr. Roth. At her appointments, Laura described her drugs as precision instruments that would eliminate her suffering, as soon as Dr. Roth found the right combination. If she had coffee with someone and became too excited and talkative, she thought, "Oh my god, I might be hypomanic right now." If she woke up with racing thoughts, she thought, "My symptoms of anxiety are ramping up. I should watch out for this. If they last more than a day, Dr. Roth may have to increase my meds." She became so skilled at diagnosing her symptoms that she said, "I'd come to the appointment having already done my analysis and just basically needing her sign-off." During the next four years, her antidepressant dosage tripled. Her dosage of Lamictal quadrupled. She also began taking Klonopin, a benzodiazepine, which has sedative effects.

She came to resemble the sort of patient described in *Love in the Ruins*, Walker Percy's 1971 novel about a small-town psychiatrist. "Every psychiatrist knows the type," Percy writes. "The well-spoken slender young man who recites his symptoms with precision and objectivity—so objective that they seem to be somebody else's symptoms—and above all with that eagerness, don't you know, as if nothing would please him more than that his symptom, his dream, should turn out to be *interesting*, a textbook case. Allow me to have a proper disease, Doctor, he all but tells me." A patient like this, Percy observes, "has so abstracted himself from himself and from the world around him, seeing things as theories and himself as a shadow, that he cannot, so to speak, reenter the lovely ordinary world."

Laura's life was increasingly devoid of interests. When Barack Obama was elected president, in 2008, Laura said,

"I didn't have an opinion or an emotion about it." She fell out of touch with her friends. "At a certain point, it was just, 'Oh my god, Laura Delano—she's ill,'" a friend from high school said. Laura gained nearly forty pounds, which she attributed to the medications. When she looked in the mirror, she felt little connection to her reflection. "All I ever want to do is lie in my bed, cuddle with my dog, and read books from writers whose minds I can relate to," she wrote a psychiatrist. She identified intensely with Sylvia Plath, another brilliant, privileged, charismatic young woman who, in her journal, accuses herself of being just another "SELFISH EGOCENTRIC JEALOUS AND UNIMAGINATIVE FEMALE." To avoid madness, Plath wonders if she should devote "the rest of my life to a cause—going naked to send clothes to the needy, escaping to a convent, into hypochondria, into religious mysticism, into the waves."

THE DAY BEFORE THANKSGIVING, when she was twenty-five, Laura drove to the southern coast of Maine, to a house owned by her late grandparents. Her extended family was there to celebrate the holiday. She noticed her family tensing their shoulders when they talked to her. "She seemed muted and tucked away," her cousin Anna said. When Laura walked through the house and the old wooden floorboards creaked beneath her feet, she felt ashamed to be carrying so much weight.

On her third day there, her parents took her into the living room, closed the doors, and told her that she seemed trapped. They were both crying. Laura sat on a sofa with a view of the ocean and nodded, but she wasn't listening. "The first thing that came into my mind was: you've put everyone through enough."

She told her parents she was going outside to write. She went to her bedroom and poured the contents of her Klonopin, Lexapro, and Lamictal bottles into a winter mitten. Then she snuck into the pantry and grabbed a bottle of merlot and put the wine, along with her laptop, into a backpack. Her sisters and cousins were getting ready to go to a Bikram yoga class. Her youngest sister, Chase, asked her to join, but Laura refused. "She looked so dead in her eyes," Chase said. "There was no expression. There was nothing there, really. I remember holding her shoulders and saying, 'It's going to be okay.'" Her other sister, Nina, was exasperated that Laura wouldn't go to yoga. Nina said, "I remember thinking, 'Why aren't you doing things that are going to make you feel better? What's so hard in life? Why is it so hard for you?'"

As Laura walked out of the house, she felt thankful that her grandmother was no longer alive. She imagined her saying, "Oh God, Laura, snap out of it. Don't be ridiculous." There were two trails to the ocean, one leading to a sandy cove and the other to the rocky coast, where Laura and her sisters used to fish for striped bass. Laura took the path to the rocks, passing a large boulder that Nina, a geology major in college, had written her thesis about. The tide was low, and it was cold and windy. She leaned against a rock, took out her laptop, and began typing. "I will not try to make this poetic, for it shouldn't be," she wrote. "It is embarrassingly cliché to assume that one should write a letter to her loved ones upon ending her life."

She reflected on a study showing that people who compose suicide notes are less likely to complete the act. Nevertheless, she wrote, "in all the analysis I've been doing in my head (for years now, but today in particular), I realize that, in the long run, it's better for all of you." She went on, "I would never have a life of normality."

She swallowed three large handfuls of pills, washing down more than thirty pills with wine. "I feel incoherene coming on, so typos and potentially incomprehensible words are going to follow," she wrote. She found it increasingly hard to sit upright, and her vision began to narrow. She felt grateful to be ending her life in such a beautiful place. She fell over and hit her head on a rock. Although she heard the sound, she felt no pain.

WHEN LAURA HADN'T returned by dusk, her father went to the shore with a flashlight. It took him twenty minutes to walk along the coast. Then he saw Laura's laptop sitting on a boulder. He walked to the other side of the rock. "There she was, stooped over," he said. "I jumped down and tried to shake her and slap her and wake her up, but it was impossible." He ran back to the house and called an ambulance.

Laura was airlifted to Massachusetts General Hospital, but the doctors said they weren't sure if she would ever regain consciousness. She was hypothermic, her body temperature having fallen to nearly ninety-four degrees. "They told us that even if she did survive, she could be brain-damaged," Lyman said. "They gave us the option of just letting her go."

Two days later, she woke up in the intensive care unit. Her sisters and parents watched as she opened her eyes. Tears streamed from them. "Why am I still here?" she said. Nina told me, "I suppose I had this spiritual idea that she might have passed through gates, and someone on the other side told her to come back. But it wasn't that. It was pure science. It was so cold on the rocks that her body had gone into a kind of hibernation mode. She would never have lived if her body had been warmer."

After a few days, Laura was transported by stretcher to

McLean Hospital, where she'd been excited to arrive seven years earlier. Now she was weak, dizzy, sweating profusely, and anemic. Her body ached from a condition called rhabdomyolysis, which results from the release of skeletal-muscle fibers into the bloodstream. She had a black eye from hitting the rock.

Nevertheless, a doctor wrote that "her eye contact and social comportment were intact." Although she was disappointed that her suicide attempt didn't work—she told her doctors she'd swallowed the pills after doing a "cost-benefit analysis"—she also felt guilty for having worried her family. She reported having a "need to follow rules," a doctor wrote. Another doctor noted that she did not seem to meet the criteria for major depression, despite nearly dying by suicide. The doctor proposed that she had borderline personality disorder, a condition marked by unstable relationships and self-image and a chronic sense of emptiness. According to her medical records, Laura agreed. "Maybe I'm borderline," she said.

Shortly before her discharge, she drafted a letter to the staff on her unit: "I truly don't know where to begin in putting in words the appreciation I feel for what you've all done to help me," she wrote. "It's been so many years since I've felt the positive emotions—hope, mostly—that have flooded over me." Unpersuaded by her own sentiment, she stopped the letter midsentence and never sent it.

LAURA BEGAN SEEING a new psychiatrist at McLean, who confirmed that her underlying problem was borderline personality disorder. "It is unclear whether she has bipolar (as diagnosed in the past)," he wrote.

The concept of borderline personality disorder emerged

in medical literature in the 1930s, for patients whose symptoms didn't fit any other diagnoses. Harold Searles, a psychiatrist at Chestnut Lodge, described these patients as too "audience-oriented": they patterned their sense of identity on other people's expectations. In 1980, the diagnosis was added to the DSM, which noted that "the disorder is more commonly diagnosed in women." Its defining features, which include excessive emotions, lack of self-control, and a fragmented sense of self, seem to pathologize stereotypically feminine traits. The sociologist Janet Wirth-Cauchon has described borderline personality disorder as the "new 'female malady' of late modern society."

In 2010, when she was twenty-seven, Laura moved in with her aunt, who lived outside of Boston, and attended a borderline day-treatment program in Boston. "It was another offering of what could fix me, and I hadn't tried it," she said. At her intake interview, she said that the director of the borderline program told her, "So, you went to Harvard. I bet you didn't think you'd end up at a place like this." Laura started crying, though she knew that her reaction would be interpreted as "emotional lability," a symptom of borderline disorder. A doctor there observed that Laura was "showing insight into herself but without relief from this insight." She told the doctor that she had "given up agency."

Laura had once found a kind of solace in surrendering herself to disease. She had realigned her life, consciously or not, so it more purely expressed the way she'd been classified. But now she felt betrayed when she realized that the story that was supposed to explain her life wasn't offering the kind of clarity or healing she felt she'd been promised. She'd developed insight into the wrong condition.

She had been content to be bipolar. "I fit into the DSM criteria perfectly," she said. But borderline personality disorder didn't feel blameless to her. Almost all the patients in Laura's group were women, and many had histories of substance abuse, sexual trauma, and destructive relationships. Laura, who was drinking heavily at the time, said that she interpreted the diagnosis as her doctors saying, "You are a slutty, manipulative, fucked-up person."

Her pharmacologist prescribed her naltrexone—a drug that is supposed to block the craving for alcohol. For the first time, Laura was insulted by what she'd been prescribed. If she were to quit drinking, she wanted to feel that she had done it on her own. She was already taking Effexor (an antidepressant), Lamictal, Seroquel, Abilify, Ativan, lithium, and Synthroid, a medication to treat hypothyroidism, a side effect of lithium. The medications made her so sedated that she sometimes slept fourteen hours a night.

A few months after entering the borderline clinic, she wandered into a bookstore, though she rarely read anymore. On the table of new releases there was a book with a picture of a face overlaid by the names of several medications she had taken. She bought the book, *The Anatomy of an Epidemic*, written by Robert Whitaker, a Pulitzer Prize–winning journalist who has become a guiding light for people critical of psychiatry. His book examines why, between 1987 and 2007, despite the development of new psychiatric medications like Prozac, the number of U.S. Social Security disability claims had doubled, with mental illness accounting for one of the largest portions of the rise. Whitaker argues that psychiatric medications, taken in heavy doses over the course of a lifetime, may be turning some episodic disorders, which might have otherwise resolved on their own, into chronic disabilities. (Whitaker largely ignores the social and economic reasons, like cuts to social-welfare programs and a lack of jobs for people without higher degrees, that have contributed to increasing numbers of Americans leaving the workforce and going on disability.)

The book prompted Laura to begin reading about the history of psychiatry. She hadn't realized that the idea that depression was caused by a chemical imbalance was just a theory—"at best a reductionistic oversimplification," as Schildkraut, the scientist at the National Institute of Mental Health, had put it. Nathan Kline, Ray's onetime doctor, had been confident that "we'll find a biochemical test or series of tests that will prove highly specific to a particular depressive condition." But such a test never materialized. For more than fifty years, scientists have searched for the genetic or neurobiological origins of mental illness, spending billions of dollars on research, but they have not been able to locate a specific biological or genetic marker associated with any diagnosis. It is still unclear why antidepressants work. The theory of the chemical imbalance, which had become widespread by the nineties, has survived for so long perhaps because the reality—that mental illness is caused by an interplay between biological, genetic, psychological, and environmental factors—is more difficult to conceptualize, so nothing has taken its place. In 2022, Thomas Insel, who directed the National Institute of Mental Health for thirteen years, published a book lamenting that, despite great advances in neuroscience, when he left the position in 2015, he realized, "Nothing my colleagues and I were doing addressed the ever-increasing urgency or magnitude of the suffering millions of Americans were living through—and dying from."

Laura wrote Whitaker an email with the subject line "Psychopharms and Selfhood," and listed the many drugs she had taken. "I grew up in a suburban town that emphasized the belief that happiness comes from looking perfect to others, that sadness and anger aren't legitimate feelings and should be kept to oneself," she wrote. In some sense being the perfect patient had been a form of avoidance, a way of attending to a narrow set of symptoms rather than to discontents about her social world—the goals for which she was supposed to be competing, the pristine persona she was expected to cultivate. Theories about her mind had masked what she was actually experiencing. Even in her conversations with me, Laura shied away from discussing specific details about her upbringing, because she didn't want to offend her family.

Whitaker told me that Laura reminded him of many young people who had contacted him after reading his book. He said, "They'd been prescribed one drug, and then a second, and a third, and they are put on this other trajectory where their self-identity changes from being normal to abnormal—they are told that, basically, there is something wrong with their brain, and it isn't temporary—and it changes their sense of resilience and the way they present themselves to others."

At her appointments with her pharmacologist, Laura began to raise the idea of going off her drugs. In fourteen years, she had taken nineteen different medications. "I never had a baseline sense of myself, of who I am, of what my capacities are," she said. She wanted to somehow strip away the framework that had been imposed on her identity.

The doctors at the borderline clinic initially resisted her request to stop her medications, but they also seemed to recognize that her struggles could not be fixed with technology. A few months earlier, one doctor had written on a prescription pad, "Practice Self-Compassion," and for the number of refills he'd written, "Infinite."

FOLLOWING HER PHARMACOLOGIST'S ADVICE, the first medication that Laura stopped was Ativan, the benzodiazepine. A few weeks later, she went off Abilify, the antipsychotic. After she stopped taking both drugs, the lights in her house suddenly felt too bright. She began sweating so much that she stopped wearing any color but black. If she turned her head quickly, she felt woozy. Her body ached, and occasionally she was overwhelmed by waves of nausea. Her skin pulsed with a strange kind of energy. "I never felt quiet in my body," she told me. "It felt like there was a current of some kind under my skin, and I was trapped inside this encasing that was constantly buzzing."

She worried she'd never fall asleep again. She was over-stimulated by colors and sounds. "I felt as if I couldn't protect myself from all this life lived around me," she said. She rarely went outside at all. When her aunt Sara updated the rest of the family, she joked that Laura had become part of the couch. Her family learned to vacuum around her.

A month later, she went off Effexor, the antidepressant. Within a week, Laura felt disproportionally affected by minor frustrations or slights. When a cashier at the grocery store spoke to her, she was convinced that he was only pretending to be cordial—that what he really wanted to say was, "You are a repulsive, disgusting, pathetic human." Her reactions felt artificial and out of context. "It's like you feel possessed," Laura told me. "The emotions are occupying you, and you're at their mercy, and yet, on one level, you know they are not you."

Later, she found a community of people online who were struggling to withdraw from psychiatric medications and had already invented a word to describe this experience: "neuro-emotion," an exaggerated feeling not grounded in reality. The web forum Surviving Antidepressants, visited by thousands of people each week, listed the many varieties of neuro-emotion: neuro-fear, neuro-anger, neuro-guilt, neuro-shame, neuro-regret. Another word that members used was "dystalgia," a wash of despair that one's life has been futile.

For many people on the forums, it was impossible to put the experience of withdrawing from medications into words. "The effects of these drugs come so close to your basic 'poles of being' that it's really hard to describe them in any kind of reliable way," one person wrote. Another wrote, "This withdrawal process has slowly been stripping me of everything I believed about myself and life. One by one, parts of 'me' have been falling away, leaving me completely empty of any sense of being someone."

In the past, when Laura had experienced symptoms of depression or mania, she had known what to do with them: she'd remember the details and report them to her doctor. Now this ritual seemed less purposeful. "Bipolar was a path I was on," she told me. "And then all of a sudden I wasn't on that path anymore." She felt like she was stepping into a void.

PSYCHOANALYSIS WAS ONCE a lifelong process. Now, nearly two decades after the closure of Chestnut Lodge, psychopharmacology has entered a similarly chronic mode. Today, antidepressants are taken by one in eight people in America, and a quarter of them have been doing so for more than a decade. Nathan Kline warned of this problem as early as 1964. "It is relatively simple to determine when to start treatment," he wrote, "but much more difficult to know when to stop."

Once the chemical-imbalance theory became popular, mental health became synonymous with an absence of symptoms, rather than with a return to a person's baseline, her mood or personality before and between periods of crisis. Dorian Deshauer, a psychiatrist and historian at the University of Toronto, told me, "Once you abandon the idea of the personal baseline, it becomes possible to think of emotional suffering as relapse—instead of something to be expected from an individual's way of being in the world." There's also the possibility that mental health is determined not only by symptoms but by aspirations, like, say, experiencing the "oceanic sentiment," or other forms of belonging. For adolescents who go on medications when they are still learning what it means to be their best self, they may never know if they have a baseline, or what it is. "It's not so much a question of 'Does the technology deliver?'" Deshauer said. "It's a question of 'What are we asking of it?'"

In rejecting the authority of psychoanalysis, psychiatrists had hoped to rid themselves of the sway of culture and the fundamental subjectivity it implied. But the history of biological psychiatry has been marked by biases about gender and race just as psychoanalysis had been. The benzodiazepines, a class of tranquilizer celebrated as a replacement for psychoanalysis, was marketed in the seventies especially to women, to give them personalities congenial to husbands. In ads called "35 and Single" in the *Archives of General Psychiatry* in 1970, the pharmaceutical company Roche encouraged doctors to give Valium to the kind of highly strung patient who "realizes she's in a losing pattern—and that she may *never* marry." Between 1969 and 1982, Valium was the most widely prescribed medication in America, and roughly three-quarters of its users were women. In an editorial in the French journal *L'Encéphale*, two psychiatrists from the largest psychiatric hospital in Paris warned, "Benzodiazepines have lost their status as medications . . . and become simple domestic helpers."

Serotonin reuptake inhibitors, or SSRIs—most prominently Prozac and Zoloft—were created in the eighties,

filling a gap in the market opened by concerns that benzodiazepines were addictive. They were soon prescribed for
not just depression but the anxieties that benzodiazepines
had previously addressed. Now more than one in five white
women in America take antidepressants. Peter Kramer, the
author of *Listening to Prozac*, told me that the SSRIs were
"eerily consonant with what the culture required of women:
less fragility, more juggling outside of the home." An early
advertisement for Zoloft showed a white woman in a pant-
suit, holding the hands of her two children, and the phrase
"Power that speaks softly." An ad for Prozac, which ran for
two and a half years, showed another white woman, her wedding ring visible, and the slogan "For both restful nights and
productive days."

While Black women tend to be undermedicated for depression, white women, especially ambitious ones, are often
overmedicated, in order to "have it all": a family and a thriving career. And yet, a common side effect of the drugs is loss
of sexuality, an experience perhaps more compatible with
contemporary gender roles than we would like to imagine.
Allen Frances, an emeritus professor of psychiatry at Duke
who chaired the task force for the fourth edition of the *DSM*,
in 1994, told me, "It was very apparent early on that the SSRIs
have a fairly dramatic impact on sexual interest and performance. It has always puzzled me that this was not more of a
disqualifying aspect of their wide popularity."

Audrey Bahrick, a psychologist at the University of Iowa
Counseling Service who has published papers on the way
that SSRIs affect sexuality, said she sees thousands of college
students each year, many of whom have been taking SSRIs
since adolescence. She told me, "I seem to have the expectation that young people would be quite distressed about the
sexual side effects, but my observation clinically is that these

young people don't yet know what sexuality really means or why it is such a driving force. They start to look a little behind their peers with regard to having crushes or being sexually motivated."

LAURA HAD ALWAYS felt alienated by women her age who dressed in flattering clothes. They seemed "so settled into their bodies," she said. She had never masturbated, an activity that baffled her. "I was like, 'Why do people like this?' It didn't make sense."

Eight months after Laura stopped taking her medications, she was walking down the street in Boston and felt a flicker of desire. "It was so uncomfortable and foreign to me that I didn't know what to do with it," she said. She felt exposed, as if her sexuality were visible to the public. The sensation began to occur at random times of day, often in public and in the absence of an object of attraction. "It was as if that whole part of my body was coming online again, and I had no idea how to channel it," she said.

A year later, when she was thirty-one, she began a long-distance relationship with a journalist from Victoria, Canada, named Rob Wipond, who writes about the mental-health system in Canada. Both Laura and Rob became emotional when talking with me about Laura's sexuality. Laura told me, "I felt like a newborn. I hadn't ever figured out what my body was meant to be." Rob said, "She was suddenly open and awake and looking at sexuality from an adult perspective. Everything was new to her. We were like, 'Well, gee, what is this sexuality thing—what shall we do?'"

For years, Laura had been unable to have stable relationships, a symptom, she'd assumed, of borderline personality disorder. "I honestly thought that, because I was mentally

ill, the numbness was just part of me," she told me. "I looked
at beautiful sex scenes in movies, and it never crossed my
mind that this was in the cards for me." Now she wondered
if her inability to connect was partly a consequence of the
many medications she'd been taking. "On this very sensory,
somatic level, I couldn't bond with another human being,"
she said. "It never felt real. It felt synthetic."

Laura bought a book about women's sexuality, and, when
she was thirty-one, she learned how to give herself an or-
gasm. "It took so long and I finally figured it out, and I just
broke down in tears and called Rob, and I was like, 'I did it!
I did it! I did it!'"

LAURA WROTE DR. ROTH, her former psychiatrist, and asked if
she could read her own medical records. She wanted to know
how Dr. Roth had made sense of her emotional and sexual
numbness. "The loss of my sexuality is the hardest part to
make peace with," she told me. "It feels like a betrayal."

When Laura didn't get a response, she went to Dr. Roth's
home office to hand-deliver another request for her records.
As she was walking up the driveway, she saw Dr. Roth walking her dog. "It was awkward," Laura said. "I was like, 'Oh, hi.
It's Laura Delano.' We actually hugged. I told her, 'I just want
to reassure you, I don't have any ill will here. I'm just trying to
piece together what the fuck happened.'"

Dr. Roth proposed that they set up a meeting. Laura
prepared for hours. On the appointed day, as she sat in Dr.
Roth's waiting room, she tried to focus on the questions she
would ask. She intended to begin by saying, "I'm sitting in
front of you and I'm off all these drugs, and I've never felt
more vibrant and alive and capable, and yet I had this serious mental illness. How do you make sense of that?"

But she was distracted by nostalgia: the familiar hum of the white-noise machine, the sound of the wind being sucked inside as Dr. Roth opened the front door. She had always loved Dr. Roth's presence—the way she would sit with her legs folded in an arm chair, cradling a large mug of coffee, her nails neatly polished. By the time Dr. Roth opened the door of the waiting room, Laura was crying.

They hugged. Then they took their usual positions in Dr. Roth's office. But Laura said that Dr. Roth seemed so nervous that she talked for the entire appointment, summarizing the conversations they'd had together. It was only when Laura left the office that she realized she had never asked her questions.

LAURA BEGAN A BLOG about her experience with psychopharmacology, describing the way that, over the course of a decade, she had lost the sense that she had control over what was happening to her. She'd put so much faith in "these tiny pills and capsules," she wrote, that she viewed herself as a "living and breathing medium through which they did their work." Soon, people began contacting her to ask for advice about getting off large doses of multiple medications. Some had been trying to withdraw for years. They had developed painstakingly slow methods for tapering their medications, like using grass-seed counters to dole out individual beads in the capsules.

Psychiatric drugs are brought to market in clinical trials that typically last less than twelve weeks. Few studies follow patients who take the medications for more than a year. The field has neglected questions about how to take people off drugs—a practice known as "deprescribing." Some of the earliest studies about this problem involved pregnant women told to discontinue their medications, since the drugs were thought to affect the fetus. In the nineties, both *Annals of Pharmacotherapy* and *The British Journal of Psychiatry* published case studies of pregnant women, one on Prozac and the other on Luvox, an SSRI, who tried to get off their medications but couldn't. One woman "experienced feelings of severe aggression." The other "was unable to stop" the medication, because "whenever she had tried to do so, she was overwhelmed by strong feelings of aggression (she felt that she 'could murder someone')."

Guy Chouinard, an emeritus professor of psychiatry at McGill who for ten years served as a consultant for Eli Lilly, the pharmaceutical company that makes Prozac, told me that when the SSRIs came to market, he was thrilled to see his patients, previously crippled by self-doubt and fear, living tolerable and fulfilling lives. Chouinard is considered one of the founders of psychopharmacology in Canada; he performed the first controlled studies of four different antidepressants. In the early 2000s, he began to be referred cases of patients who, after taking antidepressants for years, had stopped their medications and were now experiencing what he called "crescendo-like" anxiety and panic that went on for weeks and, in some cases, months. It was only when he reinstated their medication that their symptoms began to resolve, usually within two days.

Many people who discontinue antidepressants do not struggle with withdrawal for more than a few days. Some experience no problem at all. "The medical literature on this is a mess," Chouinard told me. "Psychiatrists don't know their patients well—they aren't following them long-term—so they don't know whether to believe their patients when they say, 'I've never had this experience in my life.'" He believes that in many cases withdrawal symptoms, misdiagnosed and

never given time to resolve, may create a false sense that patients can't function unless they go back on their drugs.

Laura immersed herself in what she described as the
"layperson withdrawal community," a constellation of web
forums and Facebook groups where people who are trying to
stop their psychiatric medications mentor one another: Surviving Antidepressants, the International Antidepressant
Withdrawal Project, Benzo Buddies, Paxil Progress, Cym-
balta Hurts Worse. The groups offer instructions for slowly
tapering from medications and a place to communicate about
emotional experiences that do not have names. The websites
attract people who, in a previous era, might have been drawn
to anti-psychiatry, a movement that reached its pinnacle
in the seventies, when psychiatrists such as R. D. Laing and
Thomas Szasz proposed that insanity was a natural response
to the madness of contemporary life. But that question—
"Am I the insane one, or is it society?"—diminishes the reality of mental disability and presumes the impossible: that the
self can be divorced from the society that shapes it.

A common theme on the forums was that people felt that
at some point, having taken numerous medications for years,
they'd become disabled, and they were no longer sure if it
was due to their underlying disorder, the heavy medications
they'd taken for it, or the way their families or communities
had responded to them—a process that sometimes coincided
with the pressure of needing to prove their disability, in order
to receive social security benefits. Swapnil Gupta, a professor at the Yale School of Medicine, told me that when her
patients express fear about stopping their medications, their
concerns are often about social and financial problems as
much as about medical ones. "Some people worry they will
lose their disability payments because being on lots of meds
has become a badge of illness," she said. For others, "the pills

represent an attachment to a physician, and taking away that medication means they are losing that attachment." She went on, "It is a loss of identity, a different way of living: suddenly everything that you are doing is yours, and not necessarily your medication."

Gupta, too, is trying to recalibrate the way she understands her patients' emotional lives. "We tend to see patients as fixed in time—we don't see them as people who have ups and downs like we all do—and it can be really disconcerting when suddenly they are saying, 'See, I'm crying—put me back on my meds.'" She said, "I have to sit them down and say, 'It's okay to cry—normal people cry.' Just today someone asked me, 'Do you cry?' And I said, 'Yes, I do.'"

~~~~~~~~

I first came across Laura's blog at a time when I was trying to understand the relationship between medication and my own self-esteem. The psychiatry that had shaped the early years of my life, in the late eighties, barely resembled the field that Laura had encountered a decade later. My hospitalization preceded the era in which it had become standard to medicate children. Instead, I had learned to see my illness as a kind of stress reaction. "The anorexia appears to be a coping style in dealing with the pressures that she has felt," my psychiatrist had written. In a sense, Laura and I were mirrors on which different faces of psychiatry had been reflected.

My friend Anna, who had just finished medical school, helped reacquaint me with the field. I had a sense of perpetual inadequacy about work that Anna (in an attempt to help me see my irrationality) labeled "anorexic." She recommended that I schedule an appointment with a psychiatrist, her former professor, whom she admired. At the time, I was going through a period of social anxiety that was sparked by some professional success, which had led to more interactions with people I found intimidating. Anna and I used to joke that our minds were full of "trash," the name we used to categorize circular thoughts about minor social lapses or regrettable emails. In my journal from the time, I had described my problem as one of "constantly thinking of what I am saying, how I am being perceived—not *communicating*." Returning home from a party, I wrote, "45 percent of what I said was pure throwaway." I urged myself to be more "human," instead of "hyper-contained," "impenetrable."

At my first appointment with the psychiatrist, whom I'll call Dr. Hall, he asked why I had come to see him. I did not have a particularly good answer. I offered that sometimes, after sending an email, I would become so ashamed by a phrase I'd written—as soon as I pressed "send," the wrongness of my words would become apparent—that I would rewrite the email in Microsoft Word, to assess the scale of my mistake. Dr. Hall observed that perhaps I felt isolated, and writing imaginary emails was a way to feel connected. I agreed, and referred to myself, dismissively, as the "worried well"—a phrase that had always brought to mind an image of undifferentiated worriers filling a hole of water. It wasn't until we discussed the phrase that I realized that I had been envisioning the wrong kind of "well." He suggested that I try antidepressants for a short period—less than six months. The medications, he said, could help me achieve a kind of "negative capability," by which he meant that I should learn to accept that I cannot control, nor can I know, what impression I have made on another person. The poet John Keats described negative capability as the state "when a man is capable of being in uncertainties, mysteries, doubts, without any irritable reaching after fact and reason." I left the appointment with a prescription for 10 milligrams of Lexapro, an SSRI.

I was in the process of writing a story for *The New Yorker* about teenagers who are homeless in New York City. For months, I had struggled with the piece, worrying that the interviews weren't adding up to anything. The stakes seemed uncomfortably high, in part because I was longing for some sense of community, a professional or social world that made me feel less alone, and I was somehow under the impression that, if my next article was good enough, I might find it. I remember the moment when the Lexapro seemed to hit: it occurred to me that it would be fine if I just wrote an informative story. It did not have to be the ideal story. I only needed to meet the requirements. And yet, at that moment, the subject suddenly became much more compelling. As I listened to audio recordings of interviews that at the time I had felt were going nowhere, I realized that these people had been saying fascinating things. It was as if previously I had been looking for something too constricted. The frame of my curiosity had widened.

My first six months on Lexapro were probably the best half year of my life. I was what psychiatrists call a "good responder." My brain suddenly felt like a fun, fresh place to be. "Today: nothing I'm feeling shame for," I wrote in my journal. I began writing jokey emails to people for no other reason than that I was brimming with warmth for them. One night, in my kitchen, I tried to imitate the way that some of the kids I'd been interviewing vogued at dance parties. My boyfriend, whom I had been dating for five years, told me, "That's the silliest thing I've ever seen you do." I had always believed myself to be a fundamentally silly person, but apparently this truth had not been obvious. When we took a trip to Portugal, I felt as if I finally understood vacations—why it is that people cherish and enjoy them.

I encouraged my friends to go on Lexapro, too. They were navigating similar forms of self-doubt, and some of them took my suggestion. Two weeks after beginning the medication, my friend Helen, a novelist, told me in an email, "It is making me infinitely nicer to my family." Riding the subway one day, she realized she would like to have a baby. "But I hate babies," she wrote. Another friend reported that Lexapro had made her more moderate: "The drug put on brakes after four or five hours of work where in the past I would have gone on, unprofitably, for nine or ten." Helen and I, along with two other friends, went out for dinner every few weeks, and the evenings felt electric. I contributed to the conversations with such exuberance that I wondered at times if I was accidentally shouting. I enjoyed their company without reservation, a phenomenon that reminds me of an observation from one of Nathan Kline's colleagues, from a 1958 paper in the *Journal of Clinical and Experimental Psychopathology*. After giving a patient iproniazid, he wrote, "For the first time in fifteen years, [the patient] could have his coffee breaks and engage in casual conversation with his co-workers without fear of wasting his time."

Helen and I kept discovering new Lexapro users, both colleagues and friends. We became unnerved by how many of us—mostly white women—were taking the same drug. "These more and more seem like Make The Ambitious Ladies More Tolerable pills," Helen wrote me. When I told Dr. Hall that nearly all my female friends were on Lexapro and thriving, a fact that made me think we were swept up in a cultural phenomenon, rather than suffering from the same disease, he joked of my concern about being relegated to what he called the "red tent"—a reference, I assume, to the tent in which women of Jacob's tribe find solace and sisterhood while menstruating and giving birth. Dr. Hall seemed to recognize that this drug was speaking particularly to females, but he seemed incurious about why. I remember telling him, before the Lexapro took full effect, that I often worried that I had inadvertently been "brassy"—that somehow secret parts of me (ones that even my boyfriend didn't know about) were bursting out too loudly and sloppily and aggressively. Recently I asked Helen how she understood the source of our anxiety, and she wrote, "We are all 'good girls' in every sense of the word (but also, bad girls)."

Anna, the friend who had recommended Dr. Hall, took Lexapro, too, and she helped me justify my drug use in existential terms. Even if I had never been clinically depressed, she suggested, perhaps there was some misalignment between my mind and the rhythms of contemporary life. The bioethicist Carl Elliott writes that for some people antidepressants do not address an inner psychic state so much as "an incongruity between the self and external structures of meaning—a lack of fit between the way you are and the way you are expected to be." Elliott wonders if "at least part of the nagging worry about Prozac and its ilk is that for all the good they do, the ills that they treat are part and parcel of the lonely, forgetful, unbearably sad place where we live."

But there is a difference, of course, between lonely sadness and the kinds of deprivations that defined Naomi's history—and the cognitive dissonance when those wrongs were not acknowledged, the sense that reality could not be trusted. Yet psychiatry approaches these sets of troubles in the same way, adopting a position of neutrality that can feel violent. What can a psychiatrist say, Elliott asks, to "an alienated Sisyphus as he pushes the boulder up the mountain? That he would push the boulder more enthusiastically, more creatively, more insightfully, if he were on Prozac?"

TO SOME DEGREE, Lexapro had been a social drug, a collective experience. After a sense of uncanny flourishing for several months, my friends and I began wondering if we should quit. Helen was the first to stop taking Lexapro. She felt the effect within days. "I was irritable and enraged basically from the moment I went off," she emailed me, adding (condescendingly, I suspected), "whereas you seemed more relaxed than I'd ever seen you." Now that she was off Lexapro, she reported, "I no longer feel inclined to hang out. And when I am hanging out (for example with my family, who want me back on the meds), I feel that terrible itch to get back home and start doing something worthwhile."

When Helen went off, I somehow felt I should do the same. My six-month trial was over, and the medication had worked—I was out of my impasse. During the course of a week, I tapered the drug. Two weeks later, for the first time in my life, I experienced depression the way that it has been described in textbooks: as an inability to move or to act. Whatever illusion sustains the belief that one's work has meaning and relevance dissolved. I experienced a layer of self-consciousness that was new to me: sometimes when I talked, I became distracted by the sensation of my lips moving. One sunny day, after spending the afternoon outside with a friend, I noted all the things in life that I should be grateful for. "But without Lexapro I become greedy and can't appreciate any of it," I wrote.

I went back on Lexapro and felt better within two weeks. During the next two years, I tried to go off Lexapro three more times, but each time I felt immobilized and disconnected, as if I had lost my motivational core. Dr. Hall never suggested that these experiences could be related to withdrawal, and I never stayed off the drug for more than six weeks to find out. I worried that my baseline self was not who I'd been in the years before taking Lexapro but the more dysfunctional self that had occasionally resurfaced—most visibly when I was six and hospitalized. Or perhaps the medications had changed me so much that my baseline self was no longer mine to reclaim. The sociologist Alain Ehrenberg writes that long-term treatment with antidepressants has become a cure for people who feel inadequate. The drugs create a "paradoxical situation, in which the medication is invested with magical powers while the pathology becomes chronic." Helen, who stayed off Lexapro, believed there had been something phony about her sudden desire, while medicated, to be part of the world. I, too, found it foreign. But it also felt true. "It is joy to be hidden," the British psychoanalyst D. W. Winnicott wrote, "but disaster not to be found."

The Swedish neuropharmacologist Arvid Carlsson observed that when people took Zimelidine, a precursor of Prozac, their income rose. The same could be said of me. Lexapro tracks closely with the development of my career. It also corresponds with the period in which my boyfriend and I decided to get married. Perhaps I would have reached those milestones anyway, but I cannot cleanly separate them from the medication. In *Listening to Prozac*, Peter Kramer writes, "Seeing how poorly patients fared when they were cautious and inhibited, and how the same people flourished once medication had made them assertive and flexible, I developed a strong impression of how our culture favors one interpersonal style over another."

Three years after going on Lexapro, I got pregnant. Despite my troubles withdrawing from the drug, I immediately stopped taking the medication, because I worried it might affect the fetus. Within two weeks, I lost access to the reasons that had made me want to be a mother. My pregnancy suddenly felt accidental, though it was planned. I remember flipping through a book about newborns and learning that, in the early weeks of the infant's life, a baby does not know the difference between himself and his mother. I found this alarming. I told my friends that I was afraid I wouldn't love my child. When I am honest with myself, I realize that I feared the opposite: my love would be so massive that I'd become unrecognizable to myself. In high school and early college, I'd had a boyfriend to whom my devotion nearly subsumed all other interests and goals. I imagined that, as a parent, I'd become depleted in the same way. The psychoanalyst Adam Phillips has said that "everybody is dealing with how much of their own aliveness they can bear." It was as if Lexapro directly acted on this capacity. Without the drug, I lacked the courage to try something new. In Roland Kuhn's terms, I had lost the "power to experience."

After seeing me off the medication, six weeks into pregnancy, Dr. Hall asked me if I was considering an abortion. The thought had occurred to me, but my body felt so uninhabitable that I believed a miscarriage might resolve the question. A few days later, Dr. Hall told me that he'd discussed my case with the chief of child psychiatry at his medical school: "I described the clinical picture to him," he wrote, "and he said that if it were his wife, he'd restart it." I was taken aback by the idea of two men discussing what drugs they'd tell their wives to take, but I followed the advice. I went back on Lexapro. Within three weeks, I felt connected again to my reasons for having a baby.

When I met Laura, I told her I may have experienced something akin to a "neuro-abortion": a false desire to terminate a pregnancy. A 2001 paper in the *Journal of Psychiatry & Neuroscience* chronicled thirty-six women who were on either antidepressants, benzodiazepines, or a combination of the two, and who stopped their drugs abruptly when they became pregnant. A third of the patients said they felt suicidal, and four were admitted to a hospital. One had an abortion because "she did not feel that she could go through the pregnancy feeling so awful," though the pregnancy was "otherwise wanted." The authors didn't follow up with this woman, but I wonder if she, too, withdrew too quickly from the medications. Once she went back on her pills, did she want her baby again, too?

MY SIX-MONTH EXPERIMENT with Lexapro has now spanned more than a decade. For years, I have been slowly and unsystematically tapering, because I fear that if I don't I will be on this drug for the rest of my life. I worry about unknown side effects later in life, but not enough to give up on the drug completely. I had a second child and stayed on Lexapro through that pregnancy, too. For a few years, I tapered down to 2.5 milligrams of Lexapro, a quarter of my original dose. I was not depressed, but I was less social, flexible, and spontaneous. It seemed I had reached my baseline personality. I noticed how similar that personality was to my father's—it has always been clear that I inherited his temperament—and I imagined how he might have handled certain moments in our lives better had he been on this drug. I decided to increase my dose again, because with the next generation I'd like to avoid those mistakes.

In *Listening to Prozac*, Kramer asks whether some people might feel pressure to take medications, as they watch their colleagues and friends take the drugs and become, in a social and emotional sense, upwardly mobile. I told Laura that I was struggling with a slightly different dilemma: to continue as the person I'd become I needed a drug. I wanted my children to remember the version of me that took Lexapro. On the medication, I was more capable of giving my husband the kind of feedback required for an enduring relationship. I was less inclined to feel agitated about little things, like, for instance, the fact that no matter how many times I objected, my son still put his hand on my head as if it were a handrail, so he could balance while I helped him take off his socks. "On 7.5 milligrams, I'm a better family member," I told her.

"Isn't it possible it could actually be withdrawal, that maybe you need to go slower?" Laura asked me.

I found the question reductive, and a little insulting. It occurred to me that she was still devoted to the same idea—that the answer to an individual's distress can be found in medications—but from the opposite angle. If medications are the central question—to take or not—then one has permission again to ignore the context, the kinds of social worlds that create and perpetuate disabilities. One explanation was still holding too much power.

In her book *Depression: A Public Feeling*, the scholar Ann Cvetkovich writes that if depression can be "conceived of as blockage or impasse or being stuck, then its cure might lie in forms of flexibility or creativity more so than in pills." I am drawn to this idea, though I don't think these two strategies are in opposition. I also realize that I've endowed my pill of choice with mystical capacities—it contains the things I'm not but wish I was—and merely the idea of swallowing such a thing has healing power. I wish I had a more flexible approach toward my feelings of inadequacy ("I want to be someone better than me," I had written in my second-grade diary), but I also feel closer to that space of flexibility when I take

Lexapro; it seems to relieve the cognitive rigidity that often accompanies anxiety and depression—the sense that one's story can unfold only one way.

~~~~~~~~~

The doctors at Chestnut Lodge had once described their hospital as a lighthouse crashing into an advancing tide. The history of psychiatry is a chronicle of these sorts of crashes, one model of treatment, a source of promise, giving way to the next. Over time, I found myself disagreeing with the way Laura seemed to frame her story—the idea of freedom from medication as the lighthouse at the end of a long journey. I wondered if it wasn't the withdrawal from drugs that created the conditions for Laura's recovery so much as something less novel: a new story about what ailed her, one without the illusion that a seamless life is possible; a community who could affirm that, yes, it is okay to cry. She had discovered that "real loneliness," as Fromm-Reichmann writes, is "potentially a communicable experience, one which can be shared."

After I had been meeting with Laura for nearly a year, her sister Nina texted me to say: "10 years to the day, Laura has some news for you that may be a great ending to your story." Laura had recently moved to Hartford to live in an apartment a block away from a new boyfriend, Cooper, who worked at an agency that supported people with psychiatric and addiction histories. They had met at a mental-health conference. Cooper had recovered from an addiction to Adderall, which he'd been prescribed when he was seventeen. As an adolescent, he said, he'd been made to believe "I am not set up for this world. I need tweaking, I need adjusting."

Standing in Cooper's kitchen, Laura told him that wood and thin plastic utensils can't go in the dishwasher. Cooper asked if a number of different household items were safe for the dishwasher, before asking one last question. He pulled an engagement ring out of his pocket. He had been planning to propose for several weeks, and he hadn't realized that the moment he'd chosen was precisely a decade after her suicide attempt.

Shortly after their engagement, a twenty-three-year-old from Montreal named Bianca Gutman flew to Hartford to spend the weekend with Laura. Bianca's mother, Susan, had discovered Laura's blog two years earlier and had emailed her right away. "I feel like I'm reading my daughter's story," she wrote. Susan had paid Laura for Skype conversations, so Laura could guide her daughter through the withdrawal process. Eventually, Laura told her to stop paying; she had come to think of Bianca, who had been diagnosed as having depression when she was twelve, as a little sister.

Laura and Bianca spent the weekend taking walks in frigid weather. Bianca, who is barely five feet tall, moved and talked more slowly than Laura, as if many more decisions were required before she converted a thought into words. She had been on 40 milligrams of Lexapro—double the recommended maximum dose—for nearly nine years. She'd taken Abilify, an antipsychotic, for six years. Now, after talking to Laura, Bianca's father, an emergency-medicine doctor, had found a pharmacy in Montreal that was able to compound decreasing quantities of her medication, dropping 1 milligram each month. Bianca, who worked as an assistant at an elementary school, was down to 5 milligrams of Lexapro. Her mother said, "I often tell Bianca, 'I see you coping better,' and she's like, 'Calm down, Mommy. It's not like being off medication is going to wipe me clean and you're going to get the daughter you had before'"—the hope she harbored when Bianca first went on medication.

Like Laura, Bianca had always appreciated when her psychiatrists increased her dosage. She said, "It was like they were just matching my pain," which she couldn't otherwise express. She described her depression as "nonsensical pain. It's so shapeless and cloudy. It dodges all language." She said that, in her first conversation with Laura, there was something about the way Laura said "mm-hmm" that made her feel understood. "I hadn't felt hopeful in a very long time. Hopeful about what? I don't know. Just hopeful, I think, because I felt that connection with someone." She told Laura, "Knowing that you know there's no words—that's enough for me."

At my request, Laura had dug up several albums of childhood photographs, and the three of us sat on the floor going through them. Laura looked radically different from one year to the next. There was no continuity. She had had a phase of wearing pastel polo shirts that were too small for her, and in this period, when Laura was pictured among friends, Bianca and I struggled to tell which girl was her. It wasn't just that she was fatter or thinner; her face seemed to be structured differently. In her debutante photos, she looked as if she were wearing someone else's features. Bianca kept saying, "I don't see you."

Since I'd known Laura she had always had a certain shine, but on this day she seemed nearly luminous. She had taken a newfound interest in clothing and was wearing trousers from Sweden with a tucked-in T-shirt that accentuated her waist. When Cooper returned to the apartment, after an afternoon spent with his family, she exclaimed, "Oh, Cooper is back!" Then she became self-conscious and laughed at herself.

I told Laura I was wary of repeating her sister's sentiment that marriage was the end of her story, as if the only curative form of connection was a groom—a convention that shaped the early history of psychiatry. In his case studies of women, Freud claimed therapeutic victory by resolving the case with marriage. "Years have again gone by since her visit," his case study of Dora concludes. "In the meantime the girl has married." In his case history of Fräulein Elisabeth von R., Freud writes that the last time he saw her was at a private ball in which "I did not allow the opportunity to escape me of seeing my former patient whirl past in a lively dance. Since then, by her own inclination, she has married someone unknown to me."

Laura shared my discomfort with the marriage plot. "It's not like 'Laura has finally arrived,'" she said. "If anything, these trappings of whatever you want to call it—life?—have made things scarier." She still felt overwhelmed by daily routines, like too many emails accumulating, and she cried about five times a week. She was too sensitive. She let situations escalate. Cooper said that his tendency in moments of tension was to withdraw, which exacerbated Laura's impulse to hash out the problem immediately. Laura had not seen a therapist since she left the borderline clinic, but she said, "If I actually sat in front of a psychiatrist and did an evaluation, I would totally meet the criteria for a number of diagnoses." But the diagnostic framework no longer felt meaningful to her.

Bianca, who was still struggling to let go of the idea that depression explained who she was, said, "It's like your darkness is still there, but it's almost like it's next to you as opposed to your totality of being." She added, "But I know you haven't come out the other side."

"It's not like I'm good to go," Laura agreed. "Literally every day I am still wondering how to be an adult in this world."

EPILOGUE: HAVA

"Stranger to myself"

A few years ago, I emailed Thomas Koepke, the psychologist who had treated me for anorexia at Children's Hospital of Michigan three decades ago. We hadn't spoken since. I asked for an interview, and he proposed that I also meet with three of his colleagues, psychologists who had known me when I was six and hospitalized. In the eighties and nineties, they had been part of a research team that received funding from the National Institute of Mental Health to test treatments for anorexic adolescents. I was too young to be included in their study, but my treatment drew from the same protocol. "The prognosis is positive if an adolescent's eating disorder is treated soon after its onset," they wrote. "Otherwise, the disorder may become a chronic condition."

We met at an office in Bloomfield Hills, a suburb of Detroit, where one of the psychologists worked. The doctors all stood up and greeted me warmly, like prep-school teachers proud and curious to see how an old student, back on a visit from college, was faring in the larger world. For the occasion, Koepke's wife had baked a coffee cake, which he served us.

At Koepke's recommendation, I had brought him a photo from when I was six, to help spark his memories. In the photo, I wore a purple bathing suit that looked a little baggy, and my hair was stringy and mane-like. "Oh, yes," Koepke said. "Yes, yes, yes." He passed the photo to his colleagues. "Your parents were going through quite an ordeal at the time, I do remember that," he said. He recalled that my mom was an English teacher and always seemed to be either grading papers or writing in a journal. "You gained weight rather well. You didn't argue with me, as I recall." He described anorexia as a way to "avert the pressure that you felt in your family onto yourself. You may have thought it would bring some homeostasis into your family's life, because your parents were separate and chaotic."

For some reason I found myself insufficiently interested in the conversation. I kept worrying that Ray Osheroff's son Joe, whom I was supposed to meet the next day in Ann Arbor, where he lives, was not texting me back. When I heard the ring of an incoming text, I was filled with hope that the interview would happen. But it was just my sister, Sari, asking me how the conversation with my old doctors was going. What these psychologists were saying felt true and right and, at the same time, generic. If this was my story, I somehow didn't feel a personal connection to it.

"This is just from an old therapist who hasn't worked in a long time and might have very bad insight into things," one of the psychologists, who had retired, told me. "But I am feeling that you really didn't like the intervention that you experienced with us."

"I felt the same thing," Koepke said.

"Do other people say that it was a great experience?" I asked.

"No, no," a psychologist named Ann Moye said. "In the first place, anorexia is thought of as a friend. 'This helps me—you're trying to take it away from me.'"

I said I wasn't sure if I had ever been anorexic, at least not at first; it felt like I had been taught to have the illness. "I still remember admiring this girl named Hava," I said. "I wanted to be like her. I thought she was so beautiful."

They were silent. "Is it appropriate to tell you about Hava?" Moye asked. "Is that appropriate?"

"No, I don't know if it would be," Koepke said.

Moye didn't elaborate. But at the end of the meeting, as I left the office, she told me, "You know, you and Hava did look so much alike. You looked like you could be Hava's younger sister."

WHEN I GOT HOME, I searched for Hava online and saw her obituary. She had died ten weeks earlier. After having discussed my encounter with anorexia so casually, I felt chastened. Mental disorder can feel uncertain and liminal, but it can also be more straightforward, a tragedy that overwhelms people's capacity to think and connect. "This was a long time coming," her father, David, said at the funeral service, which the funeral home had streamed online. "We were living on borrowed time."

Several months later, I called David, an oncologist and a critical-care physician who was no longer practicing. When I explained who I was, he asked me a number of questions to make sure I had not been sent on some sinister quest by his ex-wife. "I have some idea of who you are," he told me, after I'd described my time in the hospital. "Let me guess: your mother was probably reasonably bright but frustrated, academically and intellectually. She wasn't achieving what she'd hoped."

I agreed.

"And your father was likely a professional sort, highly skilled and demanding."

"Right."

"And there was a tremendous amount of discord."

"How did you know?" I asked him.

"It's not an infrequent story," he said.

My mom had once told me that a doctor at Children's Hospital had written a case study of me, and, though there is no published evidence of this, for a second I wondered if this text existed after all. I felt a little deflated upon realizing that David's thumbnail sketch of my childhood was not particular to me. I was among a large class of girls finding the same misguided solution to roughly the same type of tensions, often in similar social settings. Over the course of the past forty years, David had become an expert in eating disorders. "I've done just a little bit of reading," he said, laughing.

Once he was satisfied that I had called of my own volition, he told me that Hava had read some of my writing. "You were mentioned in the context of, 'Here's someone who was ill, who was hospitalized, who was younger than me, and who ended up doing okay,'" he said. "Hava wasn't a young lady that felt envy. She felt respect and legitimate pleasure for others. Had Hava been able to do what she liked, she would have wanted to bring recognition to her struggles and to the stigma of the illness."

"I'll give you one anecdote," he went on. When Hava was in her late teens, she went to a party, after having spent much of her adolescence in institutions, and saw a friend from one of her hospital stays. The friend had struggled with an eating disorder too. "Hava sought her out," he said. "She was feeling out of place, and she wanted to reminisce about things that happened while they were institutionalized. But this girl was trying to escape. She told Hava, essentially: 'I'm doing better now. I'm assimilating into what I'd like to think is a normal existence. And I don't want contact with the prior life. You make me vulnerable.'" David went on, "I don't think what this girl said was wrong—it's not an inappropriate thing to say from a psychologist's point of view—but it was devastating for Hava. She was inconsolable."

I sensed that on some level this story was also about me, and I asked which aspect of the encounter hurt Hava most. "Children with significant psychiatric illness are tolerated for a period of time when they are cute and cuddly and small," he responded. "But once it goes beyond that period, it is tremendously upsetting for older people, in terms of their own anxieties. And then, at some magical point—I'm not sure you can define it—these children, instead of generating empathy, become uncomfortable freaks."

"DEAR PRESIDENT CLINTON," Hava wrote in 1993, when she was seventeen. "I know our country is short on money, but don't cut mental health funds!" She told him, "I've spent 5 years in and out of hospitals dealing with an eating disorder. But every place I've left has crumbled behind me!" In the nineties, Michigan's governor, John Engler, a fiscal conservative who didn't think the state should be in the business of mental-health care, hastily shut down ten psychiatric hospitals. Hava wrote the president from the Hawthorn Center, the state's only remaining psychiatric hospital for children, where fifteen staff members had just been laid off. "These staff that work with us day in and day out are people we've learned to trust," she wrote. "Someone in our lives that for the first time we can depend on and believe that they'll be there for us."

Not long after writing the letter, Hava was discharged from the Hawthorn Center because she had exceeded her insurance cap for inpatient mental-health care. Anorexia is the most fatal of all mental illnesses, but insurance companies tend to consider anorexics "the 'wrong' kind of sick," writes the anthropologist Rebecca Lester. They require protracted periods of treatment and often still don't improve. "They are poor economic investments," Lester explains. According to one survey, 97 percent of eating-disorder specialists said that their patients had been put in situations that threatened their lives, because their insurance wouldn't pay for more care, and one in five specialists said that insurance companies were responsible for the death of a patient. The companies may feel justified in their stinginess, Lester writes, because "eating disorders continue to occupy a space in the popular imagination as a choice," a sickness for which the sufferer bears responsibility.

Often, Hava began new notebooks with a pledge to become a different sort of person. "A new beginning!" she wrote when she was twenty. She got a part-time job caring for three children. "I suppose you could label me as a professional babysitter or a nanny if you must," she wrote. She realized she had to make a decision: "Either deal with the initial pain of loneliness and emptiness and start building a life from scratch, or resort back to the familiarity of my eating disorder." But as she gained weight she felt dislocated. "I would give anything to get my identity back!" she wrote. "My identity as the dependent anorexic." She was convinced that people found her more compelling and pleasant when she was visibly starving. She was desperate for a new way to interpret her sense of alienation, to give it some meaning, and felt angry at God for being "an intangible object rather than something I could physically grasp onto."

She drifted away from her brother and sister. Her brother told me, "I didn't blame her. I wasn't angry. I just didn't know really how to talk to her anymore." By her twenties, Hava had become bulimic. Her journals entered a new register: there were long lists of the foods she had consumed in a kind of altered state, before throwing up. "I've gotten to the point where the only thing I can focus on is food," Hava wrote. "Constantly food!"

In a laboratory simulation of famine, conducted at the end of World War II, researchers at the University of Minnesota, hoping to guide treatment for victims of famine, studied how thirty-six men, placed on a severe diet for twenty-four weeks, developed semi-starvation neurosis. Eating became the main topic of their conversations, even after the experiment had ended. The men read menus, collected recipes, and took vicarious pleasure in watching others eat. In her essay "The Ascetic Anorexic," the anthropologist Nonja Peters observes that anorexics, too, find their interests narrowing, but they are never told that "these food images and obsessions are involuntary, produced by the body's survival instinct."

Once, when Hava was briefly hospitalized after taking too many laxatives, she was jolted to see a thirty-nine-year-old patient whom she recognized from a hospitalization more than a decade earlier. After a group therapy session at the hospital, she wrote, "Great, there are 30 girls in the same room as me stuck in the same sinking boat. Where do we go from here? Talking is the easy part. Where do I set down my foot? I seem to be suspended in the air." She kept in touch with friends from previous hospital stays, and she was troubled to realize that "each person that was doing well was attributing their newfound life to God." They were able to move on, it seemed, because they had reoriented their lives around a new story.

———

THE FIRST TIME I met Hava's mother, Gail, I was seven months pregnant, and she immediately began talking about her desire for grandchildren. I felt self-conscious about the idea of suddenly appearing in her life as a reminder of what might have been. We met in her hotel room in Brooklyn— her son lives there, and she had traveled from Michigan to see him—and she sat on the hotel bed, her back propped against stiff, ornamental pillows, with three of Hava's note-books beside her. She told me that in the storage room of her basement she had dozens of Hava's diaries. She had never read them. She'd only flipped through the pages quickly, long enough to see a reference to a six-year-old ("the snarled hair falls upon the slumped shoulders") that she guessed was me. I assumed she'd feel protective of her daughter's remaining words, but she seemed exhausted by the idea of them. "The writing was part of her sickness," Gail told me.

In the journals, Hava had composed outlines of her plans for exercise; schedules planning what she would eat and when; and contracts, signed and dated. "I, Hava," she wrote, "will eat only when hungry as rarely as possible and as little as possible." There were also vivid, almost anthropological, accounts of the hospital unit where we'd lived when I was six. At the time, I had felt some sense of collectivity—the other girls had seemed to be my friends and mentors—but now I saw the machinery behind the structure of our days. There was something cutthroat, a kind of perverse American individualism, about the way the girls compared stats: weight, blood pressure, heart rate. Hava's numbers didn't feel low enough, she wrote, "if someone else had accomplished the same."

She seemed to have two different modes of writing, de-pending on her weight. When she felt fat, her language became clichéd and repetitive. She was constantly chastising herself for not being disciplined, and she seemed to lose other ways of interpreting her life. Like Ray, who had paced the halls of Chestnut Lodge, fantasizing about the great man he once was, Hava described weight loss as a way of holding on to an ideal and impossible version of herself.

But as she approached the ideal—to be skinny was to enter a "complete and utter state of euphoria"—she seemed to reevaluate what it was she had been striving for all along. "My life flies by and I sacrifice everything that has ever had any meaning to me," she wrote.

WHEN HAVA WAS TWENTY-FIVE, she accidentally got pregnant. She hoped that her boyfriend, a personal trainer, would start a family with her, but he wasn't interested, and she didn't feel she could raise a child on her own. Hava and her mother, Gail, began looking for adoptive parents on Adoption.com. They met a childless couple in New York who seemed caring and supportive, and Hava decided to give her baby to them. But when Hava revealed the details of her mental illness, "They said, 'Oh, forget it,'" Gail told me. "They were concerned about genetics and didn't want anything to do with her baby."

Hava found a new couple, Ann and Larry, who lived in Virginia. Ann said, "During our first conversation, Hava told me, 'I need to know that you guys will love this child regardless of whether or not he has a mental illness.'" They promised they would.

They agreed to an open adoption that would allow Hava to be a part of her child's life. As part of their arrangement, Hava could keep the baby for the first few days after she gave birth, so she could say goodbye. In a 2007 *Washington Post* article about open adoptions, Hava described how Ann and Larry had wanted to come to the hospital for the birth, but she said no. "My feeling was: Don't ask me," Hava said. "I'll be damned if you're going to take away the one thing that's mine."

She gave birth to her son, Jonathan, in 2002. Less than a week later, she and Gail delivered him to his new family. "We sat on the floor and sobbed and sobbed and sobbed," Gail told me. "That was the most painful thing I have ever done: giving that baby away." Hava later described the adoption as "the one good thing I feel I did on the face of this Earth."

For the first few years of Jonathan's life, Hava visited her son's family in Virginia a few times a year, sleeping over at their house. *The Washington Post* described how Jonathan grew up viewing Hava as "a mythical cat woman." She wore cat earrings; her socks were embroidered with cats; her coffee mug said "CATfeinated." But as Jonathan increasingly gravitated toward his adoptive mother, Hava found the visits more painful. Jonathan had a speech delay, and Hava blamed herself for not being able to decipher his words.

When Jonathan was eleven, his family moved to Christchurch, New Zealand, for Larry's work. Years later, I spoke with Jonathan's parents on video chat, and I asked if they saw Hava in their son.

"Oh yeah," they both said at the same time.

"Genetics does still work," Larry said.

"He's very sweet, like her," Ann said. "And he thinks out of the box. He thinks differently."

"He has the anxiety," Larry said. "He has a lot of that."

"The anxiety and the perfectionist thing," Ann continued. "And he's really gentle. He's very loving. A lot of that we definitely see from Hava."

Jonathan, who was eighteen, was in the next room. "Jonathan, do you want to come say hi?" Ann asked.

He had rosy cheeks, black rectangular glasses, and wavy dirty-blond hair that fell over his eyes. It was morning in New Zealand, and he had just woken up. "Rachel actually met Hava when she was a young girl," Ann said. She encouraged him to share his memories of Hava.

Jonathan stared at the computer screen, clearly uncomfortable. After a few seconds, he turned to his mom and quietly said, "I don't want to say."

"She played trains with you," Ann offered. She reminded him about Hava's cats.

"I'm fully aware she's family and all," he said in a surprisingly deep voice. "I don't know how to describe it. I haven't spent enough time with her."

When Jonathan walked away, Ann began crying. "I just feel so much empathy on the birth mother's side," she said. "To make that decision to be torn apart from your child, because you know, intellectually, that it's best for him."

THE POET LOUISE GLÜCK, who was anorexic, wrote, "The tragedy of anorexia seems to me that its intent is not self-destructive, though its outcome so often is. Its intent is to construct, in the only way possible when means are so limited, a plausible self." On these terms, perhaps my experience with this illness could be viewed as a success. After I left the hospital, my parents were a little afraid of me. They deferred to my opinions, and everyone established clearer boundaries. At the same time, I was given latitude to behave as oddly as I pleased, standing up in the classroom and at the dinner table—when we went to my mom's friend's house for Thanksgiving, the friend didn't even bother putting a chair at my table setting—without feeling judged. Maybe I was too young to process the way that people at the table were exchanging annoyed glances, but I never felt stuck in a particular story that others had created for me. I had the freedom to get bored of my behavior and to move on.

It wasn't until middle school, when I had friends who were experimenting with anorexia, that I grasped the kinds of meanings that the diagnosis carried. But by then, the illness no longer felt compelling. I had built a life in which I found meaning elsewhere. "Dear Journal," I wrote in second grade, in large letters, fitting only a few words on each page.

Things that our important:

>ice skating
>having fun
>Stuart little
>Matilda Every part
>of my body
>Trees

I remember trying to decide whether I'd be willing to live my childhood all over again, if it meant getting to avoid the part where I had anorexia, so my personal history could be wiped clean of that embarrassment. But the episode put me in contact with a category of experience that I might not have recognized if I hadn't been there myself. There is one moment from the hospital that has always haunted me, because I've never been able to describe it. I was standing near the open door of my hospital room when I heard a voice. I listened closely and the sound grew fainter, as if it were somehow folding in on itself. There was a kind of taunting echo, like the noise that can be heard when you hold a conch shell to your ear. This noise was categorically different from anything I had ever heard before and anything I've heard since. It was what William James, in his essay on the "unclassified residuum," might have described as one of those "wild facts, with no stall or pigeon-hole."

When I try to form a clear picture of the experience, I find myself thinking about what a young woman whom I interviewed years ago told me about her attempt to translate symptoms of psychosis into language: "It's like trying to explain what a bark sounds like to someone who's never heard of a dog."

I sometimes think of that voice as a potential entry into a different realm of experience, an alternative path that for reasons I don't fully understand I never took. It may have been that I was too young for anorexic behavior to stick to me. I was moving through developmental phases too quickly. If I had been a little older, it's possible that I would have had more social reinforcement and would have gone on to develop an anorexic "career." The difference between my illness and Hava's may have simply been a few years. I am overwhelmed by the meagerness of this fact.

I feel tied to Hava, but also to all the people I've written about here, through the pages we've left behind: "Here let me explain something about me," I wrote in a diary when I was eight. "I had a diseas called anexexia." Ray, Bapu, Naomi, and Laura also felt compelled to write about their illnesses, even as they realized that the language on offer wasn't quite right. They described their psychological experiences with deep self-awareness, but they also needed others to confirm whether what they were feeling was real. It didn't matter whether they believed they were married to God or saving the world from racism—they still looked to authorities (mystics for Bapu, doctors for the others) to tell them how and why they were feeling this way. Their distress took a form that was created in dialogue with others, a process that altered the path of their suffering and their identities too.

WHEN HAVA WAS THIRTY-ONE, she moved into her father's condominium. "There was nowhere else to go," her father, David, told me. "Her insurance was out." She had previously lived in subsidized housing, but after a suicide attempt that left her in a coma for several weeks she needed more individual attention. Some days she never got out of bed. David treated his daughter like his patient, keeping detailed daily records of her medical care. He essentially ran an intensive care unit for one person.

To understand his life with Hava, David recommended that I read *The Curious Incident of the Dog in the Night-Time*, a novel about a boy with behavioral difficulties who is raised by his father. "The father, in particular, is touching," David told me. "He is destroying his life as a sacrifice for his sick child. He is trying to achieve sainthood for what he perceives as prior crimes."

In her journals, Hava framed the problem in opposite terms. She was the one taking care of her dad, who had become estranged from the rest of her family. No longer a practicing doctor, he found purpose in caring for her. "I am the only one with the power to bring him out of his world for a time," she wrote. "He seems so much happier in it, that I simply oblige and encourage it."

She lived in her father's condominium for twelve years. "I talk about myself as though I were some case study," she wrote. She could recite the factors that contributed to the onset of her illness ("agitating my chemical imbalance," she wrote), but she didn't know where to go from there. Despite her deep knowledge about her illness, she still felt unknown. "I suppose I am one of those people that thoroughly understands myself yet am a stranger to myself," she wrote. "I'm not completely convinced I want to be rescued. Maybe it is just because I don't quite know who I am and what kind of person I am going to be."

IN AN ESSAY on the nature of recovery, the psychologist Pat Deegan, who was diagnosed with schizophrenia when she was seventeen, criticized the messaging of a popular advertising campaign for antidepressants. In an ad that circulated in the late nineties, a smiling girl races up the stairs to greet her mother. "I got my Mommy back," reads a note in crayon. Deegan challenges the idea that, after the disruption of mental illness, people can slip back into their former identities. "For those of us who have struggled for years, the restitution storyline does not hold true," she writes. In another essay, comparing herself to a friend who was paralyzed from the neck down, Deegan writes, "Recovery does not refer to an end product or result. It does not mean that the paralyzed man and I were 'cured.' In fact, our recovery is marked by an ever-deepening acceptance of our limitations." She proposes that "transformation rather than restoration becomes our path."

Deegan acknowledges that some phases of recovery require planning and work, but not every part of the process can be consciously orchestrated. "All of the polemic and technology of psychiatry, psychology, social work, and science cannot account for this phenomenon of hope," she writes. "But those of us who have recovered know that this grace is real. We lived it. It is our shared secret."

When Hava was forty-one, she drove from her father's house to Panera Bread for a date with a financial analyst named Tim. They had met online. She ordered a bagel and talked for three hours, telling the story of her illness. "From her perspective it was strategic in that she wanted to get everything out right away," Tim told me. "It was like, this is what you are dealing with—yea or nay." He, too, had gone through periods of hopelessness. In high school, the idea of going to class required so much energy that for a month he rarely left his bed. As an adult he had similar bouts of paralysis. "I came to the relationship from the place of understanding how difficult it is to put yourself out there," he told me. "I could tell she was a nervous wreck. She had been stuck in her dad's condo for years and years, and she wanted more."

They began dating, and, as the relationship became more serious, Hava took Tim to meet her psychiatrist, a doctor whom she'd known since she was fourteen. "Do you understand the extent of her eating disorder?" the psychiatrist asked him.

"The best word I can come up with is 'very,'" Tim responded.

Tim entered the dates of all her hospitalizations in an Excel sheet. She had a circular, tangential way of talking, and he wanted to clearly visualize her life. He added dates whenever she relayed a new anecdote. The final entry was "We met."

Sometimes, after sharing a meal together, Hava would go to the bathroom and throw up. "Yes, I did question it: Why do you do that to yourself?" Tim said. Perhaps a unique stigma attaches to the adult anorexic woman, as if she brought the whole problem on herself through vanity. Tim seemed surprised when I asked if he had ever judged Hava for vomiting. "It never even occurred to me to be judgmental," he said. "I did my little readings on bulimia, and I just came to the conclusion that this is how she had to deal with her anxieties. It was a routine, unfortunately. There is no judging about that. No more than I would want someone judging me for getting anxious and not wanting to go out." He seemed to embody the negative capability—the state of "being in uncertainties"—that Keats had described. As their relationship progressed, Hava had more tolerance for feelings of discomfort, too. She sat with the emotions rather than finding ways to immediately dispense with them.

She began sleeping over at Tim's apartment nearly every night. Once, when he came back from work at the end of the day and she was still in bed, nine hours later, he gently suggested that tomorrow she should try to move to the couch. "I talked about my own struggles and how even if I don't want to do anything all day I'll get dressed," he said. "I'll make myself food—it's the tiniest, tiniest little things. You're never going to have a big breakthrough. But there are a lot of tiny breakthroughs, and they add up."

Years before, during a period of semi-recovery, Hava had written in her journal that she felt like the turtle in *The Grapes of Wrath* who attempts to cross a highway. With "old humorous frowning eyes," the turtle drags himself across the hot pavement, even after his shell is clipped by a speeding truck and he flips onto his back and off the road. The turtle rights himself and slowly inches forward. "How good it would be to absorb a rain or even a light drizzle," Hava wrote. "But for now he travels on."

Hava's family and friends said that with Tim she seemed happier than she'd ever been in her life. Her son's parents, with whom she often talked on the phone, attributed her well-being to the connection that she and Tim had formed through shared vulnerabilities. "We all strive to fill our cups alone," Larry said, "but often we can't." She was living on disability benefits and volunteering for an organization that provided shelter to people without homes, and "she was thriving," Ann said. Decades of illness had transformed her values, her understanding of what a good life can be. Tim told me, "She didn't use the word 'recovery.' She wouldn't give it any technical term, but she did say, 'I'm in a better spot than I've ever been.'"

In an essay called "Remarks on the Philosophy of Mental Disorder," Fromm-Reichmann, the Lodge psychiatrist, described a patient crying in her office because she was about to be released from the Lodge and was terrified of rejoining her relatives and friends. Fromm-Reichmann reassures her patient, "You have gathered during these years a tremendous amount of human experience, having had the opportunity to observe practically all types of emotional experience in your fellow patients and in yourself. And what are these emotional experiences of the mentally disturbed other than human experiences of the kind we all go through, seen as if under a magnifying glass?"

ON APRIL 11, 2019, Tim made coffee, got dressed for work, and then, as was his routine, came back to bed to kiss Hava goodbye. She didn't respond. She didn't seem to be breathing. Tim called 911 while trying to perform CPR. When paramedics arrived, they couldn't resuscitate her, either. It appeared that she had thrown up in her sleep and asphyxiated. After years of bulimia, the muscles in her esophagus had been stretched. "I know that my eating disorder is a 'slow suicide,'" Hava had once written. But during this phase in her life she had plans for the future. She and Tim had just signed a lease on an apartment and planned to move in two weeks. Their belongings were already in boxes. Hava had been saving money for a trip to New Zealand, to visit her son there for the first time. Whenever she had extra money at the end of the month, she put her cash in a sock. "She talked about her son every day," Tim said.

When Tim and I spoke, on Zoom, he was sitting in the basement of his parents' house, where he'd moved after Hava's death. The walls were made of linoleum painted the hue of wood. Behind him was a Beatles poster and a still life of a baseball bat and mitt. He was pale and handsome, with a rectangular face and a buzz cut. He sipped a red energy drink. After Hava's death, he told me, he'd gone through the worst depression of his life. "You wouldn't know it from talking to me now," he said. "I look at her suffering—the way she handled her life—and that's what gets me through the day."

After his first period of depression, as a teenager, Tim, who is Catholic, had begun reciting a prayer at night: "Please help me use my sufferings to help others. Please don't let my suffering be wasted." In the last year, he had amended the prayer for the first time in more than twenty years: "I say to God, 'Please help me be as strong as Hava,'" he said. "'Please help me to be as forgiving as Hava'—that's the harder part." Although on paper it looked as if her diagnosis determined her path, he admired how she resisted the story that had been told about her life. The ending was different than others realized.

He began crying, and I apologized for asking him to recount events that were still so fresh. "And I hope it never goes away," he said. "A lot of times your own sufferings—how you deal with your suffering—helps people. More than you will ever know."

I saw my square image in the corner of our Zoom window and I felt self-conscious about hovering over a life that wasn't mine. My hair looked wavy and a little wild, like Hava's, and I wondered if he, too, saw me as her sister.

Notes

PROLOGUE: RACHEL

7 *"reading disorder"*: Abigail Bray, "The Anorexic Body: Reading Disorders," *Cultural Studies* 10, no. 3 (1996): 413.

8 *"The eight-letter-word"*: Takayo Mukai, "A Call for Our Language: Anorexia from Within," *Women's Studies International Forum* 12, no. 6 (1989): 613.

8 *"Lady Anorexia"*: Elaine Showalter, *Hystories: Hysterical Epidemics and Modern Media* (New York: Columbia University Press, 1997), 20.

8 *"blind search for a sense of identity"*: Hilde Bruch, *The Golden Cage: The Enigma of Anorexia Nervosa* (Cambridge, MA: Harvard University Press, 1978), xxii.

8 *"The illness used to be the accomplishment"*: Bruch, xxiv.

10 *"For god's sake the girl's only 6"*: Hava's mother shared more than a dozen of Hava's handwritten notebooks, beginning in 1988, as well as Hava's letters and emails, hundreds of which Hava had printed out and stored in folders. Her mother keeps Hava's old writing in boxes in her basement.

13 *"'digitalized' world, where everything was understood"*: Mukai, "A Call for Our Language," 634.

13–14 *the disease unfolds in distinct phases*: Nonja Peters, "The Ascetic Anorexic," *Social Analysis: The International Journal of Social and Cultural Practice*, no. 37 (April 1995): 44–66.

14 *"Maybe, yes"*: Mukai, "A Call for Our Language," 620.

14 *"Once the ascetic path is taken"*: Peters, "The Ascetic Anorexic,"
    51–52.

14 *"holy anorexia"*: Rudolph M. Bell, *Holy Anorexia* (Chicago: Uni-
    versity of Chicago Press, 1985), xii.

14 *"the desire not to be a saint"*: René Girard, "Eating Disorders and
    Mimetic Desire," *Contagion* 3 (Spring 1996): 16.

14 *"There is great irony in the fact"*: Girard, 9. Regarding anorexia and
    sainthood: A 2014 paper in *Case Reports in Psychiatry* describes
    a young girl, raised in a suburb of Chicago, who wanted to be a
    saint and starved herself while studying at a Catholic convent.
    "While occurring in modern time, her reasons for voluntary self-
    starvation and the cultural context in which she was raised are
    more similar to those individuals described in history as having
    anorexia mirabilis," the authors wrote. The girl did not have ac-
    cess to a full-length mirror—only to a tiny one that she used to
    adjust her habit. She never stepped on a scale, either. When the
    supervisors at her convent asked her to see a psychiatrist, "she did
    not understand why she needed to do this as she thought that she
    was being pious by restricting what she ate." See Amelia A. Davis
    and Mathew Nguyen, "A Case Study of Anorexia Nervosa Driven
    by Religious Sacrifice," *Case Reports in Psychiatry* (2014), 512–764.

19 *a condition known as "resignation syndrome"*: Rachel Aviv, "The
    Trauma of Facing Deportation," *The New Yorker*, March 17, 2017.

20 *"looping effect"*: Ian Hacking, *The Social Construction of What?*
    (Cambridge, MA: Harvard University Press, 1999), 34.

21 *"the space of possibilities for personhood"*: Ian Hacking, "Making Up
    People," in *Reconstructing Individualism: Autonomy, Individuality
    and the Self in Western Thought*, ed. Thomas C. Heller and Morton
    Sosna (Stanford, CA: Stanford University Press, 1987), 229.

21 *"We make ourselves in our own scientific image"*: Ian Hacking,
    "Kinds of People: Moving Targets," *Proceedings of the British Acad-
    emy* 151 (2007): 305.

21 *"have 'learned' or—better—'acquired' a new psychic state"*: Ian
    Hacking, "Pathological Withdrawal of Refugee Children Seeking
    Asylum in Sweden," *Studies in History and Philosophy of Biological
    and Biomedical Sciences* 41 (December 2010): 317.

21 *"recruited"*: Joan Jacobs Brumberg, *Fasting Girls: The History of
    Anorexia Nervosa* (New York: Vintage Books, 2000), 40.

21 *"career"*: Brumberg, 41.

22 *"correct attitude to a morbid change"*: Aubrey Lewis, "The Psycho-

pathology of Insight," *The British Journal of Medical Psychology* 14 (December 1934): 332–48.

22 *people of color are rated*: Laurence J. Kirmayer, Ellen Corin, and G. Eric Jarvis, "Inside Knowledge: Cultural Constructions of Insight in Psychosis," in *Insight and Psychosis: Awareness of Illness in Schizophrenia and Related Disorders*, ed. Xavier F. Amador and Anthony S. David (New York: Oxford University Press, July 2004), 197–232.

23 *"the misguided split"*: Department of Health and Human Services, *Mental Health: A Report of the Surgeon General*, National Institute of Mental Health (1999), 6.

23 *"no scientific justification for distinguishing"*: David Satcher, "Statement at Release of the Mental Health Report," December 13, 1999. See also: Colleen L. Barry and Richard G. Frank, "Economic Grand Rounds: Economics and the Surgeon General's Report on Mental Health," *Psychiatric Services* 53, no. 4 (April 1, 2002), ps.psychiatryonline.org/doi/full/10.1176/appi.ps.53.4.409.

23 *people who see mental illness as biological*: Amy Loughman and Nick Haslam, "Neuroscientific Explanations and the Stigma of Mental Disorder: A Meta-analytic Study," *Cognitive Research: Principles and Implications* 3, no. 1 (November 2018): 43.

23 *"being told that whatever had gone wrong"*: Elyn Saks, *The Center Cannot Hold: My Journey Through Madness* (New York: Hyperion, 2007), 168.

24 *There are stories that save us*: I owe the formulation of this idea to Tanya Luhrmann, who read a draft of this prologue. Thanks to Rachael Bedard, Anna Goldman, and Alice Gregory, who also helped me see much more clearly what I was trying to say in these sections.

25 *"the ideal of every science"*: William James, *Essays in Psychology* (Cambridge, MA: Harvard University Press, 1984), 247. In the essay, James also writes, "Round about the accredited and orderly facts of every science there ever floats a sort of dust-cloud of exceptional observations, of occurrences minute and irregular, and seldom met with, which it always proves less easy to attend to than to ignore."

RAY

29 *"How many miles"*: This chapter draws from some 250 pages of medical records that Ray's former lawyer, Philip J. Hirschkop,

shared with me. He stored Ray's files in his garage. A handful of medical records were also given to me by Ray's Silver Hill psychiatrist, Joan Narad.

29 *"mechanism of self-hypnosis"*: This chapter also draws from more than fifteen hundred pages of drafts of Ray's unpublished memoir as well as hundreds of pages of letters, emails, memos, and transcriptions of audio recordings of Ray talking to himself. Ray would sometimes speak into a tape recorder and then have a secretary transcribe the tapes. I obtained some of these pages from Hirschkop and some from Ray's high school friend Henry Kellerman, a psychoanalyst in Manhattan. A few excerpts of the memoir were given to me by Ray's friend Andy Seewald, a lawyer in New Jersey.

31 *founded in 1910*: Walter Freeman, *The Psychiatrist: Personalities and Patterns* (New York: Grune & Statton, 1968), 243–52.

31 *"I knew the psychotic"*: Quoted in David McK. Rioch, "Dexter Bullard, Sr., and Chestnut Lodge," *Psychiatry* 47 (February 1984): 2–3.

32 *"no therapeutic stone unturned"*: Freeman, *The Psychiatrist*, 243–52.

32 *His goal was to create an institution*: Dexter M. Bullard, "The Organization of Psychoanalytic Procedure in the Hospital," *The Journal of Nervous and Mental Disease* 91, no. 6 (June 1940): 697–703.

32 *"We don't know enough yet"*: Alfred H. Stanton and Morris S. Schwartz, *The Mental Hospital: A Study of Institutional Participation in Psychiatric Illness and Treatment* (Basic Books, 1954), 44.

32 *"No single word used"*: Stanton and Schwartz, 194.

32 *"getting better"*: Stanton and Schwartz, 149.

32 *"What occurred at the hospital"*: Stanton and Schwartz, 193. Stanton and Schwartz also observed that the Lodge psychiatrists restricted their "attention to 'deep' interpretation," often ignoring literal meanings—a tendency "so frequent as to amount almost to an occupational illness." Formal rules were regarded as "imposed by the demands of a society which feared and defended against the 'really vitally human.'"

32 *"pharmacology has no place"*: Dexter M. Bullard, interview by Robert Butler, January 17, 1963, page 23, transcript, American Psychiatric Association Foundation: Melvin Sabshin, M.D., Library and Archives.

32 *"You can't say that!"*: Quoted in Paul A. Offit, *Pandora's Lab: Seven Stories of Science Gone Wrong* (Washington, D.C.: National Geographic, 2017), 142.

32   *"queen of Chestnut Lodge"*: Gail A. Hornstein, *To Redeem One Person Is to Redeem the World: The Life of Frieda Fromm-Reichmann* (New York: Other Press, 2000), 278. Hornstein's book offers a vivid and rigorous portrait of the spirit of the Lodge during Fromm-Reichmann's tenure and beyond.

33   *"we know"*: Quoted in *Psychoanalysis and Psychotherapy: Selected Papers of Frieda Fromm-Reichmann*, ed. Dexter M. Bullard (Chicago: University of Chicago Press, 1959), 335.

33   *"one of the least satisfactorily conceptualized"*: Frieda Fromm-Reichmann, "Loneliness," *Contemporary Psychoanalysis* 26 (1990): 306. Originally printed in *Psychiatry: Journal for the Study of Interpersonal Processes* 22 (1959).

33   *"fact that there were people"*: Fromm-Reichmann, 310.

33   *"naked existence"*: Fromm-Reichmann, 318. She is referring to a definition of loneliness formulated in Ludwig Binswanger, *Grundformen und Erkenntnis Menschlichen Daseins* (Zürich: Niehans, 1942), 130.

33   *"substitute mothers"*: Ann-Louise S. Silver, "A Personal Response to Gail Hornstein's *To Redeem One Person Is to Redeem the World: The Life of Frieda Fromm-Reichmann*," *Psychiatry* 65, no. 1 (Spring 2002): 9. Silver also shared memories of the Lodge in a conversation with me not long before she died.

33   *"part of a dysfunctional family"*: Ann-Louise S. Silver, "Thorns in the Rose Garden: Failures at Chestnut Lodge," in *Failures in Psychoanalytic Treatment*, ed. Joseph Reppen and Martin A. Schulman (Madison, CT: International Universities Press, 2003), 37–63.

33   *"Have a good hour!"*: Quoted in Richard M. Waugaman, "The Loss of an Institution: Mourning Chestnut Lodge," in *The Therapist in Mourning: From the Faraway Nearby*, ed. Anne J. Adelman and Kerry L. Malawista (New York: Columbia University Press, 2013), 162.

34   *"The world was sick"*: Quoted in Ran Zwigenberg, "Healing a Sick World: Psychiatric Medicine and the Atomic Age," *Medical History* 62, no. 1 (January 2018): 28.

34   *"The greatest prerequisite for peace"*: Quoted in Anne Harrington, *Mind Fixers: Psychiatry's Troubled Search for the Biology of Mental Illness* (New York: W. W. Norton, 2019), 119.

34   *"The world will be saved"*: Quoted in Zwigenberg, "Healing a Sick World," 28.

34 *compared the case's significance*: Peter D. Kramer, *Ordinarily Well: The Case for Antidepressants* (New York: Farrar, Straus and Giroux, 2016), 46.

34 *"showdown between two forms of knowledge"*: Quoted in James L. Knoll IV, "The Humanities and Psychiatry: The Rebirth of Mind," *Psychiatric Times* 30, no. 4 (April 2013): 29. Originally from M. Robertson, "Power and Knowledge in Psychiatry and the Troubling Case of Dr. Osheroff," *Australasian Psychiatry* 13, no. 4 (2005): 343–50.

35 *"we would walk all the way"*: This quote is from Dotty Smith's testimony at Ray's hearing before the State of Maryland Health Claims Arbitration Board. The hearing was video recorded and kept in storage at the office of one of Ray's former lawyers, David J. Fudala. This chapter draws from more than twenty VHS tapes Fudala shared with me from the two-week hearing.

36 *"some disarray in the biochemical tides"*: Nathan S. Kline, *From Sad to Glad: Kline on Depression* (New York: Ballantine Books, 1974), 2.

36 *"Do not try to dredge up"*: Kline, 157.

36 *photograph from 1953*: Mark Caldwell, *The Last Crusade: The War on Consumption, 1862–1954* (New York: Atheneum, 1988), 242–47.

36 *"I couldn't quite bring myself"*: Quoted in Maggie Scarf, "From Joy to Depression: New Insights into the Chemistry of Moods," *The New York Times*, April 24, 1977.

37 *"caring for her household"*: Nathan Kline, "Clinical Experience with Iproniazid (Marsilid)," *Journal of Clinical and Experimental Psychopathology & Quarterly Review of Psychiatry and Neurology* 19 (1958): 73.

37 *"He produced a profusion"*: Kline, 75.

37 *"There was a large and adamant"*: Kline, *From Sad to Glad*, 57.

37 *"regarded as somewhat peculiar"*: Solomon Snyder, *Brainstorming: The Science and Politics of Opiate Research* (Cambridge, MA: Harvard University Press, 1989), 10.

37 *"For you were not born"*: Quoted in Kline, *From Sad to Glad*, epigraph.

38 *"felt he was God"*: Quoted in Meredith Platt, *Storming the Gates of Bedlam: How Dr. Nathan Kline Transformed the Treatment of Mental Illness* (New York: DePew Publishing, 2012), 104.

38 *"The chemicals produce"*: Nathan S. Kline, "The Challenge of the Psychopharmaceuticals," *Proceedings of the American Philosophical Society* 103, no. 3 (June 1959): 458.

38 *"cookbook-type operation"*: Quoted in Summary of Transcript of James L. Wellhouse Deposition, Raphael J. Osheroff, M.D., v. Chestnut Lodge, Inc., et al. (hereafter cited as *Osheroff v. Chestnut Lodge*), 490 A.2d 720 (Circuit Court for Montgomery County, Maryland, April 10, 1985).

38 *"participate mechanically"*: Testimony of Raphael Osheroff, *Osheroff v. Chestnut Lodge*, November 26, 1986. All the quotations in the following two sections come from VHS tapes of the hearing, provided to me by Ray's former lawyer David J. Fudala.

39 *"The symptoms and the sickness"*: Joanne Greenberg, *I Never Promised You a Rose Garden* (New York: Henry Holt, 1964), 209.

40 *"I don't care to stay"*: Testimony of Louis Bader, *Osheroff v. Chestnut Lodge*, November 26, 1986.

40 *"pull back and become more distant"*: Transcript of Staff Conference, Chestnut Lodge, March 12, 1979, 14. The quotes in this section draw from a staff conference among twelve medical professionals on the Lodge staff. The transcript of the meeting, which had been recorded, is twenty-two pages single-spaced.

41 *"The time that I spent"*: Transcript of Staff Conference, 11.

43 *"sprinkling of under-achieving"*: Morton M. Hunt, "A Report on the Private Mental Hospital: Survival Through Evolution," *Trends in Psychiatry* (1964): 15.

45 *"For three days now"*: Roland Kuhn, "The First Patient Treated with Imipramine," in *A History of the CINP*, ed. Thomas A. Ban and Oakley S. Ray (Brentwood, TN: J. M. Productions, 1996), 436. The book identifies Kuhn's note as a "Photocopy from medical history #21502 of the 'Kantonal Treatment and Care Clinic in Münsterlingen,' concerning female patient Paula F.J., born April 30, 1907." In March 2020, a report by historians at the University of Zurich found that Kuhn (who experimented with many compounds beyond imipramine) had failed to comply with methodological requirements that were common at the time. For instance, some experimental substances were given to patients without having passed through all the stages of preliminary testing. Also, Kuhn did not adhere to the start and end dates for clinical trials. See Marietta Meier, Mario König, and Magaly Tornay, *Testfall Münsterlingen: Klinische Versuche in der Psychiatrie, 1940–1980* (Zürich: Chronos, 2019). See also Marietta Meier, press release, September 23, 2019, in "Pierre Baumann and Francois Ferrero: An Official Inquiry on the Clinical Research Activities (1946–1972) of

Roland Kuhn (1912–2005)," International Network for the History of Neuropsychopharmacology website, inhn.org/fileadmin /user_upload/User_Uploads/INHN/Controversies/MEIER_Press _release__of_Kuhb_report.pdf.

45 *Kuhn was Nathan Kline's rival*: David Healy, *The Antidepressant Era* (Cambridge, MA: Harvard University Press, 1997), 49–62. See also Kramer, *Ordinarily Well*, 3–6.

45 *"whereas previously they were continually tortured"*: Roland Kuhn, "The Treatment of Depressive States with G-22355 (Imipramine Hydrochloride)," *The American Journal of Psychiatry* 115 (1958): 459.

45 *"I don't think of it anymore"*: Quoted in Kuhn, 460.

46 *"completely restores"*: Roland Kuhn, "The Imipramine Story," in *Discoveries in Biological Psychiatry*, ed. Frank J. Ayd and Barry Blackwell (Philadelphia: J. B. Lippincott, 1970), 216.

46 *"letting the things themselves speak"*: Roland Kuhn, "On Existential Analysis" (paper presented at the Philadelphia Psychiatric Society's Symposium on Psychiatric Therapies in Europe, March 23, 1959). See also Louis A. Sass, "Phenomenology as Description and as Explanation: The Case of Schizophrenia," *Handbook of Phenomenology and Cognitive Science* (December 2009): 635–54.

46 *"a machine that just runs faster or slower"*: Quoted in Nicholas Weiss, "No One Listened to Imipramine," in *Altering American Consciousness: The History of Alcohol and Drug Use in the United States, 1800–2000*, ed. Sarah W. Tracy and Caroline J. Acker (Amherst: University of Massachusetts Press, 2004), 329–52.

46 *"not dealing with a self-contained, rigid object"*: Roland Kuhn, "Artistic Imagination and the Discovery of Antidepressants," *Journal of Psychopharmacology* 4, no. 3 (1990): 129.

47 *"a piece of burned meat"*: Jane Kenyon, "Having It Out with Melancholy," in *Constance: Poems* (Minneapolis, MN: Graywolf Press, 1993).

48 *"Within a week the miracle"*: Percy Knauth, *A Season in Hell* (New York: Pocket Books, 1977), 118.

48 *"No fears, no worries"*: Knauth, 83.

48 *"There is little doubt"*: Knauth, 120.

48 *"at best a reductionistic oversimplification"*: Joseph Schildkraut, "The Catecholamine Hypothesis of Affective Disorders: A Review of Supporting Evidence," *The Journal of Neuropsychiatry and*

Clinical Neurosciences 7, no. 4 (November 1995): 530. The article originally appeared in *The American Journal of Psychiatry* 122, no. 5 (1965): 509–22.

48 *"The new style of thought"*: Nikolas Rose, *The Politics of Life Itself: Biomedicine, Power, and Subjectivity in the Twenty-First Century* (Princeton, NJ: Princeton University Press, 2007), 192.

49 *He called his colleague Robert Greenspan*: Memorandum Opinion, Robert Greenspan, M.D., et al. v. Raphael J. Osheroff, M.D., et al. (hereafter cited as *Greenspan v. Osheroff*), 232 Va. 388 (Circuit Court for the City of Alexandria, Virginia, February 8, 1983).

50 *the head nurse described Ray as a "lunatic"*: Testimony of Margaret Hess, *Greenspan v. Osheroff*, 11.

50 *"excessive reaction"*: *Diagnostic and Statistical Manual of Mental Disorders, Second Edition (DSM-II)* (Washington, D.C.: American Psychiatric Association, 1968), 300.

51 *"science over ideology"*: Quoted in Rick Mayes and Allan V. Horwitz, "DSM-III and the Revolution in the Classification of Mental Illness," *Journal of the History of the Behavioral Sciences* 41, no. 3 (Summer 2005): 250.

51 *"literary legerdemain"*: Raphael Osheroff, email message to Henry Kellerman, February 2, 2009.

51 *"pharmacological Calvinism"*: Quoted in Healy, *The Antidepressant Era*, 227.

51 *"if a drug makes you feel good"*: Gerald L. Klerman, "Drugs and Social Values," *International Journal of the Addictions* 5, no. 2 (1970): 316

52 *"blessing for mankind"*: Quoted in Emily Martin, "Pharmaceutical Virtue," *Culture, Medicine and Psychiatry* 30, no. 2 (June 2006): 157.

52 *"most important and dramatic epics"*: Quoted in Robert Whitaker, *Anatomy of an Epidemic: Magic Bullets, Psychiatric Drugs, and the Astonishing Rise of Mental Illness in America* (New York: Broadway Paperbacks, 2010), 64.

52 *"no advantage is gained"*: Quoted in Aaron T. Beck, *Depression: Causes and Treatment* (Philadelphia: University of Pennsylvania Press, 1967), 313. The pharmaceutical company Merck, which produces Elavil, bought fifty thousand copies of Ayd's book to distribute to doctors. The company also hired a musicologist to compile an album of blues songs—the word "Elavil" was printed

on the jacket—that would be a "beautiful expression of how life and the problems of life create depression."

52 *"dealing with a sincere honest"*: Frank Ayd Testimony before the State of Maryland Health Claims Arbitration Board, December 7, 1983.

53 *"If the diagnosis and treatment"*: Ray attended the 1989 American Psychiatric Association convention in San Francisco, and this quote comes from his notes. He reflects on the experience in chapter 27 of one of the later drafts of his memoir.

54 *" 'externalization,' that is, the tendency"*: Thomas G. Gutheil, M.D., "Preliminary Report on *Osheroff v. Chestnut Lodge et al.*," undated, 1–2.

54 *"insistence on the biological nature"*: Gutheil, "Preliminary Report," 4.

54 *"It's a demeaning comment"*: Testimony of Raphael Osheroff, *Osheroff v. Chestnut Lodge*.

54 *"The sheer mechanical banging"*: Testimony of Raphael Osheroff.

56 *"the outcome of the Osheroff case"*: Joel Paris, *The Fall of an Icon: Psychoanalysis and Academic Psychiatry* (Toronto: University of Toronto Press, 2005), 96.

56 *"the conventional belief"*: Miriam Shuchman and Michael S. Wilkes, "Dramatic Progress Against Depression," *The New York Times*, October 7, 1990, www.nytimes.com/1990/10/07/archives /dramatic-progress-against-depression.html.

56 *"determine to a great extent"*: Sifford D, "An Improper Diagnosis Case That Changed Psychiatry," *Philadelphia Inquirer*, March 24, 1988, 4E.

56 *the medical equivalent of a "Miranda rule"*: Gerald L. Klerman, "The Psychiatric Patient's Right to Effective Treatment: Implications of *Osheroff v. Chestnut Lodge*," *The American Journal of Psychiatry* 147, no. 4 (April 1990): 409. The original article referenced is Sifford D, "An Improper Diagnosis Case That Changed Psychiatry."

57 *"nothing could be said"*: Michael Robertson and Garry Walter, *Ethics and Mental Health: The Patient, Profession and Community* (Boca Raton, FL: CRC Press, 2014), 180.

57 *"Art kills"*: Quoted in Abigail Zuger, "New Way of Doctoring: By the Book," *The New York Times*, December 16, 1997, www.nytimes .com/1997/12/16/science/new-way-of-doctoring-by-the-book.html.

58 *The Lodge doctors felt chastened*: Thomas H. McGlashan, "The

Chestnut Lodge Follow-Up Study I. Follow-Up Methodology and Study Sample," *Archives of General Psychiatry* 41, no. 6 (June 1984): 573–85. See also Thomas H. McGlashan, "The Chestnut Lodge Follow-Up Study II. Long-Term Outcome of Schizophrenia and the Affective Disorders," *Archives of General Psychiatry* 41, no. 6 (June 1984): 586–601.

58 *roughly the same percentage of patients*: J. D. Hegarty et al., "One Hundred Years of Schizophrenia: A Meta-Analysis of the Outcome Literature," *The American Journal of Psychiatry* 151, no. 10 (October 1994): 1409–16.

58 *"The data is in"*: Quoted in Ann-Louise S. Silver, "Chestnut Lodge, Then and Now: Work with a Patient with Schizophrenia and Obsessive Compulsive Disorder," *Contemporary Psychoanalysis* 33, no. 2 (April 1997): 230.

59 *"Madness has become an industrialized product"*: A. Donald, "The Wal-Marting of American Psychiatry: An Ethnography of Psychiatric Practice in the Late Twentieth Century," *Culture, Medicine, and Psychiatry* 25 (2001): 435.

59 *"The real patient"*: Donald, 433.

60 *"We are not so different"*: Quoted in "Money Woes May End Mission of Historic Hospital," *Psychiatric News* 36, no. 8 (April 20, 2001): 9.

60 *"A great listing lighthouse"*: Silver, "A Personal Response to Gail Hornstein," 2.

61 *"ghost hunters"*: Nesa Nourmohammadi, "A Year Later, Historic Chestnut Lodge Still Mourned," *The Washington Post*, June 17, 2010, www.washingtonpost.com/wp-dyn/content/article/2010/06/16/AR2010061603175.html.

61 *"A Belated Obituary"*: Sharon Packer, "A Belated Obituary: Raphael J. Osheroff, MD," *Psychiatric Times*, June 28, 2013, www.psychiatrictimes.com/view/belated-obituary-raphael-j-osheroff-md.

64 *"illusory or medically-useless treatments"*: Plaintiff Complaint, Government Employees Insurance Co. et al. v. Prescott et al., Case No. 1:14-cv-00057-BMC (U.S. District Court for the Eastern District of New York, January 6, 2014).

65 *a man's "unfinished business"*: Samuel Osherson, *Finding Our Fathers: How a Man's Life Is Shaped by His Relationship with His Father* (Chicago: Contemporary Books, 2001), 1. (Osherson is not related to Osheroff, despite the odd similarity of their names.)

66 *"passed away in his sleep"*: "Dr. Raphael J. Osheroff," *The Star-*

Ledger, March 20, 2012, obits.nj.com/us/obituaries/starledger/name
/raphael-osheroff-obituary?id=22024016.

66   *"it is a matter of indifference":* Sigmund Freud, *Writings on Art and
     Literature* (Stanford, CA: Stanford University Press, 1997), 247.

BAPU

70   *"scorpion":* This chapter draws from more than eight hundred
     pages of handwritten journals, composed largely in Tamil (with
     some Sanskrit interspersed, too), that Bapu's daughter-in-law
     discovered in a cabinet in Bapu's house after she died. I also read
     some ninety pages of letters (as well as bank memos, a police
     report, and other miscellany) that Bhargavi discovered in her
     father's briefcase after his death. Both the journals and the let-
     ters were translated by Vidya Mohan, a Tamil language lecturer
     at the University of Michigan, and by Tyler Richard, a lecturer
     in Sanskrit and Tamil languages at Columbia. Sruthi Durai, a
     student at Berkeley, also assisted with the translations. Addi-
     tionally, Vidya, who grew up in a Brahmin family in Chennai
     at roughly the same time as Bhargavi, provided extraordinarily
     helpful context.

72   *"god intoxication":* Vijaya Ramaswamy, *Walking Naked: Women,
     Society, Spirituality in South India* (Shimla, India: Indian Institute
     of Advanced Study, 1997), 3.

72   *she escaped her in-laws' house:* Kumkum Sangari, "Mirabai and the
     Spiritual Economy of Bhakti," *Economic and Political Weekly* 25,
     no. 27 (July 1990): 1464–75.

73   *"To me":* Quoted in Ramaswamy, *Walking Naked,* 33.

73   *"Like the pure river Ganges":* From Sri Nambudiri's foreword to
     Bapu's book titled *Red-Eyed One, Open Your Red Eyes* (Chennai:
     Madras Two, 1970), 1. Vidya Mohan translated the book for me.

75   *"limping on the right leg":* Letter from Rajamani to the Madras po-
     lice, June 9, 1970.

75   *"my Elder brother in religion":* Quoted in V. K. Subramanian, *101
     Mystics of India* (New Delhi: Abhinav Publications, 2001), 221.

76   *"wandering at large":* The Mental Healthcare Act, Act No. 10,
     Ministry of Law and Justice, New Delhi, 2017.

77   *"doctrine of the abyss":* Louis A. Sass, *Madness and Modernism: In-
     sanity in the Light of Modern Art, Literature, and Thought* (New
     York: Basic Books, 1992), 16.

77   *"When faced with such people":* Quoted in Angela Woods, *The*

Sublime Object of Psychiatry: Schizophrenia in Clinical and Cultural Theory (Oxford: Oxford University Press, 2011), 51.

77 *The earliest phase of schizophrenia*: Zeno Van Duppen and Rob Sips, "Understanding the Blind Spots of Psychosis: A Wittgensteinian and First-Person Approach," *Psychopathology* 51, no. 4 (2018): 4.

78 *"crystal-clear sight"*: Sass, *Madness and Modernism*, 44.

79 *Jal Dhunjibhoy, one of the first*: Waltraud Ernst, *Colonialism and Transnational Psychiatry: The Development of an Indian Mental Hospital in British India, c. 1925–1940* (London: Anthem Press, 2013), xvii–xx.

79 *"nation-building programme"*: Quoted in Waltraud Ernst, "Crossing the Boundaries of 'Colonial Psychiatry': Reflections on the Development of Psychiatry in British India, c. 1870–1940," *Culture, Medicine, and Psychiatry* 35 (August 2011): 539.

79 *"onward march to civilization"*: Quoted in Ernst, 539.

79 *"a point on which all students"*: George Devereux, "A Sociological Theory of Schizophrenia," *The Psychoanalytic Review* 26 (January 1939): 317.

79 *it was claimed that the Parsis*: Ernst, *Colonialism and Transnational Psychiatry*, 14. See also T. M. Luhrmann, *The Good Parsi: The Fate of a Colonial Elite in a Postcolonial Society* (Cambridge, MA: Harvard University Press, 1996).

80 *"If we are to advise"*: Quoted in Ernst, *Colonialism and Transnational Psychiatry*, 12.

80 *"in India, European civilization"*: Quoted in Amit Ranjan Basu, "Emergence of a Marginal Science in a Colonial City: Reading Psychiatry in Bengali Periodicals," *The Indian Economic and Social History Review* 41, no. 2 (2004): 131.

80 *"It will recall to my mind"*: Quoted in Christiane Hartnack, *Psychoanalysis in Colonial India* (New Delhi: Oxford University Press, 2001), 1.

80 *"oceanic sentiment"*: Quoted in William B. Parsons, "The Oceanic Feeling Revisited," *The Journal of Religion* 78, no. 4 (October 1998): 503.

80 *"I shall now try"*: Quoted in Sudhir Kakar, *The Analyst and the Mystic: Psychoanalytic Reflections on Religion and Mysticism* (New Delhi: Viking, 1991), 6.

81 *"mystical quest is not apart"*: Kakar, ix.

81 *"depressive core at the base"*: Kakar, x.

81   *"reality of being utterly and agonizingly alone"*: Quoted in Kakar, *Analyst*, 25. Originally from Paul C. Horton, "The Mystical Experience: Substance of an Illusion," *Journal of the American Psychoanalytic Association* 22 (1974): 364–80.

81   *"We will end up"*: N. C. Surya and S. S. Jayaram, "Some Basic Considerations in the Practice of Psychotherapy in the Indian Setting," *Indian Journal of Psychiatry* 38 (1996): 10.

81   *"statistical norm"*: Quoted in N. N. Wig, "Dr. N. C. Surya—The Lone Rider," *Indian Journal of Psychiatry* 38 (1996): 7.

81   *"like every other John"*: Quoted in Wig, 7.

81   *"completely out of tune"*: Quoted in Wig, 4.

81   *he quit the field*: Wig, 2.

81   *"One cannot discover"*: Quoted in Sudhir Kakar, "Reflections on Psychoanalysis, Indian Culture and Mysticism," *Journal of Indian Philosophy* 10 (1982): 293.

82   Rauwolfia serpentina: Edward Shorter, *A Historical Dictionary of Psychiatry* (New York: Oxford University Press, 2005), 256.

82   *"Ayurvedic drugs, easily available"*: W. K., "Indian Drugs for Mental Diseases," *The New York Times*, May 31, 1953.

82   *decided to give an extract*: Nathan S. Kline, "Use of *Rauwolfia serpentina* Benth. in Neuropsychiatric Conditions," *Annals of the New York Academy of Sciences* 59, no. 1 (April 1954): 107–27.

82   *"She was not suddenly cured"*: Nathan S. Kline, *From Sad to Glad: Kline on Depression* (New York: Ballantine Books, 1974), 66.

82   *the hospital's glazier noticed*: David Healy, *The Creation of Psychopharmacology* (Cambridge, MA: Harvard University Press, 2002), 105.

82   *New York's commissioner of mental health*: Elliot S. Valenstein, *Blaming the Brain: The Truth About Drugs and Mental Health* (New York: Free Press, 1988), 70.

82   *"It was my peculiar distinction"*: Kline, *From Sad to Glad*, 59.

82   *"just another curious aspect"*: Kline, 62.

82   *"swing the emotional pendulum"*: Kline, 117.

82   *"greatly reinforced the case"*: "Chlorpromazine for Treating Schizophrenia," Lasker Foundation website, laskerfoundation.org/winners/chlorpromazine-for-treating-schizophrenia/.

82   *"keystone of psychopharmacology"*: Quoted in Alain Ehrenberg, *Weariness of the Self: Diagnosing the History of Depression in the Contemporary Age* (Montreal: McGill–Queen's University Press, 2009), 176.

83 *To dramatize the premedicated state*: Jonathan M. Metzl, *The Protest Psychosis: How Schizophrenia Became a Black Disease* (Boston: Beacon Press, 2009), 103.

83 *"It makes them cooperative"*: Quoted in Mat Savelli and Melissa Ricci, "Disappearing Acts: Anguish, Isolation, and the Reimagining of the Mentally Ill in Global Psychopharmaceutical Advertising (1953–2005)," *Canadian Bulletin of Medical History* 35, no. 2 (Fall 2018): 259.

84 *"At a time when only men"*: Rajesh Govindarajulu, "The Chellammal Effect," *The Hindu*, August 1, 2014, www.thehindu.com /features/metroplus/the-chellammal-effect/article6272190.ece.

84 *"A woman of her age"*: Lakshmi Narayan, "The Kesavardhini 'Mami,'" *Femina*, May 23, 1975, 15.

87 *"She is to look upon him"*: Quoted in Andrew O. Fort, *Jīvanmukti in Transformation: Embodied Liberation in Advaita and Neo-Vedanta* (Albany: State University of New York Press, 1998), 162.

90 *The Upanishads*: Quoted in Josef Parnas and Mads Gram Henriksen, "Mysticism and Schizophrenia: A Phenomenological Exploration of the Structure of Consciousness in the Schizophrenia Spectrum Disorders," *Consciousness and Cognition* 43 (May 2016): 79.

91 *"A perfect knower"*: Quoted in David R. Kinsley, *The Divine Player: A Study of Kṛṣṇa Līlā* (Delhi: Motilal Banardidass, 1979), 226.

92 *"In heaven there is a fair"*: Quoted in David Kinsley, "'Through the Looking Glass': Divine Madness in the Hindu Religious Tradition," *History of Religions* 13, no. 4 (May 1974): 293.

92 *"deprived of the sight"*: Quoted in Vijaya Ramaswamy, "Rebels— Conformists? Women Saints in Medieval South India," *Anthropos* 87, no. 1/3 (1992): 143.

92 *"sad every moment"*: Robert Bly and Jane Hirshfield, *Mirabai: Ecstatic Poems* (Boston: Beacon Press, 2004), 25.

94 *"epistemic injustice"*: Miranda Fricker, *Epistemic Injustice: Power and the Ethics of Knowing* (New York: Oxford University Press, 2007), 1.

95 *ECT could be administered*: Chittaranjan Andrade, "The Practice of Electroconvulsive Therapy in India: Considerable Room for Improvement," *Indian Journal of Psychological Medicine* 15, no. 2 (July 1992): 1–4. See also Chittaranjan Andrade, "ECT in India: Historical Snippets," *Convulsive Therapy* 11, no. 3 (1995): 225–27.

98 *"So great is my desire"*: Quoted in Sisir Kumar Das, *A History of Indian Literature, 500–1399: From the Courtly to the Popular* (New Delhi: Sahitya Akademi, 2005), 50.

99 *"Her blouse is badly stitched"*: Bhargavi V. Davar, "The Fugitive." The play is unpublished. Bhargavi shared a thick pile of old printouts of her writing, including stories and poems, composed mostly in her teens and twenties, when I visited her apartment in Pune.

100 *"One wants to know"*: Bhargavi V. Davar and Parameshwar R. Bhat, *Psychoanalysis as a Human Science: Beyond Foundationalism* (New Delhi: Sage Publications, 1995), 20.

100 *a revival of the phenomenological tradition*: A phenomenological approach to schizophrenia has undergone a modest renaissance in recent years. See Louis Sass, Josef Parnas, and Dan Zahavi, "Phenomenological Psychopathology and Schizophrenia: Contemporary Approaches and Misunderstandings," *Philosophy, Psychiatry, and Psychology* 18, no. 1 (March 2011): 1–23.

100 *"A 'depressive' does not"*: Bhargavi V. Davar, "Writing Phenomenology of Mental Illness: Extending the Universe of Ordinary Discourse," in *Existence, Experience, and Ethics*, ed. A. Raghuramaraju (New Delhi: DK Printworld, 2000), 61–62.

100 *"in the writing of history"*: Davar, 75.

104 *"there is a sense"*: Bhargavi V. Davar, "From Mental Illness to Disability: Choices for Women Users/Survivors of Psychiatry in Self and Identity Constructions," *Indian Journal of Gender Studies* 15, no. 2 (May 2008): 270.

105 *the Buddha enduring*: J. Moussaieff Masson, *The Oceanic Feeling: The Origins of Religious Sentiment in Ancient India* (Dordrecht, Holland: D. Reidel Publishing Company, 1980), 6.

105 *a mother has gone mad*: Gananath Obeyesekere, "Depression, Buddhism, and the Work of Culture in Sri Lanka," in *Culture and Depression: Studies in the Anthropology and Cross-Cultural Psychiatry of Affect and Disorder*, ed. Arthur Kleinman and Byron Good (Berkeley: University of California Press, 1985), 144–45.

106 *"Some were sitting up"*: Barry Bearak, "25 Inmates Die, Tied to Poles, in Fire in India in Mental Home," *The New York Times*, August 7, 2001, www.nytimes.com/2001/08/07/world/25-inmates-die-tied-to-poles-in-fire-in-india-in-mental-home.html.

106 *"sent to doctors"*: "SC Orders Inspection of Mental Asylums," *Times of India*, February 6, 2002, timesofindia.indiatimes.com/india/sc-orders-inspection-of-mental-asylums/articleshow/12409583.cms.

107 *"there seems to be"*: Asha Krishnakumar, "Beyond Erwadi," *Frontline*, July 20, 2002, frontline.thehindu.com/other/article30245597 .ece.

107 *"culturally valued refuge"*: Ramanathan Raguram et al., "Traditional Community Resources for Mental Health: A Report of Temple Healing from India," *British Medical Journal* 325, no. 7354 (July 2002): 38.

107 *"We should welcome"*: Ramanathan Raguram et al., "Rapid Response: Author's Response," *British Medical Journal* website, August 12, 2002, www.bmj.com/rapid-response/2011/10/29/authors -response-0.

107 *"I am appalled"*: Santhosh Rajagopal, "Rapid Response: Misleading Study," *British Medical Journal* website, July 19, 2002, www.bmj .com/rapid-response/2011/10/29/misleading-study.

108 *"The much talked about 'stigma'"*: Davar, "Writing Phenomenology," 62.

108 *"credibility gap"*: Patel also writes eloquently about this dilemma in "Rethinking Mental Health Care: Bridging the Credibility Gap," *Intervention* 12, no. 1 (2014): 15–20.

108 *"doctors of the soul"*: Bhargavi V. Davar and Madhura Lohokare, "Recovering from Psychosocial Traumas: The Place of Dargahs in Maharashtra," *Economic and Political Weekly* 44, no. 16 (April 2009): 63.

109 *"Psychiatry and psychology have described"*: Bhargavi Davar, unpublished report on faith healing (which I made a copy of when I visited the Bapu Trust library in Pune), 120.

109 *series of studies conducted*: T. V. Padma, "Developing Countries: The Outcomes Paradox," *Nature* 508 (April 2014): 14–15. See also G. Harrison et al., "Recovery from Psychotic Illness: A 15- and 25-Year International Follow-Up Study," *The British Journal of Psychiatry* 178 (June 2001): 506–17.

109 *"If I become psychotic"*: Quoted in Kim Hopper, "Outcomes Elsewhere: Course of Psychosis in 'Other Cultures,'" in *Society and Psychosis*, ed. Craig Morgan, Kwame McKenzie, and Paul Fearon (Cambridge: Cambridge University Press, 2008). For reflections on the WHO studies and their implications, see Ethan Watters, *Crazy Like Us: The Globalization of the American Psyche* (New York: Free Press, 2010).

109 *large Indian families may be more supportive*: Another theory for the WHO findings is that in Western cultures a disorganized or

dispersed sense of self might feel more distressing and patholog-
ical than in cultures where individual autonomy is less intensely
valued. Tanya Luhrmann, a medical anthropologist at Stanford,
studied people in three cities—Chennai; Accra, Ghana; and San
Mateo, California—who hear voices. The Americans experienced
their voices as an invasion that made them feel violated. The Africans and Indians were more comfortable imagining "mind and
self as interwoven with others," Luhrmann found. They were more
likely to describe their voices as a positive force, the bearers of useful guidance. They "interpreted them, in effect, as people—who
cannot be controlled," she wrote. See: T. M. Luhrmann et al., "Differences in Voice-Hearing Experiences of People with Psychosis in
the U.S.A., India and Ghana: Interview-Based Study," *The British
Journal of Psychiatry* 206, no. 1 (January 2015): 41–44.

110   *"his benign look"*: Quoted in Fort, *Jīvanmukti in Transformation*,
      145.

110   *"There is something"*: Paul Brunton, *A Search in Secret India* (Lon-
      don: Rider, 1934), 141.

110   *"desire to regain"*: Quoted in Ramaswamy, *Walking Naked*, 8.

117   *"I am mad with love"*: Bly and Hirshfield, *Mirabai*, 38.

NAOMI

120   *"target the 'undesirable' elements"*: Milton William Cooper, *Behold
      a Pale Horse* (Flagstaff, AZ: Light Technology Publishing, 1991),
      168.

120   *"ruling elite"*: Cooper, 167.

121   *"Our stars and stripes"*: Saul Williams, "Amethyst Rocks," in *The
      Dead Emcee Scrolls: The Lost Teachings of Hip-Hop* (New York:
      Pocket Books, 2006), 54.

121   *hundreds of others*: Incident report, Saint Paul Police Department,
      July 4, 2003.

121   *"I'm hurting inside"*: Transcript of interview of Naomi Gaines by
      Officer Sheila Lambie, July 4, 2003. I also drew from more than
      a hundred pages of police and medical records to describe the
      events leading up to Lambie's interview.

123   *When the Homes were built*: Audrey Petty, *High Rise Stories: Voices
      from Chicago Public Housing* (San Francisco: McSweeney's Books,
      2013), 19.

123   *Twenty-eight identical*: D. Bradford Hunt, "What Went Wrong

with Public Housing in Chicago? A History of the Robert Taylor Homes," *Journal of the Illinois State Historical Society (1998–)* 94, no. 1 (2001): 96.

123 *covered ninety-two acres*: William Julius Wilson, "The Urban Underclass," in *The Urban Reality*, ed. Paul E. Peterson (Washington, D.C.: Brookings Institution, 1985), 137.

123 *twenty-seven thousand people*: Wilson, 138.

123 *"The world looks on"*: Quoted in Devereux Bowly Jr., *The Poorhouse: Subsidized Housing in Chicago* (Carbondale: Southern Illinois University Press, 1978), 109.

123 *"Anyone who has seen"*: Prentiss Taylor, "Research for Liberation: Shaping a New Black Identity in America," *Black World*, May 1973, 13.

123 *"A modest dose"*: Frances E. Kuo, "Coping with Poverty: Impacts of Environment and Attention in the Inner City," *Environment and Behavior* 33, no. 1 (January 2001): 28.

124 *the Hole—three buildings*: "Taylor Homes: The Demo of the 'Hole,'" *South Street Journal* 5, no. 3, Summer 1998, 1.

124 *"It's a hell hole"*: Linnet Myers, "Hell in the Hole," *Chicago Tribune*, April 12, 1998.

124 *By the nineties*: Pam Belluck, "End of a Ghetto: A Special Report; Razing the Slums to Rescue the Residents," *The New York Times*, September 6, 1998.

124 *"Goddamn public aid penitentiary"*: Quoted in Belluck, 26.

125 *"gunfire might just as well"*: George Papajohn and William Recktenwald, "Living in a War Zone Called Taylor Homes," *Chicago Tribune*, March 10, 1993.

127 *Illinois had the nation's highest rate*: Arthur Horton, "Disproportionality in Illinois Child Welfare: The Need for Improved Substance Abuse Services," *Journal of Alcoholism and Drug Dependence* 2, no. 1 (2013): 145.

128 *"I was in book heaven"*: Naomi Gaines, "Victory: A Memoir," 49. Naomi's manuscript is 264 pages and dedicated to her twin sons. She wrote most of it in prison.

130 *"a useful place of healing"*: bell hooks, *Rock My Soul: Black People and Self-Esteem* (New York: Atria Books, 2002), 205. hooks also writes, "I have found myself saying again and again that mental health is the revolutionary antiracist frontier African Americans must collectively explore."

130 *For a Black patient to reveal her fears*: John Head, *Standing in the Shadows: Understanding and Overcoming Depression in Black Men* (New York: Broadway Books, 2004), 3.

130 *"Many black folks worry"*: hooks, *Rock My Soul*, 23.

130 *"Black people's skin"*: Kelly M. Hoffman et al., "Racial Bias in Pain Assessment and Treatment Recommendations, and False Beliefs About Biological Differences Between Blacks and Whites," *Proceedings of the National Academy of Sciences* 113, no. 16 (April 2016): 4296.

130 *"Dysaesthesia Aethiopica"*: Christopher D. E. Willoughby, "Running Away from Drapetomania: Samuel A. Cartwright, Medicine, and Race in the Antebellum South," *Journal of Southern History* 84, no. 3 (August 2018): 579.

130 *"indifferent to punishment or even to life"*: Quoted in Cathy McDaniels-Wilson, "The Psychological Aftereffects of Racialized Sexual Violence," in *Gendered Resistance: Women, Slavery, and the Legacy of Margaret Garner*, ed. Mary E. Frederickson and Delores M. Walters (Urbana: University of Illinois Press, 2013), 195. Cartwright also coined another mental disorder called "Drapetomania, or the diseases causing slaves to run away." For more context on Cartwright, see Jonathan Metzl's *The Protest Psychosis*, which offers a groundbreaking discussion of racism in Civil Rights–era psychiatry.

130 *"partial insensibility of the skin"*: Quoted in Bob Myers, "'Drapetomania': Rebellion, Defiance and Free Black Insanity in the Antebellum United States" (PhD diss., UCLA Electronic Theses and Dissertations, 2014), 7. See also Samuel A. Cartwright, "Report on the Diseases and Physical Peculiarities of the Negro Race," *New Orleans Medical and Surgical Journal* (1851).

131 *more Black Americans were migrating*: John Biewen, "Moving Up: Part Two," broadcast by Minnesota Public Radio, August 7, 1997.

132 *"Black women have either been"*: Simone Schwarz-Bart and André Schwarz-Bart, *In Praise of Black Women: Ancient African Queens* (Houston: Modus Vivendi Publications, 2001), vii.

132 *the coffee-table book*: James Allen et al., *Without Sanctuary: Lynching Photography in America* (Santa Fe, NM: Twin Palms Publishers, 1999).

132 *originally part of an exhibition*: "Death by Lynching," *The New York Times*, March 16, 2000, www.nytimes.com/2000/03/16/opinion /death-by-lynching.html.

133 *"any notion of self-coherence"*: Joseph R. Winters, *Hope Draped in Black: Race, Melancholy, and the Agony of Progress* (Durham, NC: Duke University Press, 2016), 18.

133 *"Melancholy registers the experience"*: Quoted in Winters, 19–20. Winters is paraphrasing an argument made by Anne A. Cheng in *The Melancholy of Race: Psychoanalysis, Assimilation and Hidden Grief* (New York: Oxford University Press, 2000).

133 *Barred from full recognition*: For more on racial melancholy, see José Esteban Muñoz, *Disidentifications: Queers of Color and the Performance of Politics* (Minneapolis: University of Minnesota Press, 1999), 74; David L. Eng and Shinhee Han, "A Dialogue on Racial Melancholia," *Psychoanalytic Dialogues* 10, no. 4 (2000): 667–700; Cheng, *The Melancholy of Race*.

133 *"That's what makes it"*: Quoted in Louise Bernard, "National Maladies: Narratives of Race and Madness in Modern America" (PhD diss., Yale University, 2005), 8.

134 *"She believes her depression"*: This chapter draws from thousands of pages of Naomi's records: from emergency rooms and hospitals, Ramsey County Jail, Shakopee Correctional Facility, and the Minnesota Security Hospital. Many of these documents were sent to me in response to FOIA requests to the Ramsey County Attorney's Office. With Naomi's permission, Dennis Gerhardstein, the public information officer there, worked for half a year to help collect and then share these pages with me.

135 *"insanity was very rare"*: Martin Summers, "'Suitable Care of the African When Afflicted with Insanity': Race, Madness, and Social Order in Comparative Perspective," *Bulletin of the History of Medicine* 84, no. 1 (2010): 68. The original study referenced is "Exemption of the Cherokee Indians and Africans from Insanity," *The American Journal of Insanity* 1 (1845): 288.

135 *"Where there is no civilization"*: George M. Beard, *American Nervousness: Its Causes and Consequences* (New York: G. P. Putnam's Sons, 1881), 164.

135 *"prior to the war"*: Quoted in John S. Hughes, "Labeling and Treating Black Mental Illness in Alabama, 1861–1910," *The Journal of Southern History* 58, no. 3 (August 1993): 437.

135 *"insane and idiots"*: Quoted in Albert Deutsch, "The First U.S. Census of the Insane (1840) and Its Uses as Pro-Slavery Propaganda," *Bulletin of the History of Medicine* 15, no. 5 (May 1944): 471. See also Calvin Warren, "Black Interiority, Freedom, and the

Impossibility of Living," *Nineteenth-Century Contexts* 38, no. 2 (2016): 113.

135 *"The African is incapable"*: Quoted in Warren, 113.

135 *"are not only far happier"*: "Reflections on the Census of 1840," *Southern Literary Messenger* 9, no. 6 (June 1843): 350.

136 *"furnish little else"*: "Reflections on the Census of 1840," 350.

136 *the census was riddled with mistakes*: Warren, "Black Interiority," 114.

136 *"one of the most amazing tissues"*: Deutsch, "The First U.S. Census," 475.

136 *"civilization is not to be donned"*: Arrah B. Evarts, "Dementia Precox in the Colored Race," *The Psychoanalytic Review* 1 (January 1913): 393.

136 *"strangers within our gates"*: Arrah B. Evarts, "The Ontogenetic Against the Phylogenetic Elements in the Psychoses of the Colored Race," *The Psychoanalytic Review* 3 (January 1916): 287.

136 *"demanded an adjustment"*: Evarts, "Dementia Precox," 394.

136 *Like the Parsis*: Waltraud Ernst, *Colonialism and Transnational Psychiatry: The Development of an Indian Mental Hospital in British India, c. 1925–1940* (London: Anthem Press, 2013).

136 *"They never reproduce"*: Mary O'Malley, "Psychoses in the Colored Race," *The American Journal of Psychiatry* 71 (October 1914): 314.

136 *"Their sorrows and anxieties"*: O'Malley, 327.

137 *the suicide rate for African American adults*: Warren Breed, "The Negro and Fatalistic Suicide," *Pacific Sociological Review* 13, no. 3 (September 1970): 156–62. See also James A. Weed, "Suicide in the United States: 1958–1982," in *Mental Health, United States 1985*, ed. Carl A. Taube and Sally A. Barrett (Washington, D.C.: National Institute of Mental Health, 1985), 135–45; Judith M. Stillion and Eugene E. McDowell, *Suicide Across the Life Span: Premature Exits* (New York: Taylor & Francis, 1996), 18–20; "Racial and Ethnic Disparities," Suicide Prevention Resource Center website, sprc.org/scope/racial-ethnic-disparities; Ronald W. Maris, Alan L. Berman, and Morton M. Silverman, *Comprehensive Textbook of Suicidology* (New York: Guilford Press, 2000), 75; Centers for Disease Control and Prevention, National Center for Health Statistics, National Vital Statistics System, *National Vital Statistics Reports* 52, no. 3 (September 2003): 10; Deborah M. Stone, Christopher M. Jones, and Karin A. Mack, "Changes in Suicide Rates—United States, 2018–2019," *Morbidity and Mortality Weekly Report* 70 (2021): 261–68.

137 *Suicides may end up classified*: Head, *Standing in the Shadows*, 30.

137 *suicide has historically been*: Keven E. Early and Ronald L. Akers, "'It's a White Thing': An Exploration of Beliefs About Suicide in the African-American Community," *Deviant Behavior* 14, no. 4 (1993): 277.

137 *"some veteran southern psychiatrists"*: Arthur J. Prange and M. M. Vitols, "Cultural Aspects of the Relatively Low Incidence of Depression in Southern Negroes," *International Journal of Social Psychiatry* 8, no. 2 (1962): 105.

137 *"As a rule blacks don't"*: Quoted in Kevin E. Early, *Religion and Suicide in the African-American Community* (Westport, CT: Greenwood Press, 1992), 42.

137 *"almost a complete denial"*: Early, 81.

137 *"bold up, brace our shoulders"*: Quoted in Early, 43.

137 *"Negro self-esteem"*: Abram Kardiner and Lionel Ovesey, *The Mark of Oppression: Explorations in the Personality of the American Negro* (New York: W. W. Norton, 1951), 387.

137 *"There is only one way"*: Kardiner and Ovesey, 387.

138 *"Modern psychiatry got on its feet"*: Richard Wright, "Psychiatry Comes to Harlem," *Free World* 12, no. 2 (September 1946): 51.

138 *"chronic human need"*: Wright, 49.

138 *Wright helped found*: Dennis A. Doyle, *Psychiatry and Racial Liberalism in Harlem, 1936–1968* (Rochester, NY: University of Rochester Press, 2016), 108.

138 *"the Negroes of Mississippi"*: Wright, "Psychiatry Comes to Harlem," 49.

138 *"the will to survive"*: Wright, 51.

138 *the clinic shut down*: Gabriel N. Mendes, *Under the Strain of Color: Harlem's Lafargue Clinic and the Promise of an Antiracist Psychiatry* (Ithaca, NY: Cornell University Press, 2015), 160.

138 *"brutal awareness"*: Quoted in George Ritzer and Jeffrey Stepnisky, *Sociological Theory: Tenth Edition* (Thousand Oaks, CA: Sage, 2018), 562.

138 *"may ask what we have"*: Frantz Fanon, *Black Skin, White Masks* (London: Pluto Press, 1986), 138.

138 *"I know nothing about her"*: Quoted in Rey Chow, "The Politics of Admittance: Female Sexual Agency, Miscegenation, and the Formation of Community in Frantz Fanon," in *Frantz Fanon: Critical Perspectives*, ed. Anthony C. Allessandrini (London: Routledge, 1999), 39.

138 *Five Percent Nation*: Felicia M. Miyakawa, *Five Percenter Rap: God Hop's Music, Message, and Black Muslim Mission* (Bloomington: Indiana University Press, 2005), 68.

140 *"most extreme suspension"*: Iris Marion Young, *On Female Body Experience: "Throwing Like a Girl" and Other Essays* (New York: Oxford University Press, 2005), 49.

140 *"It feels somewhat like a gas bubble"*: Young, 48.

141 *the largest public-housing complex*: Sudhir Venkatesh, "Midst the Handguns' Red Glare," *Whole Earth* 97 (Summer 1999): 41.

141 *Four years earlier*: Dirk Johnson, "6 Children Found Strangled After Mother Confesses to 911," *The New York Times*, September 5, 1998, www.nytimes.com/1998/09/05/us/6-children-found-strangled -after-mother-confesses-to-911.html.

141 *"I don't know why"*: Quoted in Lourdes Medrano Leslie, Curt Brown, and staff writers, "A Young Mother Accused of Murder," *Star Tribune*, November 15, 1998.

141 *The McDonough Homes housed*: "Choice, Place and Opportunity: An Equity Assessment of the Twin Cities Region," Twin Cities Metropolitan Council website, metrocouncil.org/Planning /Projects/Thrive-2040/Choice-Place-and-Opportunity/FHEA /CPO-Sect-5.aspx.

141 *particularly South Asian refugees*: Bruce T. Downing et al., "The Hmong Resettlement Study: Site Report, Minneapolis–St. Paul, Minnesota" (Washington, D.C.: U.S. Department of Health and Human Services, Office of Refugee Resettlement, October 1984), 3.

141 *among the most segregated*: "Most to Least Segregated Cities," Othering & Belonging Institute website, belonging.berkeley.edu/most -least-segregated-cities.

141 *communities with less "ethnic density"*: Sophie J. Baker et al., "The Ethnic Density Effect in Psychosis: A Systematic Review and Multilevel Meta-Analysis," *The British Journal of Psychiatry* (2021): 1–12.

141 *For people of color, the risk*: T. M. Luhrmann, "Social Defeat and the Culture of Chronicity: Or, Why Schizophrenia Does So Well Over There and So Badly Here," *Culture, Medicine, and Psychiatry* 31 (May 2007): 135–72.

144 *Kenyan activist Wangarĩ Muta Maathai*: Sophie Mbugua, "Wangari Maathai: The Outspoken Conservationist," Deutsche Welle website, March 6, 2020, www.dw.com/en/wangari-maathai-the -outspoken-conservationist/a-52448394.

144 *"speculate directly"*: Lorna A. Rhodes, *Emptying Beds: The Work of an Emergency Psychiatric Unit* (Berkeley: University of California Press, 1995), 40.

144 *"can be described"*: Rhodes, 14.

144 *"the 'unconscious' of psychiatry"*: Rhodes, 31.

145 *psychoanalytic insight was often achieved*: Critiquing a rigid approach, D. W. Winnicott writes, "The patient is not helped if the analyst says: 'Your mother was not good enough . . . your father really seduced you . . . your aunt dropped you.' Changes come in an analysis when the traumatic factors enter the psycho-analytic material in the patient's own way, and within the patient's omnipotence." See D. W. Winnicott, "The Theory of the Parent-Infant Relationship," *The International Journal of Psychoanalysis* 41 (1960): 585.

148 *"the accused was laboring"*: Quoted in "Insanity Defense," Legal Information Institute website, www.law.cornell.edu/wex/insanity _defense.

148 *"Remuneration with him"*: Quoted in Benjamin F. Hall, *The Trial of William Freeman for the Murder of John G. Van Nest, Including the Evidence and the Arguments of Counsel, with the Decision of the Supreme Court Granting a New Trial, and an Account of the Death of the Prisoner, and of the Post-mortem Examination of His Body by Amariah Brigham, M. D., and Others* (Auburn, NY: Derby, Miller & Co., 1848), 502.

148 *"You have been tried for killing"*: Kenneth J. Weiss and Neha Gupta, "America's First M'Naghten Defense and the Origin of the Black Rage Syndrome," *The Journal of the American Academy of Psychiatry and the Law* 46, no. 4 (December 2018): 509.

149 *"shocked beyond the power of expression"*: William H. Seward, *Argument of William H. Seward, in Defence of William Freeman, on His Trial for Murder, at Auburn, July 21st and 22d, 1846* (Auburn, NY: H. Oliphant, printer, 1846), 4.

149 *"in the abstract"*: Seward, 8.

149 *"I have never seen"*: Quoted in Hall, *The Trial of William Freeman*, 501.

149 *"When the framers of the Constitution"*: Rule 20 Evaluation, written by Gregory A. Hanson, assistant director of psychological services, and Jennifer Service, Minnesota Security Hospital clinical director, October 7, 2003, 1–29.

151 *"hesitant, quiet"*: This chapter draws from more than six hundred

pages of notes and assessments from mental-health staff at Sha-kopee, obtained through a records request (with Naomi's permission) from the Minnesota Department of Corrections and from the Minnesota Department of Human Services.

151 *Minnesota's state governor Luther Youngdahl*: Susan Bartlett Foote, *The Crusade for Forgotten Souls: Reforming Minnesota's Mental Institutions, 1946–1954* (Minneapolis: University of Minnesota Press, 2018), xiii.

151 *A quarter of them*: Albert Q. Maisel, "Scandal Results in Real Reforms," *Life*, November 12, 1951, 152.

151 *"particeps criminis"*: Luther W. Youngdahl, "The New Frontier in Mental Health," speech at the American Psychiatric Association convention, Detroit, Michigan, May 4, 1950, mn.gov/mnddc/past/pdf/50s/50/50-NFM-LWY.pdf.

152 *"The roots of demonology"*: Luther W. Youngdahl, "Statement by Governor Luther W. Youngdahl at the Burning of Restraints" (speech), Anoka, Minnesota, October 31, 1949, mn.gov/mnddc/past/pdf/40s/49/49-SGL-Youngdahl.pdf.

152 *"There is no such thing as a rich patient"*: Youngdahl, "The New Frontier," 6.

152 *"cold mercy of custodial isolation"*: John F. Kennedy, *Message from the President of the United States Relative to Mental Illness and Mental Retardation*, 88th Cong., 1963, H. Doc., serial 12565, 3.

152 *"predictable problems of living"*: D. G. Langsley, "The Community Mental Health Center: Does It Treat Patients?," *Hospital and Community Psychiatry* 12 (December 1980): 815.

152 *"socially maladjusted"*: E. Fuller Torrey, *American Psychosis: How the Federal Government Destroyed the Mental Illness Treatment System* (New York: Oxford University Press, 2014), 78.

152 *"For the most massive movement"*: Torrey, 93.

153 *more than two-thirds of women incarcerated*: Jennifer Bronson and Marcus Berzofsky, "Indicators of Mental Health Problems Reported by Prisoners and Jail Inmates, 2011–12," U.S. Department of Justice special report. Open-file report available at www.themarshallproject.org/documents/3872819-Indicators-of-Mental-Health-Problems-Reported-by. For a great overview of the intersection between mental-health care and criminal justice, see Alisa Roth, *Insane: America's Criminal Treatment of Mental Illness* (New York: Basic Books, 2018).

153 *the number of women incarcerated*: "Incarceration Trends in Min-

nesota," Vera Institute of Justice website, www.vera.org/downloads /pdfdownloads/state-incarceration-trends-minnesota.pdf.

153 *"Freedom is the test"*: Quoted in Thomas M. Daly, *For the Good of the Women: A Short History of the Minnesota Correctional Facility Shakopee* (Daly Pub.: 2004), 7.

153 *helped found the prison*: Daly, 7.

154 *roughly 16 percent of the women*: "Minnesota Correctional Facility: Shakopee Inmate Profile," Minnesota Department of Corrections website, coms.doc.state.mn.us/tourreport/04FacilityInmateProfile .pdf.

154 *"Dear Paper"*: This line comes from a 120-page notebook that Naomi titled "My Journal." Naomi periodically cleaned out her cell at Shakopee and mailed letters, notebooks, drawings, and books to her sister Toma, who kept the items in storage in her house in Chicago. By the time Naomi was released, Toma had transferred all of Naomi's letters and other writings into three enormous garbage bags. This chapter draws from the contents of two of those bags—the third was hidden under other storage and too hard for Toma to access—which Naomi invited me to read when I met her in Chicago in February 2021.

155 *"the burdens in the world"*: Khoua Her, "Khoua Her's Story: Part IV," *Hmong Times*, January 1, 2001, 13.

155 *"The more I felt"*: Her, 9.

155 *"Please listen to your inner self"*: Khoua Her, "Khoua Her's Story: Part I," *Hmong Times*, November 16, 2000, 1.

155 *after death a person's soul*: Christopher Thao Vang, *Hmong Refugees in the New World Culture, Community and Opportunity* (Jefferson, NC: McFarland, 2016), 168. See also Youhung Her-Xiong and Tracy Schroepfer, "Walking in Two Worlds: Hmong End-of-Life Beliefs and Rituals," *Journal of Social Work in End-of-Life and Palliative Care* 14, no. 4 (2018): 291–314.

155 *"concerns among some"*: Mara H. Gottfried, "'This Can Never Happen Again': 1998 Slayings of Six Children in St. Paul by Their Mother Led to Changes in Mental Health Assistance," *Bemidji Pioneer*, September 1, 2018.

156 *"Not a house in the country"*: Toni Morrison, *Beloved* (New York: Vintage Books, 1987), 6.

158 *the Ida B. Wells Homes*: Bowly Jr., *The Poorhouse*, 24.

161 *"the capacity to integrate"*: Arthur Blank, "Apocalypse Terminable and Interminable: An Interview with Arthur S. Blank Jr.," in

Listening to Trauma: Conversations with Leaders in the Theory and Treatment of Catastrophic Experience, ed. Cathy Caruth (Baltimore, MD: Johns Hopkins University Press), 288.

161 *"As a clinician"*: Blank, 284.

161–62 *"White clinicians may unconsciously withdraw"*: William H. Grier and Price M. Cobbs, *Black Rage: Two Black Psychiatrists Reveal the Full Dimensions of the Inner Conflicts and the Desperation of Black Life in the United States* (New York: Basic Books, 1968), 156.

162 *"The patient needs an experience"*: Quoted in Rollo May, *The Discovery of Being* (New York: W. W. Norton, 1983), 158.

164 *"regardless of age, race"*: Elizabeth Hawes, "Incarcerated Women Are Punished for Their Trauma with Solitary Confinement," Solitary Watch website, December 24, 2020, solitarywatch.org/2020/12/24/incarcerated-women-are-punished-for-their-trauma-with-solitary-confinement/.

164 *"Putting someone in seg"*: Quoted in Hawes, 7.

164 *"Walls breathe"*: Quoted in Elizabeth Hawes, "Women's Segregation: 51 Interviews in 2019" (unpublished), Solitary Confinement Reporting Project, 9.

164 *"I was suicidal"*: Quoted in Hawes, 9.

166 *"Hello Naomi"*: Letter from Carl to Naomi, April 29, 2004. I found this letter (along with more correspondence with Carl and others) in the large garbage bags where Toma kept Naomi's belongings from prison. See the *"Dear Paper"* note on page 265 for more context.

170 *preoccupation with her ancestors*: Hearing transcript, "In the Matter of Naomi Gaines: Findings of Fact and Recommendation," Department of Human Services, Special Review Board, Saint Paul, Minnesota, September 17, 2015.

171 *"By having doctors and staff"*: Quoted in Andy Steiner, "Her Sentence Complete, Naomi Gaines-Young Wants to Talk About Mental Illness," *MinnPost*, September 3, 2019, www.minnpost.com/mental-health-addiction/2019/09/her-sentence-complete-naomi-gaines-young-wants-to-talk-about-mental-illness/.

171 *Naomi attended therapy groups*: Details about the Minnesota Security Hospital come from more than two thousand pages of records sent to me by the Minnesota Department of Human Services in response to a request for records (granted with Naomi's permission).

173 *studies with twins suggest*: Falk W. Lohoff, "Overview of the Genetics of Major Depressive Disorder," *Current Psychiatry Reports* 12,

no. 6 (December 2010): 539–46. See also Elsevier, "Largest Twin Study Pins Nearly 80% of Schizophrenia Risk on Heritability," *ScienceDaily*, www.sciencedaily.com/releases/2017/10/171005103313 .htm.

LAURA

177 *"excellent at everything"*: This chapter draws from roughly three hundred pages of medical records, spanning from 1996 to 2010, that Laura shared with me. A different version of this story was originally published in *The New Yorker* on April 1, 2019, and titled "The Challenge of Going Off Psychiatric Drugs."

178 *"affective storms"*: Joseph Biederman, "The Evolving Face of Pediatric Mania," *Biological Psychiatry* 60, no. 9 (November 2006): 901–902.

178 *Between 1995 and 2003*: Carmen Moreno et al., "National Trends in the Outpatient Diagnosis and Treatment of Bipolar Disorder in Youth," *Archives of General Psychiatry* 64, no. 9 (September 2007): 1032.

178 *"real self underneath"*: Laura Delano interviewed by Charles Eisenstein, "Laura Delano: Sanity in an Insane World," *A New and Ancient Story*, podcast, charleseisenstein.org/podcasts/new-and-ancient -story-podcast/laura-delano-sanity-in-an-insane-world-e28/.

179 *"Why do I have these extra layers"*: This chapter draws from a journal that Laura kept during her Outward Bound trip in 2004. It also quotes from dozens of emails and letters that Laura shared with me.

179 *"utter agony"*: "Eleanor Roosevelt Facts," Franklin D. Roosevelt Presidential Library and Museum website, www.fdrlibrary.org/er -facts.

180 *"best mental hospital"*: Quoted in Alex Beam, *Gracefully Insane: The Rise and Fall of America's Premier Mental Hospital* (New York: PublicAffairs, 2001), 152.

180 *"seems to be the goal"*: Quoted in Ernest Samuels, *Henry Adams* (Cambridge, MA: Harvard University Press, 1989), 200.

181 *roughly a third of patients*: A. John Rush et al., "Acute and Longer-Term Outcomes in Depressed Outpatients Requiring One or Several Treatment Steps: A STAR*D Report," *The American Journal of Psychiatry* 163, no. 11 (November 2006): 1905–17.

182 *up to 65 percent of people*: Elizabeth Jing and Kristyn Straw-Wilson, "Sexual Dysfunction in Selective Serotonin Reuptake

Inhibitors (SSRIs) and Potential Solutions: A Narrative Literature Review," *Mental Health Clinician* 6, no. 4 (July 2016): 191–96. See also Tierney Lorenz, Jordan Rullo, and Stephanie Faubion, "Antidepressant-Induced Female Sexual Dysfunction," *Mayo Clinic Proceedings* 91, no. 9 (September 2016): 1280–86.

183 *"epistemic goods"*: Miranda Fricker, *Epistemic Injustice: Power and the Ethics of Knowing* (New York: Oxford University Press, 2007), 1.

186 *"Every psychiatrist knows the type"*: Quoted in Carl Elliott, "On Psychiatry and Souls: Walker Percy and the Ontological Lapsometer," *Perspectives in Biology and Medicine* 35, no. 2 (Winter 1992): 238.

187 "SELFISH EGOCENTRIC JEALOUS": Sylvia Plath, *The Journals of Sylvia Plath* (1982; repr., New York: Anchor Books, 1998), 35.

187 *"the rest of my life"*: Plath, 61.

191 *"audience-oriented"*: Harold F. Searles, *My Work with Borderline Patients* (Lanham, MD: Rowman & Littlefield, 1986), 59.

191 *"the disorder is more commonly diagnosed"*: *Diagnostic and Statistical Manual of Mental Disorders, Third Edition (DSM-III)* (Washington, D.C.: American Psychiatric Association, 1980), 322.

191 *"new 'female malady'"*: Janet Wirth-Cauchon, *Women and Borderline Personality Disorder: Symptoms and Stories* (New Brunswick, NJ: Rutgers University Press, 2000), 2.

192 *a book with a picture of a face*: Robert Whitaker, *The Anatomy of an Epidemic: Magic Bullets, Psychiatric Drugs, and the Astonishing Rise of Mental Illness in America* (New York: Broadway Paperbacks, 2010).

192 *Whitaker largely ignores*: Helena Hansen, Philippe Bourgois, and Ernest Drucker, "Pathologizing Poverty: New Forms of Diagnosis, Disability, and Structural Stigma Under Welfare Reform," *Social Science & Medicine* (February 2014): 76–83. See also Sandra Steingard, "A Conversation with Nev Jones," *Mad in America: Science, Psychiatry, and Social Justice*, September 22, 2020, www .madinamerica.com/2020/09/a-conversation-with-nev-jones/.

193 *"at best a reductionistic oversimplification"*: Joseph Schildkraut, "The Catecholamine Hypothesis of Affective Disorders: A Review of Supporting Evidence," *The Journal of Neuropsychiatry and Clinical Neurosciences* 7, no. 4 (November 1995): 530. The article originally appeared in *The American Journal of Psychiatry* 122, no. 5 (1965): 509–22.

193 *"we'll find a biochemical test"*: Nathan S. Kline, *From Sad to Glad: Kline on Depression* (New York: Ballantine Books, 1974), 37.

193 *For more than fifty years*: Brett J. Deacon, "The Biomedical Model of Mental Disorder: A Critical Analysis of Its Validity, Utility, and Effects on Psychotherapy Research," *Clinical Psychology Review* 33 (2013). See also Falk W. Lohoff, "Overview of the Genetics of Major Depressive Disorder," *Current Psychiatry Reports* 12, no. 6 (December 2010).

193 *Despite great advances in neuroscience:* Thomas Insel, *Healing: Our Path from Mental Illness to Mental Health* (New York, Penguin Press, 2022), xvi.

193 *"I grew up in a suburban town"*: Laura Delano, email message to Robert Whitaker, September 28, 2010.

196 *"The effects of these drugs"*: Anonymous forum comment, "Narcissus: just another Effexor story," Surviving Antidepressants website, September 28, 2012, www.survivingantidepressants.org/topic/3027 -narcissus-just-another-effexor-story/?tab=comments#comment -33092.

196 *"This withdrawal process"*: Anonymous forum comment in reply to "Identity crisis," Surviving Antidepressants website, www .survivingantidepressants.org/topic/7497-identity-crisis/.

196 *one in eight people in America*: Amir Raz, "Perspectives on the Efficacy of Antidepressants for Child and Adolescent Depression," *PLOS Medicine* 3, no. 1 (2006): e9.

196 *"It is relatively simple"*: Nathan S. Kline, "The Practical Management of Depression," *The Journal of the American Medical Association* 190, no. 8 (1964): 738.

197 *"realizes she's in a losing pattern"*: Quoted in Jonathan Metzl, *Prozac on the Couch: Prescribing Gender in the Era of Wonder Drugs* (Durham, NC: Duke University Press, 2003), 147. Metzl has written persuasively about the ways that "psychotropic medications often redeploy all the cultural and social baggage of the psychoanalytic paradigms," particularly gender, sexual, and racial norms. See also Jonathan Metzl, "Selling Sanity Through Gender: Psychiatry and the Dynamics of Pharmaceutical Advertising," *Journal of Medical Humanities* 24, no. 1 (2003): 79–103; Jonathan Metzl, "Prozac and the Pharmacokinetics of Narrative Form," *Signs: Journal of Women in Culture and Society* 27, no. 2 (Winter 2002): 347–80; Jonathan M. Metzl, Sara I. McClelland, and Erin Bergner, "Conflations of Marital Status and Sanity: Implicit Heterosexist Bias in Psychiat-

ric Diagnosis in Physician-Dictated Charts at a Midwestern Medical Center," *Yale Journal of Biology and Medicine* 89, no. 2 (June 2016): 247–54.

197 *Valium was the most widely prescribed medication*: Lara Magro, Marco Faccini, and Roberto Leone, "Lormetazepam Addiction," in *Neuropathology of Drug Addictions and Substance Misuse Volume 3: General Processes and Mechanisms, Prescription Medications, Caffeine and Areca, Polydrug Misuse, Emerging Addictions and Non-Drug Addictions*, ed. Victor R. Preedy (London: Academic Press, 2016), 273.

197 *"Benzodiazepines have lost their status"*: Quoted in Alain Ehrenberg, *Weariness of the Self: Diagnosing the History of Depression in the Contemporary Age* (Montreal: McGill–Queen's University Press, 2009), 199.

197 *Serotonin reuptake inhibitors*: Todd M. Hillhouse and Joseph H. Porter, "A Brief History of the Development of Antidepressant Drugs: From Monoamines to Glutamate," *Experimental and Clinical Psychopharmacology* 23, no. 1 (February 2015): 1–21.

198 *more than one in five white women*: Debra J. Brody and Qiuping Gu, "Antidepressant Use Among Adults: United States, 2015–2018," *Centers for Disease Control and Prevention: National Center for Health Statistics Data Brief* no. 277 (September 2020), 2.

198 *"Power that Speaks Softly"*: Quoted in Metzl, *Prozac on the Couch*, 61.

198 *"For both restful nights and productive days"*: Quoted in Metzl, 154.

201 *"these tiny pills and capsules"*: Laura's blog was called *Recovering from Psychiatry*. The URL was recoveringfrompsychiatry.com, but the website is now defunct.

201 *The field has neglected questions*: Giovanni A. Fava, a professor of psychiatry at the University of Buffalo, is one of the few psychiatrists to have closely studied the complications of withdrawing from SSRIs. He recently published a book on the subject, *Discontinuing Antidepressant Medications* (New York: Oxford University Press, 2021).

202 *In the nineties*: L. Pacheco et al., "More Cases of Paroxetine Withdrawal Syndrome," *The British Journal of Psychiatry* 169, no. 3 (1996): 384.

202 *"experienced feelings of severe aggression"*: Andrea L. Lazowick and Gary M. Levin, "Potential Withdrawal Syndrome Associated with SSRI Discontinuation," *Annals of Pharmacotherapy* 29 (December 1995): 1285.

202 *"was unable to stop"*: E. Szabadi, "Fluvoxamine Withdrawal Syndrome," *The British Journal of Psychiatry* 160, no. 2 (February 1992): 284.

205 *"when a man is capable"*: John Keats to George and Tom Keats, letter, December 21–27, 1817, British Library website, www.bl.uk/romantics-and-victorians/articles/john-keats-and-negative-capability.

206 *"good responder"*: Peter Kramer, *Listening to Prozac: A Psychiatrist Explores Antidepressant Drugs and the Remaking of Self* (New York: Penguin Books, 1993), 270–71.

207 *"For the first time in fifteen years"*: Nathan S. Kline, "Clinical Experience with Iproniazid (Marsilid)," *Journal of Clinical and Experimental Psychopathology & Quarterly Review of Psychiatry and Neurology* 19 (1958): 79.

208 *"at least part of the nagging worry"*: Carl Elliott, "Pursued by Happiness and Beaten Senseless: Prozac and the American Dream," *Hastings Center Report* 30, no. 2 (2000): 9.

208 *"an alienated Sisyphus"*: Elliott, 11.

210 *"paradoxical situation"*: Ehrenberg, *Weariness of the Self*, 200.

210 *The Swedish neuropharmacologist*: Carl Elliott, introduction to *Prozac as a Way of Life*, ed. Carl Elliott and Tod Chambers (Chapel Hill: University of North Carolina Press, 2004), 3.

210 *"Seeing how poorly patients fared"*: Kramer, *Listening to Prozac*, xv.

211 *"everybody is dealing with"*: Adam Phillips, "The Art of Nonfiction No. 7," interview by Paul Holdengräber, *The Paris Review*, no. 208 (Spring 2014), www.theparisreview.org/interviews/6286/the-art-of-nonfiction-no-7-adam-phillips.

211 *lacked the courage*: In *Listening to Prozac*, Peter Kramer writes that Prozac "catalyzes the precondition for tragedy, namely participation," 258.

211 *"power to experience"*: Roland Kuhn, "The Imipramine Story," in *Discoveries in Biological Psychiatry*, ed. Frank J. Ayd and Barry Blackwell (Philadelphia: J. B. Lippincott, 1970), 215.

212 *"she did not feel that she could"*: Adrienne Einarson, Peter Selby, and Gideon Koren, "Abrupt Discontinuation of Psychotropic Drugs During Pregnancy: Fear of Teratogenic Risk and Impact of Counselling," *Journal of Psychiatry & Neuroscience* 26, no. 1 (2001): 46.

212 *pressure to take medications*: Kramer, *Listening to Prozac*. See also Peter Kramer, "Incidental Enhancement," *Human Nature and Self Design* (January 2011): 155–63.

214 *hospital as a lighthouse crashing*: Ann-Louise S. Silver, "A Personal Response to Gail Hornstein's *To Redeem One Person Is to Redeem the World: The Life of Frieda Fromm-Reichmann*," *Psychiatry* 65, no. 1 (Spring 2002): 2.

214 *"real loneliness"*: Frieda Fromm-Reichmann, "Loneliness," *Contemporary Psychoanalysis* 26 (1990): 306. Originally printed in *Psychiatry: Journal for the Study of Interpersonal Processes* 22 (1959).

217 *"Years have again gone by"*: Sigmund Freud, "Fragment of an Analysis of a Case of Hysteria (1905 [1901])," in *The Standard Edition of the Complete Psychological Works of Sigmund Freud, Volume VII (1901–1905): A Case of Hysteria, Three Essays on Sexuality and Other Works (1905)* (London: Hogarth Press, 1975), 122.

217 *"I did not allow the opportunity"*: Quoted in Susan Katz, "Speaking Out Against the 'Talking Cure': Unmarried Women in Freud's Early Case Studies," *Women's Studies: An Interdisciplinary Journal* 13, no. 4 (1987): 298. Originally from Sigmund Freud and Josef Breuer, *Studies on Hysteria*, trans. James Strachey (New York: Basic Books, 2000), 160. Originally published in 1895.

EPILOGUE: HAVA

219 *"The prognosis is positive"*: Arthur L. Robin and Patricia T. Siegel, "Family Therapy with Eating-Disordered Adolescence," in *Handbook of Psychotherapies with Children and Families*, ed. Sandra W. Russ and Thomas H. Ollendick (New York: Kluwer Academic/Plenum Publishers, 1999), 301.

221 *Mental disorder can feel uncertain*: Thanks to Nev Jones, who articulated this point after reading the manuscript. Her writing on the nature of psychosis and identity has been a source of inspiration. See Awais Aftab, "Phenomenology, Power, Polarization, and the Discourse on Psychosis: Nev Jones, PhD," *Psychiatric Times*, October 8, 2020, www.psychiatrictimes.com/view/phenomenology-power-polarization-psychosis. See also Nev Jones et al., "'Did I Push Myself Over the Edge?': Complications of Agency in Psychosis Onset and Development," *Psychosis: Psychological, Social and Integrative Approaches* 8, no. 4 (January 2016): 324–35.

223 *shut down ten psychiatric hospitals*: David Milne, "Michigan Continues to Cut Public Psychiatry Beds," *Psychiatric News*, February 7, 2003, psychnews.psychiatryonline.org/doi/full/10.1176/pn.38.3.0008.

223–24 *Anorexia is the most fatal*: Jon Arcelus et al., "Mortality Rates in Patients with Anorexia Nervosa and Other Eating Disorders: A

Meta-analysis of 36 Studies," *Archives of General Psychiatry* 68, no. 7 (2011): 729.

224 *"the 'wrong' kind of sick"*: Rebecca J. Lester, *Famished: Eating Disorders and Failed Care in America* (Oakland: University of California Press, 2019), 16.

224 *97 percent of eating-disorder specialists*: "Facts About Eating Disorders: What the Research Shows," Eating Disorders Coalition for Research, Policy & Action (EDC) website, eatingdisorders coalition.org.s208556.gridserver.com/couch/uploads/file/Eating %20Disorders%20Fact%20Sheet.pdf.

224 *one in five specialists*: "Facts About Eating Disorders."

224 *"eating disorders continue to occupy"*: Lester, *Famished*, 16.

225 *"semi-starvation neurosis"*: Ancel Keys, Josef Brozek, and Austin Henschel, *The Biology of Human Starvation* (Minneapolis: University of Minnesota Press, 1950), 908.

225 *"these food images and obsessions"*: Nonja Peters, "The Ascetic Anorexic," *Social Analysis: The International Journal of Social and Cultural Practice*, no. 37 (April 1995): 49. See also Ancel Keys, *The Biology of Human Starvation* (Saint Paul: University of Minnesota Press, 1950).

228 *"My feeling was: Don't ask me"*: Quoted in Liza Mundy, "Open (Secret)," *The Washington Post*, May 6, 2007, W18. Liza Mundy also generously corresponded with me about her encounters with Hava and her family.

229 *"The tragedy of anorexia"*: Louise Glück, *Proofs and Theories: Essays on Poetry* (Hopewell, NJ: Ecco Press, 1994), 10.

231 *"wild facts, with no stall"*: William James, *Essays in Psychology* (Cambridge, MA: Harvard University Press, 1984), 247–68.

231 *"It's like trying to explain"*: Rachel Aviv, "Which Way Madness Lies: Can Psychosis Be Prevented?," *Harper's Magazine* (December 2010), 41.

233 *"I got my Mommy back"*: Quoted in Patricia E. Deegan, "Recovery as a Self-Directed Process of Healing and Transformation," *Occupational Therapy in Mental Health* 17 (2002): 18.

233 *"For those of us who have struggled"*: Deegan, 19.

233 *"Recovery does not refer"*: Patricia E. Deegan, "Recovery: The Lived Experience of Rehabilitation," *Psychosocial Rehabilitation Journal* 11, no. 4 (1988): 14.

233 *"transformation rather than restoration"*: Deegan, "Recovery as a Self-Directed Process," 18.

233 *"All of the polemic"*: Deegan, "Recovery: The Lived Experience of Rehabilitation," 14.

235 *"old humorous frowning eyes"*: John Steinbeck, *The Grapes of Wrath* (New York: Viking Press, 1939), 15.

236 *"You have gathered during these years"*: Frieda Fromm-Reichmann, "Remarks on the Philosophy of Mental Disorder," *Psychiatry: Interpersonal and Biological Processes* 9 (1946): 294.

Acknowledgments

Thank you to Bhargavi, Karthik, Naomi, Laura, and Hava's family for knowing that your experiences would help others feel less alone and for sharing so much because of that hope.

To Eric Chinski, who somehow has always known exactly what I should hold in mind as the ideal; to PJ Mark, who has been so patient and steady that a long time ago I forgot to be afraid he might judge me; to David Remnick, for his generosity and spirit of trust for the past decade; and to Willing Davidson, whose perspective is so bound up in my idea of good writing that I don't entirely believe my writing exists until he's read it.

To Rachael Bedard, Anna Goldman, Alice Gregory, and Tanya Luhrmann, for reading chapters so closely that they grasped what I was trying to say much before I did. I am also grateful for incredible feedback and insights (on the manuscript and beyond) from Yelena Akhtiorskaya, Kate Axelrod, Carla Blumenkranz, Gareth Cook, Emily Cooke, Chloe Cooper-Jones, Jiayang Fan, Sarah Goldstein, Brian Goldstone, zakia henderson-brown, Amy Herzog, Patrick Radden Keefe, Gideon Lewis-Kraus, Rose Lichter-Marck, George Makari and Cornell's Psychiatry, Psychoanalysis, and Society workgroup, Cleuci de Oliveria (who wisely suggested that

I write about Naomi), Ed Park, Kate Rodemann, Christine Smallwood, and—the gift of adulthood—my sisters, Sari, Stephanie, and Lizzie (and Alex Kane). My conversations with Nev Jones more than a decade ago sparked many of the questions that this book explores.

To New America for helping me start this book and to the Whiting Foundation for helping me finish it. David Kortava, Teresa Matthews, and Alejandra Dechet were ideal companions in fact-checking; Vidya Mohan and Tyler Richard helped translate Bapu's letters and gave new meaning to the social world she was navigating. At FSG, thanks to Tara Sharma and her secret subtitle talents, among many others, and to Carrie Hsieh and Brian Gittis. Eugene Lancaric graced me with his empty apartment, the first time I've ever had an "office."

To Alex for being the inspiration (even when I fall short) for working up the bravery to try new kinds of experiences, including this book. Writing it gave me a new kind of respect for my mom, dad, Linda, and David for making so much feel possible. I hope that one day our children, Rafael and Sonia, will be able to say the same.

A NOTE ABOUT THE AUTHOR

Rachel Aviv is a staff writer at *The New Yorker*, where she writes about medicine, education, and criminal justice, among other subjects. In 2022, she won a National Magazine Award for Profile Writing. A 2019 national fellow at New America, she received a Whiting Creative Nonfiction Grant to support her work on this book. She lives in Brooklyn, New York.